Folens

GCSE RELIGIOUS STUDIES
FOR OCR B

PHILOSOPHY
and APPLIED
ETHICS

SHIPLAKE COLLEGE

This book is issued ON LOAN. If lost or maltreated
its holder will be charged the cost of a new book. As
soon as you receive it, ensure that the last name has
been cancelled and write in your name in ink.

NAME	HOUSE	FORM	DATE
Oliver J. Gerrard	(s)	10B	18-10-2012

LIBBY AHLUWALIA
ALEX & JAYNE MARKLEW

Acknowledgements

©a Alpha Course p223, Alamy 240(b), Alamy/Aliki Sapountzi p107(b), Alamy/Andre Jenny p99, Alamy/Andrew Fox p220,Alamy/APG p127,Alamy/Ark Religion p68(t),Alamy/Art Kowalsky p23(t),Alamy/Asia Images pp144(c), 217, Alamy/Brownstock p126(t),Alamy/Charles Sturge p64,Alamy/Charlotte Thege p165, Alamy/Clive Sawyer p202(b),Alamy/Coaster p124,Alamy/Countryside Collections/Homer Skyes p102,Alamy/Cymru p197,Alamy/David Grossman p218, Alamy/David Hoffmann p48(t),Alamy/David Wolf-Young p234,Alamy/Fabienne Fossez p117(t),Alamy/Frantzesco Kangaris p117(b),Alamy/Geopic p171,Alamy/Gordon Scammell p143,Alamy/GregBalfour p86(t),Alamy/Image Source Black p126(b), Alamy/Indykb p141,Alamy/Interfoto p194,Alamy/Israel Images pp178,181(tl),190, Alamy/Jennie Hart p189(tl),Alamy/Jenny Matthews p215,Alamy/Jeremy Horner p256, Alamy/jim Batty p213,Alamy/Jim West pp108, 208, Alamy/Joe Fox Tunisia p79, Alamy/John Warburton-Lee p48,Alamy/Jon Arnold Images p71,Alamy/Jorge Fernandez p33, Alamy/Kirk Treakle p62,Alamy/L Zacherie p255, Alamy/Leonid Serebrennikov p68(b),Alamy/Libby Welch p211,Alamy/Libby Welsh p146, Alamy/Lifestyle p216, Alamy/Look Studio p229, Alamy/Louise Batalla Duran p78, Alamy/Marta Demartini p210, Alamy/Marco Secchi p12 (b),Alamy/Mario Ponta p130,Alamy/Mark Baigent p49(b), Alamy/Mark Downey p53, Alamy/Martin Norris p186,Alamy/Mega Press p225, Alamy/Mira p90,Alamy/MMP p243,Alamy/Nathan Benn p180(tl),Alamy/Network Photographers p92(l), Alamy/Nick Hanna p135, Alamy/Paula Solloway p19,Alamy/Paula Solloway p259, Alamy/Philip Wolmouth p76,Alamy/Louise Batalla Duran p32,Alamy/Photolocation Ltd p144(b),Alamy/Ray Roberts p182(c),Alamy/Robert Harding Picture Library p69(b),Alamy/Ros Drinkwater p201,Alamy/S&R Greenhill p48(cl),49(bl), Alamy/Sally & Richard Greenhill p156(tl), Alamy/Steven May p46,Alamy/Stock Connection Blue p144(tl),Alamy/Superstock p252, Alamy/Tibor Bognar p70,Alamy/Trinity Mirror/Mirrorpix p152, Alamy/Graham Harrison p148, Alamy/Witold Skrypczak p69(t), Alamy/World Religions Photo Library p70, Alamy/Yadid Levy p92(l);
Art Directors & Trip pp58,63,180(bl),184,188,236;
Bridgeman Art Library/Galleria degli Uffizi, Florence, Italy, Alinari pp11, 12(t); Bridgeman Art library/Museum of Fine Arts, Boston, Massachusetts, USA p127(tl);
CAFOD p172;
Corbis/Ariel Skelley p14,Corbis/Kapoor Baldev/Sygma p13,Corbis/Sylvia Morara p182(tl),Corbis/Tim Wright p30(b);
Fotolia pp43(all),53, 54,115(b),127(r),131,138,182(r),240, Fotolia/Agatha Brown p9, Fotolia/G Palmer p12 (r), Fotolia/Galina Barskaya p12(c), Fotolia/Jaren Wickland p12(cl),Fotolia/Monkey Business p15(bl);
Getty Images pp193, 199, 212, 245, 247, 251, Getty Images/AFP p201, Getty Images/Creative p94;
iStockphoto pp 22, 24 (all),26 (all), 27, 28, 29(t), 30(t), 31(t&r),44, 51(t), 60(all), 72, 73, 74, 75, 77, 89, 91(all), 92, 93, 110, 117(all), 137(all),144(l), 144(tr&br),158(br),162, 173,175,176,179,181, 185, 189, 195,222, 233, 239, iStockphoto/Aldo Murillo p6, , iStockphoto.com/Bart Coenders 115, iStockphoto/Eric Foltz p7, iStockphoto.com/Ericsphotography p240(tl), iStockphoto.com/Eduardo Jose p240 (bl), iStockphoto/G Studio p8(c), iStockphoto/Kemter p15(l), iStockphoto.com/Lise Gagne p240(r),   iStockphoto.com/Ronan pp8(t), 21, iStockphoto.com/Wilson Valentin p240(cl);
Kobal Collection/Marquis Films/Philippe Antonello p238(r), Kobal Collection/Universal/ Ralph J Nelson p233;
Mary Evans Picture Library p39,
Philip Hollis p235,
Press Association/Rickett/PA Archive p105,
Rex Features p149,155(cl),168,Rex Features p202(t), Rex Features p241(l), Rex Features p107(t), Rex Features p88, Rex Features/Cater News Agency Ltd p155(tr), Rex Features/Charles Sykes p241(r), Rex Features/Dan Towers p231, Rex Features/Everett Collections p160 Rex Features/Eye Ubiquitous p103, Rex Features/ITV p238 (l), Rex Features/Kippa Matthews p216, Rex Features/NBCU Photobank p56, Rex Features/Ray Tang p155(tl), Rex Features/Sipa Press p100, Rex Features/Sipa Press p38,
Rex Features/Solent News & Photo Agency p253;
Science Photo Library/David Gifford p111;
Wikipedia p29(b), 41.

p.105 '"I forgive you", mother tells racist thugs who killed son' by Nigel Bunyan, 1 December 2005 © Telegraph Media Group Limited 2005; p.114 *Good religion needs good science* by Rev Dr Malcolm Brown, the Church of England www.cofe.anglican.org; p.116 © PETA Europe Ltd, www.peta.org.uk; p.133 Wedding vows quoted from the Church of England www.cofe.anglican.org; p134 Wedding vows quoted from the Church of England www.cofe.anglican.org; p.204 Legal and Criminal Justice, *Criminal Justice*, from the Church of England www.cofe.anglican.org; p.206 Legal and Criminal Justice, *Capital Punishment*, from the Church of England www.cofe.anglican.org; p.215 Statement of affirmation © Trinity – St Paul's United Church Celebrating Diversity Commitee p.241 Labour Party Manifesto 'Forward not back' (2005) p.245 'Voters turn against war in Afghanistan' by Nigel Morris and Kim Sengupta, The Independent 28/07/2009, www.independent.co.uk

Bible scriptures are taken fom the *Holy Bible: New International Version* (Hodder & Stoughton, 2006)

Quotes from the Qur'an are taken from *The Meaning of the Holy Qur'an* (Amana Publications, 2004)

Quotes from the Bhagavad Gita are taken from *The Bhagavad Gita* (Nilgiri Press, The Blue Mountain Center of Meditation, 2007)

Quotes from the Catechism of the Catholic Church are taken from www.vatican.va © Libreria Editrice Vaticana

© 2009 Folens Limited, on behalf of the authors.

United Kingdom: Folens Publishers, Waterslade House, Thame Road, Haddenham, Buckinghamshire, HP17 8NT.

Email: folens@folens.com Website: www.folens.com

Ireland: Folens Publishers, Greenhills Road, Tallaght, Dublin 24.

Email: info@folens.ie Website: www.folens.ie

Editor: Jane Moses

Text design and layout: RJ Design

Picture researcher: RJ Design

Illustrator(s): Martin Sanders, Jorge Santillan, Pulsar Studio

Cover design: Form, www.form.uk.com and Rosa Capacchione

Front cover images: © Getty images (above); © Peter Zurek/Fotolia (middle left); © Geronimo/Fotolia (middle right); © Freenah/Fotolia (bottom left); © Larry Hardin/Fotolia (bottom right)

The websites recommended in this publication were correct at the time of going to press, however, websites may have been removed or web addresses changed since that time. Folens has made every attempt to suggest websites that are reliable and appropriate for student's use. It is not unknown for unscrupulous individuals to put unsuitable material on websites that may be accessed by students. Teachers should check all websites before allowing students to access them. Folens is not responsible for the content of external websites.

For general spellings Folens adheres to the *Oxford Dictionary of English*, Second Edition (Revised), 2005.

First published 2009 by Folens Limited.

Every effort has been made to contact copyright holders of material used in this publication. If any copyright holder has been overlooked, we will be pleased to make any necessary arrangements.

British Library Cataloguing in Publication Data. A catalogue record for this publication is available from the British Library.

ISBN   978-1-85008-439-6   Folens code   FD4396

Contents

PHILOSOPHY 1

Nature of God

This section will help you understand Christian beliefs about God and encourages you to decide whether you agree with them.

EXAM FOCUS

Christians are **monotheists**, which means that they believe there is only one God. They believe that God is unique: nothing else is like God. They believe that although people cannot usually detect God using any of their five senses, God exists everywhere, controls the universe and has relationships with his creation.

Christians believe God has qualities which make him different from everything else. They believe that God is **omnipresent**, **omnipotent**, **omniscient**, **omnibenevolent** and **eternal**. They believe that he is the creator of the world.

For **Discussion**

What does the word 'God' mean to you? If you met someone who had never heard the word 'God' before, how would you explain what it means?

Activity 1

How do you think you would know if God exists or not? What evidence would you look for, to find out whether there is or isn't a God?

1 Omnipresent

Omnipresent means 'present everywhere'. Christians believe that God is everywhere at all times, throughout the universe. In the story of Jonah in the Bible, Jonah tried to hide from God, because he didn't like the job God had given him to do. Jonah imagined that God lived in just one place, so he thought if he went somewhere different, he would be able to get away from God.

> *But Jonah ran away from the Lord and headed for Tarshish. He went down to Joppa, where he found a ship bound for that port. After paying the fare, he went aboard and sailed for Tarshish to flee from the Lord.*
>
> **(Jonah 1: 3)**

Of course, in the story God knew exactly where Jonah was, and Jonah ended up being swallowed by a big fish and taken back to the job God had given him. The writer of the story seems to be making fun of Jonah for not realizing that it is impossible to hide from God, because God is omnipresent.

▲ *Christians believe that God is omnipresent, so Jonah was foolish to try and hide from God.*

2 Omnipotent

Christians believe that God is omnipotent, which means all-powerful. They believe that God can do everything; nothing is beyond God's power. He can create something just by saying 'Let there be…', and it comes into existence. They believe God can perform miracles; he can heal people who are ill, and can bring the dead back to life. He has power over the natural world and can make the sun stop or the waves of the sea stand still if he wants to.

> " *I am the Lord, the God of all mankind. Is anything too hard for me?* "
>
> **(Jeremiah 32:27)**

Some people think that the whole idea of omnipotence makes no sense. Could God create a stone so heavy that he could not lift it? Or a knot that he could not untie? Christians often answer this problem by saying that God's omnipotence means that God can do anything that makes logical sense.

Could God tell a lie, or die? Perhaps there are some things that God cannot do, because of his nature. Christians say that nothing is too difficult for God, but there are many things that God would never choose to do, because God is a perfectly loving being.

3 Omniscient

Omniscient means 'all-knowing'. Christians believe that God knows everything that can be known. There is nothing which is secret or hidden from God. God knows every event that has ever happened, and every thought and idea anyone has ever had. He knows all the answers to every question, and God never makes a mistake. When Christians talk about God being all-knowing, they do not just mean that God is like the biggest encyclopaedia. They also mean that God is wise, and always knows the best thing to do.

> " *Praise be to the name of God for ever and ever; wisdom and power are his.* "
>
> **(Daniel 2:20)**

4 Omnibenevolent

Omnibenevolent means 'all-loving' or 'all-good'. Christians believe that God has perfect love for his creation. They believe that everything God does is good, even if people cannot always understand it.

Because Christians believe that all love comes from God, they believe that every loving relationship in the world has God in it. When people experience love in a family, with their friends, or with a special partner, they are also experiencing God, even if they don't realize it.

> " *And so we know and rely on the love God has for us. God is love. Whoever lives in love lives in God, and God in him.* "
>
> **(1 John 4:16)**

▲ *Christians believe that all love comes from God, and that God is in every loving relationship.*

One of the central teachings of Christianity is that God showed his love for the world in the life, teaching and death of Jesus. They believe that when Jesus was born, he was the Son of God coming to live in the world to show his love for humanity. They believe that Jesus died on the cross as a sacrifice for human sin, showing that God loves the world enough to suffer and die so that people could have everlasting life in heaven.

> " *For God so loved the world that he gave his one and only Son, that whoever believes in him shall not perish but have eternal life.* "
>
> **(John 3:16)**

Practise your **evaluation** skills.

'A good God should not punish people or get angry with them.'

Discuss the statement. You should use different, supported points of view and a personal viewpoint. You must refer to Christianity in your answer.

This should be a detailed answer. You need to think about why some people might disagree with the statement, and why other people might agree with it. You also need to remember to include a Christian point of view, and explain your own opinion.

Start by saying what a Christian might think. Does the Bible have rules in it? What does God do if people disobey the rules? Try to explain why a Christian would think that God should punish people when they do wrong.

Then give a different point of view. Perhaps someone who is not a Christian would think that God should always be forgiving, and not mind how people behave. Give reasons to support this point of view.

Then give your own opinion – do people need rules to follow, or should they just do what they like? If there is a God, should God try to make people keep to the rules?

This will help you in the exam when you answer part (e) questions.

▲ *What does it mean to say you can never step in the same river twice?*

Christians also believe that because God is all-loving, he sets the standards of goodness for the world, giving people rules so that they know what to do and how to treat each other. These rules can be found in the Bible, and in the teachings of the Church. The Bible has many stories of people who disobey God's rules and are punished because of it. Sometimes God punishes individuals for the wrong they have done, and sometimes he punishes the whole people, by sending in their enemies to conquer the country. God also rewards people when they are faithful to him, for example he promises Abraham that he will have many descendants who will have a land of their own:

> *The whole land of Canaan, where you are now an alien, I will give as an everlasting possession to you and your descendants after you; and I will be their God.*
> **(Genesis 17:8)**

Many Christians also believe that the conscience can be a good way of discovering God's rules for humanity. Christians pray about their moral choices and hope that God will help them understand the right decisions to make.

5 Eternal

All things in the universe begin and end. They have limits, and they change. The ancient Greek philosopher Heraclitus was famous for saying 'You can never step into the same river twice'. He meant that if you try and repeat an experience, it will never be quite the same. The river will have changed – and so will you. You and the river both get older and change and develop. Everything in the universe is always changing, which is why 'you can never step into the same river twice'.

But God, according to Christians, is eternal. When Christians say that God is eternal, they mean that God is outside time. God exists in the past, the present and the future. There was no time that God did not exist, and there will never be a time in the future when God does not exist any more. God has no beginning and no end, and God doesn't change or develop because he is always perfect.

In this Christian hymn, the shortness of human life is compared with the eternal nature of God:

> *Frail as summer's flower we flourish*
> *Blows the wind and it is gone,*
> *But while mortals rise and perish*
> *God endures unchanging on.*
> **(H. F. Lyte)**

Many Christians believe that God can see the past, the present and the future all at the same time, so that God knows all the choices we will make and what will happen to each of us throughout our lives.

I'm a Christian, and I believe that because God is eternal, he knows what my future will be. This makes me feel confident because I know that God has a plan for my life, and that whatever happens, it will be because that's the way God meant it to be. Even though I can't understand why bad things sometimes happen, God understands, and I know that I can trust God's plans.

Leng

However, other Christians think that if God knows the future before it happens, then we can't make real choices for ourselves. It would be as if God has already decided for us what we were going to do. So they believe that God knows the past and the present, but not the future.

I'm a Christian too, but I believe God gives us freedom to make our own choices. God gives us opportunities but lets us plan our own lives.

Sam

6 Creator of the world

Christians believe that the world is not just here by accident. They believe that it was deliberately made by God, who used his unlimited power and wisdom to create the whole universe and everything in it.

> ❝ *In the beginning God created the heavens and the earth.* ❞
>
> **(Genesis 1:1)**

Christians believe that the universe and everything in it was made by God the creator. Because Christians believe that God created the world, they think that people have a duty to look after the planet. They also believe that human life is God's creation and should be treated with great respect.

Christian belief about the Trinity

It can be difficult for people to understand the belief that God is the maker of the whole universe, but at the same time be interested in the thoughts and actions of each person. Why would such a powerful being as God care about what goes on in the life of one small human, when he has the whole universe to take care of?

Christians try to explain how God can do this through the **doctrine of the Trinity**. The doctrine of the Trinity says that God can be understood in three different ways: as God the Father, God the Son, and God the Holy Spirit. Christians sometimes refer to the Father, Son and Holy Spirit as the 'three persons of the Trinity'.

Christians sometimes use the image of the shamrock to show how one God can be three 'persons' at the same time. The shamrock has three leaves which are all separate but they are still the same plant.

This idea of God as Father, Son and Holy Spirit was developed by the early Christian Church. It can be seen in the Bible. At the end of Matthew's Gospel, for example, Jesus appears to his disciples after he has risen from the dead, and he tells them:

> **Therefore go and make disciples of all nations, baptising them in the name of the Father and of the Son and of the Holy Spirit.**
> **(Matthew 28:19)**

When Paul wrote to the new Christian Church in Corinth, he sent them this greeting:

> **May the grace of the Lord Jesus Christ, and the love of God, and the fellowship of the Holy Spirit be with you all.**
> **(2 Corinthians 13:14)**

So, from the very earliest days of Christianity, the idea of God was formed being 'three persons in one': Father, Son and Holy Spirit. Christians do not believe that there are three different gods. They believe in just one God, because they are monotheists. But they think that God has three different aspects.

In a church service, the priest might bless the people by saying 'In the name of the Father, the Son and the Holy Spirit'.

God the Father

When Christians call God 'Father', they are using a **metaphor** (a symbolic way of saying something). The idea of God being a father has several meanings:

- It means that God gives life and brought people into existence, just as a human father is needed to produce a baby.
- It means that God looks after his creation and provides for it by giving sun and rain and all the things necessary for food to grow, just as a human father provides for his children.

▲ A shamrock has three leaves but they are all part of the same plant.

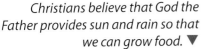

Christians believe that God the Father provides sun and rain so that we can grow food. ▼

9

- It means that God is in a position of authority, giving rules, rewards and punishments, just as a human father tries to bring up his children by teaching them what is right.

- It means that God is always ready to have a relationship with his people and wants to help them with the problems of their daily lives, just as a human father wants to have a close relationship with his children.

- It means that God loves his people, protecting them from harm, making sacrifices for them, caring about them and forgiving them when they do wrong, just as a human father loves his children.

When Christians call God 'Father', they mean that God's relationship with people is like a good father's relationship with his children.

Christians believe that God is perfect and has none of the faults a human father might have, but they still find the metaphor useful as a way of understanding something about the nature of God.

Some Christians think that calling God 'Father' can cause problems, because it might encourage people to think of God as being male and not female. In the past, the term 'Father' was a good metaphor, because the father of the household had much more authority than the mother, and had much more opportunity to provide for the children. Because society has changed since the time the Bible was written, some Christians like to refer to God as 'Mother' as well as 'Father', to show that God is not limited by gender.

God the Son

One of the central beliefs on Christianity is that Jesus came to earth as the Son of God. Christians believe that Jesus was not just an example of a very good human being. They believe that he was God **incarnate**. 'Incarnate' means 'made flesh', so when Christians say that Jesus was God incarnate they mean that he was God in a physical, human body.

> *Your attitude should be the same as that of Christ Jesus: Who, being in very nature God, did not consider equality with God something to be grasped, but made himself nothing, taking the very nature of a servant, being made in human likeness. And being found in appearance as a man, he humbled himself and became obedient to death – even death on a cross!*
>
> **(Philippians 2:5–8)**

In the Bible, when Jesus' mother Mary first found out that she was pregnant, it was an angel who gave her the news. Mary found it hard to understand how she could be pregnant because she was still a virgin. The angel explained that baby Jesus would not have a human father but would be conceived by the power of the Holy Spirit:

> *The angel answered, 'The Holy Spirit will come upon you, and the power of the Most High will overshadow you. So the holy one to be born will be called the Son of God.'*
>
> **(Luke 1:35)**

◀ *This painting by the artist Sandro Botticelli shows the angel Gabriel telling Mary that she is going to have a child through the work of the Holy Spirit.*

God the Holy Spirit

The idea of God as Holy Spirit is probably the most difficult part of the Trinity to understand. The Holy Spirit (sometimes known as the Holy Ghost) is believed to be the aspect of God that lives in the world today, working through the lives of Christians. Many Christians believe that the Holy Spirit was present during the creation of the world.

Christians believe that the Holy Spirit:

- helps them to live as Christians in all aspects of their lives

- gives them courage at difficult times

- strengthens their faith and helps them to be confident when talking to others about Christianity

- guides them to make the right decisions

- joins them together with other Christians in a community of believers

- gives them special 'spiritual gifts' such as the ability to communicate with God in prayer and the ability to understand the Bible correctly.

Christians believe that the Holy Spirit guides preachers when they lead services of worship, helping them to choose the right things to say.

The New Testament teaches that Christians should consider themselves to be 'temples' of the Holy Spirit:

> " *Don't you know that you yourselves are God's temple and that God's Spirit lives in you?* "
> **(1 Corinthians 3:16)**

For Discussion

Do you think Christians present an idea of God that is too male? Should they talk about God as 'she' as well as 'he'?

By this, they mean that they should remember that God, as the Holy Spirit, lives with them and works through them in the things that they do – so they should treat their own bodies with respect, as the place where God lives.

Exam Practice

Practise your skill in **demonstrating knowledge and understanding**.

Explain Christian teaching about the Trinity.

For this question, you need to show that you understand what Christians mean when they talk about God as 'three in one'. You should explain what they mean by each of 'Father', 'Son', and 'Holy Spirit'. In your answer, show that you understand that Christians believe these are all aspects of the same God. For high marks, try to use key terms such as monotheism.

This will help you in the exam when you answer part (d) questions.

◄ *In this painting of the baptism of Jesus, the white dove represents the Holy Spirit coming to give Jesus power to begin his teaching. In Christian art, the Holy Spirit is often shown in the form of a white dove, because in the story of Jesus' baptism, the Holy Spirit appeared like a dove as a symbol to show that Jesus had been given power from God.*

Is the doctrine of the Trinity a help in understanding God?

Ruby

I'm a Christian, and I think the doctrine of the Trinity helps me to understand God. We all have different sides to our personalities, and people relate to us in different ways. I'm a sister, and I'm a daughter, and I'm a student, and I'm a dancer, and I'm a babysitter. My brother doesn't see me in the same way that my teachers see me! But this doesn't mean I'm lots of different people. It's the same with God. Christians can relate to God in different ways at different times, but it's still only one God. We've thought of God as three in one all through Christian history, and it's a way of thinking that has helped Christians for centuries.

I'm a Hindu, and I think God can be understood in hundreds of different ways, not just three. We believe that God can take many different forms, such as Ganesha, Kali, Shiva and Krishna. So I agree with Ruby when she says that one God can have different ways of relating to people, but I don't agree that it has to be just three different ways. I think the Christian view is right, but only up to a point.

Nina

Tom

Yousif

I disagree. As a Muslim, I believe that it is wrong to think of God as anything other than one. God can't be split up into different parts like that. There is just one God; God can't be 'three in one'.

Because I don't believe in God, I don't think the doctrine of the Trinity is helpful for anything. I don't think it makes sense to talk about God being three and also being one. I don't think we need to find ways to understand God, because God doesn't exist. That's my opinion, anyway.

Practise your **evaluation** skills.

'The doctrine of the Trinity is a helpful way for Christians to understand the nature of God.'

Discuss the statement. You should use different, supported points of view and a personal viewpoint. You must refer to Christianity in your answer.

There are more marks available for this kind of question, so you need to give a longer answer with several paragraphs.

In your first paragraph, explain what a Christian might think about the doctrine of the Trinity. You might need to explain what the Trinity is, but remember that the marks here are for your skill in evaluation, so don't spend too long describing. Say why a Christian might find this doctrine helpful and give a reason, or more than one reason, supporting that point of view.

Now give a different point of view, where someone disagrees and thinks that the doctrine is not helpful at all, or not very helpful. It could be the opinion of a member of another religion, or the opinion of someone with no religious belief. Remember to give reasons explaining why someone might hold this point of view. If you have time, you could also explain a further point of view as well – but in an exam, be careful to keep to the time limit.

In the last paragraph, you need to give an evaluation of the ideas you have just been explaining. Which point of view do you think is stronger, and why? What do you think are the weaknesses of the other point of view (the one that you disagree with)? Conclude by making it clear what your own opinion is.

This will help you in the exam when you answer part (e) questions.

Belief in God

This section helps you to consider the various reasons Christians give to support their beliefs.

EXAM FOCUS

Growing up in a Christian family

Christians might believe in God because they grew up in Christian families. Perhaps their parents were Christians, and took them to church from a young age. Perhaps they went to a Christian school, where they learnt more about the Christian way of life. If children grow up in Christian families, they meet a lot of other Christians. They can see people they respect taking part in Christian worship. So a Christian way of understanding the world might come naturally to them, and they might not be able to imagine what it would be like to have no belief in God. People might have belief in the teachings of Christianity because they were brought up as Christians.

The world seems to be designed

Many Christians argue that when you look at the world, you can see that it is full of pattern and order. There are scientific laws which we can discover, such as the law of gravity or laws of magnetism. There are patterns all around us in the natural world, such as on a leaf or on the wings of a butterfly. The seasons follow in the same order every year. The planets move in ways that we can predict. Even the structure of the cells within our bodies has pattern and order.

To some people, this pattern and order is evidence for the existence of God. They argue that the world looks as if it has been designed. It does not look as if it just happened by random chance, but seems carefully planned – and the only person who could have designed a whole universe is God.

In the Bible, one of the writers explains that we only need to look at the sky to see evidence of God's design in the universe:

> The heavens declare the glory of God;
> the skies proclaim the work of his hands.
> **(Psalm 19:1)**

There must be a reason why the universe is here

The fact that the universe exists can be used as a reason to support belief in God. Christians might point out that nothing exists unless there is a cause to make it happen. Plants can exist because of seeds, sunlight, water and oxygen; rocks can exist because of the activity of volcanoes or glaciers or rivers; whatever we can think of in the world has some kind of cause which made it happen.

But what about the universe itself? Christians might argue that the universe, like everything else, must have had a cause to make it happen. If nothing had caused the universe, then the universe would not be here – but here it is. Many Christians would say that only God could cause a whole universe to begin.

Many Christians argue that the universe cannot have caused itself. There must be a reason why the universe exists, and that reason is God.

This argument for the existence of God is known as the **cosmological argument**.

We all have a sense of right and wrong

Another argument Christians might use to explain their belief in God is known as the **moral argument**. This argument says that we all have a sense of right and wrong. We know what we should do, even if we don't always do it, and we feel guilty when we do something we know is wrong. Where does this sense of right and wrong come from? According to some Christians, it comes from God. God gives us the ability to tell right from wrong, and God lets us know through our consciences which choices are the ones we should make.

Some people have personal religious experiences

Many Christians believe in God because they have had a special kind of experience, which they understood to be an experience of God. This might have taken the form of a dream, a vision, hearing a voice, or having a strong sense that God is near. Sometimes people have a strong sense that God has answered their prayers, or that God has a special job for them to do.

For Discussion

Do you think that the world looks as if someone designed it? How would you explain order and pattern in the world?

Mother Teresa of Calcutta had a personal religious experience and became convinced that God wanted her to go and work with the very poorest people of India. ▼

Exam Practice

Practise your skills in **demonstrating knowledge and understanding**.

Give three reasons why Christians might believe in God.

This is a short-answer question, so you only need to be quite brief. For example, you could say something like '1. They might believe in God because the world appears to be designed.'

This will help you in the exam when you answer part (b) questions.

Why might people disagree with Christian belief about God?

I think people used to believe in God because a lot of things in life were a mystery to them. They didn't understand where different species come from, or why the sun rises every morning, or how people naturally get better from illnesses. So they used the idea of God to explain it.

But now, science has answers to questions like these, and we don't need religious belief any more.

Other religions have different beliefs

Some people might disagree with Christian beliefs because they come from a different religious tradition. Jews and Muslims, for example, disagree with Christian beliefs about Jesus as the Son of God. Jews and Muslims argue that because there is only one God who is beyond space and time, it is impossible that God should have come into the world as a human being. God cannot be split into different parts, they argue; and a human being could never be God, because God is perfect whereas humans are not. Jews and Muslims think that Christian belief about Jesus as God in human form is **blasphemy** (saying false things about God).

But Christians might respond to this by saying that the doctrine of the Trinity shows three different ways of understanding God; it is not saying that God can be split into parts. Christians might also respond by saying that because God is omnipotent, God can come into the world in human form while still being perfect – there is nothing that God cannot do.

Lack of evidence

Some people might disagree with Christian belief about God because they might think there just isn't enough evidence that God exists. In our usual everyday lives, we can't see or hear God. Although we can see beautiful things in the world around us, and enjoy loving relationships, there are also ugly things in the world and miserable relationships. So perhaps there is just not enough evidence to show that Christians are right in their beliefs about God.

Christians might respond by saying that the evidence is there, but that people have to look for it, with faith. They might say that God has given plenty of evidence, in the world around us and especially by sending Jesus. Christians might say that God doesn't want to force people to believe in him by being too obvious. Instead, God gives people the choice to believe or not to believe.

Science can give the answers

Others might say that Christians are wrong to believe in God because scientists can explain things that people in the past used to think were caused by God. Scientists have explanations for the beginning of the universe, and for the evolution of different species. Sometimes science can explain events that might seem to be miracles.

Christians might answer this by saying that science gives one kind of explanation, and religion gives another kind, but both can go together.

I'm a scientist, and I'm also a Christian. Science helps me to understand how the world works – and the more I learn about science, the more clearly I can see evidence of God in the world.

Science shows me how things work, and my religious belief teaches me that it's all here because of the creator God.

People can be moral without being Christian

Some people might argue that the human sense of right and wrong does not have to come from God. There are plenty of good people in the world who have no religious beliefs. Perhaps our sense of right and wrong just comes from the way that we were brought up, and has nothing to do with God. They might also point out that there have been Christians who have done some terrible things. For example, some Christians in the eighteenth century made their money from trading human slaves. So belief in God does not always make you a better person.

Christians might respond by saying that because God is perfectly good, all goodness comes from God. Christians who ask for the help of the Holy Spirit should be in a better position to make right moral decisions than other people who have no beliefs.

People invent God to make themselves feel better

Some people say that religious belief is just for people who find it hard to cope with the real world. They say that believing in God is a bit like making up an imaginary friend. Perhaps Christians want to feel there is someone looking after them, and they want to believe there is life after death, so they invent a God to comfort themselves.

Christians might answer this by saying that there are a lot of very strong people who have religious belief. There are people who have done extremely brave things, and risked their lives, because of their faith. They might also say that of course a loving God will be a comfort for those who believe in him.

Exam Practice

Practise your **evaluation** skills.

'*Christians have good reasons for believing in God.*'

Discuss the statement. You should use different, supported points of view and a personal viewpoint. You must refer to Christianity in your answer.

This should be a longer answer. You need to write in paragraphs rather than just a short sentence.

Start by saying why some people might agree with the statement. Look back at the different reasons Christians give to support their belief in God, and try to write a summary, showing why Christians think they have good reasons to believe in God.

Then say why other people might disagree, and think that there are no good reasons for believing in God. Support the ideas with reasons.

In your conclusion, say what you think. Do you think that the arguments given by Christians are strong, or weak? Are the reasons against belief in God convincing? Explain your own point of view, and make sure you use the word 'because'.

This will help you in the exam when you answer part (e) questions.

Miracles

This section will help you understand Christian beliefs about how God intervenes in the world, and will help you make up your own mind about these beliefs.

EXAM FOCUS

What is a miracle?

A **miracle** is an event brought about by God which seems to happen against all odds, or which seems to break the laws of nature. For example, someone might be trapped by a fallen building after an earthquake and be pulled alive from the wreckage after several days when everyone had given up hope, this might be seen as a miracle. Or a blind person might suddenly get her sight back, and doctors might not be able to give any explanation of why it happened.

The Bible has many examples of miracle stories. The New Testament writers often show Jesus performing miracles – they wanted to show that Jesus had the power of God and that he could break the laws of nature.

◀ *This picture illustrates a miracle story from the Gospels, where Jesus meets a man who was born blind, and gives him sight.*

Activity 1

Develop your knowledge of Christian belief about miracles.

1. Use a Bible to look up these stories of Jesus performing miracles. What do the stories say that Jesus did?

Matthew 8: 2 – 3   Luke 8: 22 – 25   Luke 7: 14 – 15

This will support your answers in questions that ask for knowledge and understanding.

2. Do you believe that these events really happened? Explain why, or why not.

This will support your answers in questions that ask for evaluation.

For an event to be a called a miracle rather than just a piece of very good luck, it has to be done by God. So people who don't believe in God will not believe that miracles ever happen – they will just think that the people involved were very lucky.

Why don't some people believe in miracles?

Some people might disagree with Christian belief in miracles. An **atheist** (someone who doesn't believe in God) might argue that it is superstitious to believe in miracles. Atheists might say that when unusual things happen, there is always going to be a scientific explanation that does not involve God. If someone suddenly gets better from an illness that was said to be incurable, perhaps the diagnosis was wrong in the first place. If someone tells a story about waves parting or water turning into wine, perhaps that person was making it up, or exaggerating to get attention. Perhaps they wanted a miracle to happen so much that they convinced themselves it actually had.

People might also argue that if God can really do miracles, then he should do them more often. If God is perfectly loving and God can give blind people their sight back, then why are there still blind people in the world? If God can calm storms, then why do so many people die in floods?

God intervening in the world through Jesus

Christians believe that Jesus was God incarnate (God in a physical, human form). They believe that God was at work in the world through Jesus:

- when Jesus spoke, he gave the words of God, teaching people how to live together and telling them stories to show what the kingdom of God is like

- when Jesus healed people through miracles, he showed God's love and power

- when Jesus died on the cross, he showed God's willingness to sacrifice himself for humanity

- when Jesus rose from the dead, he showed God's promise of eternal life.

God intervening in the world through the Holy Spirit

According to Christian belief, God works in the world today through the lives of Christians, by the Holy Spirit. The Bible says that after Jesus had died, risen from the dead and gone back to heaven, Jesus' followers were scared and didn't know what to do. They had lost their leader, and they were afraid to talk about him because they might be arrested and killed. But God sent the Holy Spirit to them and, after that, they were able to go out into the world to tell people about Christianity.

Christians say that the Holy Spirit continues to work in the lives of Christians today, by:

- helping them to understand what God wants from them

- giving them the courage to do what God wants

- helping them to tell others about their faith

- helping them to work co-operatively with others

- helping them to resist doing wrong.

> *The fruit of the Spirit is love, joy, peace, patience, kindness, goodness, faithfulness, gentleness and self-control.*
>
> **(Galatians 5:22)**

Christians believe that the Holy Spirit can be seen working in the world in the lives of people who care for others. ▼

Exam Practice

Practise your skills in **demonstrating knowledge and understanding**.

Explain Christian beliefs about God intervening in the world.

In this answer, you should try to write a paragraph. You can include several different ideas. Try and explain what Christians believe about God intervening in the world through miracles; God intervening in the world through Jesus; and God intervening in the world through the Holy Spirit.

This will help you in the exam when you answer part (d) questions.

Glossary

Atheism – the belief that there is no God

Blasphemy – saying false things about God

Cosmological argument – the argument that says God must have caused the universe

Eternal – everlasting or without end. Christians believe God exists in the past, present and future

God incarnate – God in human form

Metaphor – a symbolic way of describing something

Miracle – a special event believed to have been caused by God, which breaks the laws of nature

Monotheism – the belief that there is only one God

Moral argument – the argument that says our understanding of right and wrong must have come from God

Omnibenevolent – perfectly good and perfectly loving

Omnipotent – all-powerful

Omnipresent – existing everywhere

Omniscient – all-knowing and all-wise

Trinity – three in one: Father, Son and Holy Spirit

PHILOSOPHY 1

Public and private worship

This section will help you understand Christian ideas about worshipping God.

What is worship?

For religious people it is important to believe the right things and to behave in the right way, but it is also important to them to **worship** God. To 'worship' means to give something or someone great worth; to give that person or thing a central part in your life and to recognize its importance.

Christians believe that they need to spend time worshipping God, remembering that they are created by God and that they should offer their lives to God. When Christians worship, they focus their minds on their beliefs about the greatness of God. They give praise and thanks to God, remembering the things they have done wrong and asking for forgiveness. They also try to spend quiet time listening to God and trying to understand what he wants them to do.

Worship is central in the lives of Christian believers. ▶

Exam Practice

Practice your skills in **demonstrating knowledge and understanding**.

What is meant by 'worship'?

This requires only a short answer, so you can be quite brief. You need to give a definition of the word 'worship' and then show that you understand it by giving an example.

This will help you in the exam when you answer part (a) questions.

For Christians, it is important to worship God in private and in public, by joining with other Christians at a special place of worship and taking part in a church service.

Why do Christians worship together?

In the Bible, Jesus taught that people should pray together and share their concerns, and that God would be with them as they meet:

 For where two or three come together in my name, there am I with them.
(Matthew 18:20)

Christians believe that if they meet together for worship, as well as worshipping in private, this will help them to develop their faith. Worshipping together:

- gives Christians a sense of unity with their own church and with other Christians around the world

- provides a feeling of tradition, when people worship in the same way as Christians from the past

- helps Christians to get along with each other and to find peaceful ways of resolving disagreements

- gives them the opportunity to learn from each other and look at Christianity in new ways

- enables members of a Christian community to support each other in times of difficulty.

When do Christians worship?

Sunday is the special day chosen by Christians for worship, because they believe that on Easter Sunday, Jesus rose from the dead and came back to life. They believe that one day in every seven should be set aside for rest and worship, because the Bible teaches that God wants people to do this:

 Remember the Sabbath day by keeping it holy. Six days you shall labour and do all your work, but the seventh day is a Sabbath to the Lord your God.
(Exodus 20: 8-10)

When Christians keep Sunday as a special day, they remember the commandments given to them in the Bible. They remember their belief that God created the world in six days, and rested on the seventh day. Sunday is a special day for Christians because it reminds them of their belief that Jesus rose back to life on a Sunday, after he was crucified.

Some churches hold services on other days of the week as well as Sunday; for example Roman Catholic churches usually offer extra services of **Mass** on weekdays too, so that people who have to work on Sundays can still receive Holy Communion. Christians might meet together on weekdays for activities such as Bible study, **prayer** meetings and social events.

Many Christians believe that Sunday should be made into a special time, and should be kept different from other days. They might make an effort to spend time with their families on Sundays, and avoid doing weekday chores such as shopping or making business calls.

▲ *I'm a Christian teacher, and at our school the Christian members of staff meet every Wednesday at lunchtime. We talk about different things to do with our faith, and we pray for the school and for each other. It's an important time of the week for me, because it reminds me that my faith should affect everything I do, at work as well as at home.*

Where do Christians go to worship together?

There are many different kinds of Christian places of worship. Some are enormous, beautifully decorated cathedrals that took many years to build and cost huge amounts of money. Others are simple, plain buildings that just meet the basic needs of the people who go there.

Construction of the Sagrada Familia Cathedral in Barcelona, designed by the architect Gaudí, began in 1882 and is still not completed. ▶

All different kinds of buildings can be used for Christian worship. Many Christians use buildings which were designed to be used as churches, while others use buildings which have been converted, or which are used for something else during the rest of the week; for example they might meet in a school hall. Wherever Christians meet, they believe that their place of worship is special. It provides somewhere to escape from the distractions of everyday life, and is a place where they can concentrate on God and share their faith with each other.

◀ *The church of St Peter-on-the-Wall in Essex could be the oldest church in England still used regularly for Christian worship. It dates from 654AD.*

What happens in a church service?

Within the Christian Church around the world, there are many different groups (known as denominations). For example, there are Roman Catholics, Anglicans (members of the Church of England), Methodists, Baptists, and members of the Society of Friends (more commonly known as Quakers), as well as many others. They are all Christians, but they sometimes have different ideas about which beliefs are the most important, different ideas about leadership, and different ideas about how Christianity should be understood.

There are also lots of different styles of worship. Some denominations worship in a formal way, using traditional words and prayer books. Others are less formal and more spontaneous, where the prayers are in people's own words and there is more singing.

I'm a Roman Catholic, and in my church, the service is led by the priest. We follow the service in our prayer books, so that we know what to say and when to say it. I like this style of worship, because it has a great sense of tradition. When I say the words and sing the hymns, I know that I'm joining in worship with other Catholics around the world, all saying the same thing. I'm using words my grandparents used and my grandchildren will use one day. The formal service reminds me of the greatness of God, and helps me to know I'm addressing God in the right way. If I used my own words, I might forget something important – for example, I might be distracted by what I want God to do for me, and forget to say sorry for the things I've done wrong.

I go to a Protestant church where the worship is very spontaneous and informal. We have leaders who give talks that they've prepared, but if someone in the congregation feels that the Holy Spirit wants them to speak, then that person can get up and say whatever it is that they want to say. People pray using their own words, and I like this because it gives us the opportunity to talk to God about things that are going on in our lives. Last week, we prayed for a family whose baby was born early and she's quite ill. Also, someone felt led by the Holy Spirit to remind us to keep our minds pure and be careful what we watch on television. In our services, we use a lot of music and it can get quite lively. We have guitars and drums, and often we learn new songs that have only just been written. I think this style of worship helps to keep Christianity up to date and is more attractive to young people than the old-fashioned kind.

My style of worship is very different, because I'm a member of the Society of Friends – a lot of people know us as 'Quakers'. We call our services 'meetings'. We get together in a plain and simple room, where we sit quietly, meditate and calm our minds so that God can speak to us in stillness. Sometimes, the whole meeting takes place in silence. Often, there are times when people get up and speak, but we don't have a leader or a set of words to follow. I love this kind of worship. It gives me a great sense of peace and freedom.

The interior of the church building often gives clues about the particular emphasis of a denomination. In a Roman Catholic church everyone faces the altar, which is the table where Mass is celebrated. The altar might be decorated with a special cloth, and have steps leading up to it so that everyone can clearly see it. In a church where hearing the word of God is emphasized, the **pulpit** and the lectern are prominent. The pulpit is a raised platform for the preacher, and the lectern is a stand which holds the Bible while someone reads aloud from it.

The altar in a church is the place where Holy Communion is celebrated. It reminds Christians of their belief that Jesus sacrificed himself for the sins of the world.

Many church services begin with a call to worship, where the person leading the service welcomes everyone and reminds them that they are in the presence of God, so that they can turn their minds away from other concerns and concentrate on God.

In some Christian denominations, such as the Roman Catholic Church, the most important part of worship is **Mass**, which is also known as the Eucharist or Holy Communion. This is when worshippers remember the death of Jesus, which they believe was a sacrifice for the world. They share bread (or wafers) and wine to symbolize the body and blood of Jesus. When Christians take part in this special service, they remind themselves of the last supper Jesus ate with his disciples before he was crucified.

> *For I received from the Lord what I also passed on to you: The Lord Jesus, on the night he was betrayed, took bread, and when he had given thanks, he broke it and said, 'This is my body, which is for you; do this in remembrance of me.' In the same way, after supper he took the cup, saying, 'This cup is the new covenant in my blood; do this, whenever you drink it, in remembrance of me.' For whenever you eat this bread and drink this cup, you proclaim the Lord's death until he comes.*
> **(1 Corinthians 11:23–25)**

Protestant denominations, such as the Methodist Church and the United Reformed Church, usually have an emphasis on hearing the word of God through Bible readings and in the sermon. A passage of the Bible is read out loud for everyone to hear and think about. The sermon is a talk given by the minister or another speaker, where Christian ideas are explained and people are helped to see how they can use the ideas in their own lives.

Services of Christian worship also include prayers, where believers talk to God, hymns which are a kind of prayer set to music, and times of silence. A service will usually end with a blessing or **benediction**, reminding Christians to go out into the world and put their faith into practice.

Exam Practice

Practice your skills in **demonstrating knowledge and understanding**.

Describe what Christians do when they worship together.

For this answer, you need to give an outline of the different things that happen during Christian worship. Try to use the correct terms, such as 'sermon' instead of 'talk', and try to explain them rather than simply making a list.

This will help you in the exam when you answer part (c) questions.

Christian worship at home

Christians don't just worship God on Sundays, when they go to church. They also worship on their own in private. Many Christians set aside a special time of day for quiet prayer and Bible study. They can think about their personal faith and about issues which are important to them.

◄ *I like to spend some time every day reading the Bible on my own, and praying. It helps me remember what's important, and gives me a chance to bring to God the things that matter in my life. When I read the Bible on my own, I use a study guide to help me understand and learn from the passage I'm reading.*

As a Christian, I try to worship God in everything I do. I think worship is more than just about times for prayer. Now that I'm a mum, I try and encourage the children to worship God at home by celebrating Christian festivals with them and talking to them about what it means to live a Christian life. ▼

Exam Practice

Practice your **evaluation** skills.

Do you think special buildings are necessary for Christians to worship God?

You might think that for Christians it should be possible to worship God anywhere. You could say that it does not matter whether someone is at home, at work, out in the street or in a special building, so special buildings are unnecessary. Or you might think that Christians need special buildings so that they have somewhere to meet together, and somewhere away from the distractions of everyday life.

This will help you in the exams when you answer part (e) questions.

Symbolism in Christian worship

People use symbols all the time. The words you are reading now are symbols: the shapes of the letters make up the words, and when you look at them, you understand that the shapes represent something else and have a meaning. We use symbols in mathematics: when you see a symbol such as + you know what it represents and you understand what you are supposed to do with the numbers. We use symbols on our clothes to tell us how to wash them; on our money to tell us what currency we are using; at the roadside to tell us where we can drive and how fast we should go.

Symbols are useful for several reasons:

- they give us a quick, easily recognizable way of understanding something
- they can often be understood by people who speak different languages
- they can often be understood by people who can't read
- sometimes, a symbol can 'say' more than one thing at a time
- sometimes symbols can be used to keep things secret between a small group.

For **Discussion**

Can you think of five more examples of symbols used in everyday life?

Some common Christian symbols

The best known symbol of Christianity is the cross. Christians use this symbol in all kinds of contexts. Many churches have a cross inside on the wall for Christians to look at during the service. They might also have a cross on the outside of the building, so that everyone who goes past can see that the building is a church. Crosses appear on Christian objects, such as on Bibles, church furniture and on the special clothes a priest or minister wears. Some Christians like to wear a cross on a chain around their necks.

The cross is an important symbol for Christians because it reminds them that Jesus was crucified on a wooden cross. They believe that Jesus' death took away the sin of the world and gave people the opportunity to be forgiven by God for all the wrong things they do. Christians also believe that Jesus rose back to life after his death, giving everyone who believes in him the chance of eternal life with God in heaven after they die. When Christians look at the cross, they have a lot of things to think about. They remember:

- the suffering of Jesus when he died, and this can help them to be brave during their own suffering
- the Christian belief that God forgives sins because of Jesus' death on the cross
- their hope that they will rise to a new life after death.

Other Christian symbols

Christians use the symbol of a fish as a sign to tell other people that they are Christians. The symbol dates back to the earliest days of Christianity when believers were persecuted because of their faith. They needed a secret sign so that they could recognize other Christians, so they used a code. The first letters of the Greek words for 'Jesus Christ Son of God Saviour' spell out the Greek word 'ichthus' which means 'fish'. ▼

The dove is used by Christians as a symbol of the Holy Spirit, because in the Bible story of Jesus' baptism, the Holy Spirit appeared 'like a dove'. It is also used to represent peace. ▶

The Alpha-Omega symbol is used in Christianity to show the belief that God is eternal. Alpha is the first letter of the Greek alphabet and Omega is the last letter – it is a way of saying that God is at the beginning and end of everything. ◀

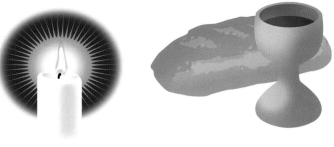
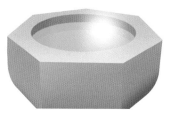

▶ Christians use the symbol of light to represent the presence of God. In the Bible, Jesus described himself as 'the light of the world', replacing evil with goodness and replacing ignorance with knowledge of God.

◀ Bread and wine are used symbolically in Christian services of Holy Communion. The bread represents the body of Jesus, and the wine represents his blood, which Christians share to remember Jesus' death on the cross.

▲ The symbol of water is used to represent cleansing. In Christianity, water is used to baptize people when they become members of the Church. It represents the washing away of sin and giving a fresh start.

For Discussion

Do you think people should be allowed to wear religious symbols to work or school?

The use of art and music to express beliefs about God

Christians have always used art and music to express their beliefs about God, although not all Christian denominations use art and music in the same way.

Art in churches

In Quaker worship (the Society of Friends) people gather in a building which is very plain and simple. There is no stained glass art, there are no statues, no needlework or paintings. Some other Protestant Christians also use buildings which are simply and plainly furnished. These Christians believe that simple surroundings help people to concentrate on God and avoid distraction. Some Christians also believe that it is better to give money to the poor than to spend it on expensive decorations for churches.

Some people think that a lot of art in a building makes it more beautiful, as a way of giving thanks to God. I can see what they mean, but I think that a very simple building is just as beautiful in its own way, and it helps me to concentrate on God.

Other Christians disagree, and think that art can be an important way of expressing religious beliefs and of giving something back to God. In the past, when not everyone could read, art was a helpful way of telling Bible stories through pictures. In a highly decorated church, everywhere Christians look they can see something which reminds them of their faith.

In Christian places of worship, art is used in many different forms:

- There might be statues of Jesus, Mary or of other Christian saints.

- Many churches have stained glass windows; sometimes they show stories from the Bible, and sometimes they are more abstract.

- Roman Catholic churches often have panels or pictures on the wall showing the stations of the cross, which are incidents from the story of the crucifixion of Jesus. Worshippers can go from one station to the next, remembering the story as they move around the church and say special prayers.

- Orthodox churches and some Roman Catholic churches use icons, which are paintings showing religious figures such as saints. These are used as a focus for prayer and worship.

- Some churches are decorated with needlework. There might be banners displaying Christian messages, or kneelers embroidered with Christian symbols. There might be embroidered cloths covering the altar or the lectern.

- Often the objects used during worship, such as the chalice for holding wine, are very beautiful works of art.

◀ *Coventry Cathedral has a beautiful tapestry showing Christian beliefs.*

Music in churches

Music also plays an important part in Christian worship. Most Christian services use some form of music as a part of worship; some churches use organ music, while others have pianos, guitars and drums. Music helps to give people a sense of belonging to a larger community when they sing hymns together, and instrumental pieces of music create an atmosphere of worship and help express feelings that might be difficult to convey in other ways.

As a church organist, I believe that making music is one of the ways that Christians can give something beautiful back to God. Music has a way of communicating feelings that are hard to put into spoken language.

Exam Practice

Practice your **evaluation** skills.

Do you think that a lot of art in a place of worship makes it difficult for believers to concentrate on God?

You might think that art should be a help for religious people. Perhaps you think it would make a place of worship seem much more special, and gives artists an opportunity to use their creativity to express their beliefs. Or you might think that a plainer building is better, so that people can focus on their thoughts without being distracted.

This will help you in the exam when you answer part (e) questions.

Music is an important part of the service in Baptist churches like this one. ▼

Prayer and meditation

This section will explain why prayer and meditation for some Christians forms an important part of their religious and spiritual experience of their faith.

Praying is talking to God, either out loud or silently, and also trying to listen to God. Christians pray when they are in church, by listening to the words of the person leading the prayers, and sometimes by saying words together with the rest of the congregation. They also pray when they are on their own, and when they are with other Christians. The best-known prayer in Christianity is one that Jesus taught and which is recorded in the Gospels of Matthew and Luke. It is known as the **Lord's Prayer**; sometimes it is said in traditional language, and sometimes in more modern language like this:

> *Our Father in heaven,*
> *hallowed be thy name.*
> *Your Kingdom come,*
> *your will be done,*
> *on earth as in heaven*
> *Give us today our daily bread.*
> *Forgive us our sins,*
> *as we forgive those who sin against us.*
> *Lead us not into temptation,*
> *but deliver us from evil.*
> *For the kingdom, the power and the glory are*
> *yours.*
> *Now and forever. Amen*

Many Christians repeat this prayer together during worship in church. The Lord's Prayer is a favourite with Christians because they are using the words of Jesus. It reminds them that they should praise God, ask for forgiveness and pray for others, as well as bringing their own needs before God. They are not just asking God to give them health, wealth and happiness, but are asking God to show them the right way to live.

Meditation involves less talking. It is about being still, emptying your mind of everyday worries, and trying to focus completely on God. Many Christians begin their times of prayer with some quiet meditation. Some try to use meditation techniques from Eastern religion as a way of listening to God and finding inner peace.

Why do people pray?

Christians pray because they believe that:

- God listens to them – they believe that God cares about each individual life, with all its worries and pleasures

- God is all-powerful, and that God can help them

- when they pray, God speaks to them

- when they take their concerns to God, God will show them a way of dealing with their problems

- praying helps them to remember to praise God and to thank God

- praying helps them to remember the things they do wrong, to ask for forgiveness and to ask for guidance in the future
- prayer unites them with other Christians around the world.

The power of prayer and answered prayers

Christians believe that prayer is a powerful way of getting things done. They believe that God answers their prayers in all kinds of ways. For example, they believe that God might answer their prayers by doing what they have asked for, such as curing someone who was ill. They believe God might answer them through their consciences, giving them a clear message about the right and wrong way to behave. Christians also believe that God answers their prayers by inspiring them to tackle issues themselves.

Many different cultures have myths and fables about people who are granted wishes by a magical creature. The character in the story is granted some wishes, which then come true. But there is often a catch. Once the wish has been granted, the character finds out that it wasn't such a good wish after all, and he wishes he had asked for something else. I think stories like these tell us lot about prayers which seem to go unanswered. I believe that God answers everyone's prayers, but he doesn't always give us the answer we want. Sometimes, he says no. We might not understand why God doesn't give us everything we ask, but as Christians we have to accept that God knows what's best for us.

Exam Practice

Practice your skills in **demonstrating knowledge and understanding.**

Explain Christian beliefs about prayer.

In your answer, show that you understand what prayer is, and why Christians think it is important to pray. You might give some examples of Christian prayers, and some examples of the kinds of things that Christians talk about in their prayers.

This will help you in the exam when you answer part (d) questions.

Food and fasting

This section will help you understand the roles of fasting and special foods in Christian belief.

EXAM FOCUS

Unlike many other religions, Christianity has no specific rules about food. Many of the earliest Christians came from a Jewish background, where they were used to following strict laws about diet (known as **kosher** rules). When the first churches began, these early Christians disagreed about food laws. Some said that Christians should carry on with the kosher laws of the Jews, while others said that Christians no longer needed to follow Jewish law. The book of Acts tells the story of a vision given to the Apostle Peter, where he was shown a wide variety of animals and was told that none of them were forbidden. This led to the Christian view that it is not necessary to keep strict food laws.

Some Christians are vegetarian, but there is no rule which says that Christians should not eat meat. Some Christians do not drink alcohol, but this is not forbidden in Christianity either. Many Christians believe that it is wrong to waste food or to spend a lot of money on luxury foods when there are hungry people in the world.

The concept of fasting

Fasting means choosing to go without food. It can involve going without any food at all, but also it can mean giving up only certain kinds of food, such as meat or sweets. In some religions, such as Islam, fasting is an important part of worship, but in Christianity there are different views about whether fasting is necessary. Some Christians fast on a regular basis, while others fast at only special times of year. Many Christians never fast for religious reasons at all.

In the Bible, fasting is sometimes used as a way for people to say they are sorry, or to show the sincerity of their prayers. In the book of Samuel, the people wanted victory over their enemies and were anxious that God should not have anything to be angry with them about:

> *On that day they fasted and there they confessed, 'We have sinned against the Lord.'*
> **(1 Samuel 7:6)**

In the book of Acts, Christians are shown fasting before they make important decisions. The Bible teaches that fasting helps them to concentrate their minds on listening to what God wants them to do:

> *While they were worshipping the Lord and fasting, the Holy Spirit said, 'Set apart for me Barnabas and Saul for the work to which I have called them'. So after they had fasted and prayed, they placed their hands on them and sent them off.*
> **(Acts 13:2-3)**

Jesus taught that if people want to fast, they should do it for the right reasons, as a way of getting close to God, rather than in order to impress their friends.

▲ *Many of the earliest Christians followed Kosher laws about food.*

> *When you fast, do not look sombre as the hypocrites do, for they disfigure their faces to show men they are fasting. I tell you the truth, they have received their reward in full. But when you fast, put oil on your head and wash your face, so that it will not be obvious to men that you are fasting, but only to your Father, who is unseen; and your Father, who sees what is done in secret, will reward you.*
> **(Matthew 6:16-18)**

Many Roman Catholics, and some members of other churches, try to fast before they take Holy Communion (Mass), so that they can think more clearly about God and show that they are sorry for the things they have done wrong.

In some Christian denominations, such as the Roman Catholic and Eastern Orthodox Churches, believers eat very simple food during Lent. They might avoid sweets, puddings, meat and alcohol, or they might have just two meals a day instead of three. They do this as a way of concentrating their minds, and they think about the time Jesus spent in the wilderness before he began his teaching. At the beginning and end of Lent, on Ash Wednesday and Good Friday, Christians might fast as a way of remembering Jesus' suffering.

Exam Practice

Practice your skills in **demonstrating knowledge and understanding**.

Explain Christian beliefs about fasting.

In your answer, explain what fasting means and show why some Christians think it can be important. For high marks, you might be able to demonstrate an understanding of different beliefs about fasting in different Christian denominations.

This will help you in the exam when you answer part (d) questions.

Food for festivals

In Christianity, as in many other religions, special foods are eaten at festival times.

Bread and wine are important for Christians when they celebrate Holy Communion. They represent the body and blood of Jesus, and remind Christians of their belief that Jesus' death was a sacrifice for the sins of the world. ▶

At Harvest festival, Christians often decorate their churches with fruits, bread and vegetables, as a way of thanking God for their food. After the services are over, the harvest gifts are given to needy people in the community. ◀

▶ *Christmas is an important festival in Christian cultures. Most Christians eat a special meal on Christmas Eve or Christmas Day, as a way of celebrating the birth of Jesus.*

◀ *Hot cross buns are often eaten at Easter; the cross shape on the top is a reminder of the crucifixion of Jesus. In the UK, traditionally people eat chocolate eggs in celebration of Easter. The egg is a symbol of new life.*

Glossary

Benediction – a blessing, often given at the end of a service of worship

Kosher – a word meaning 'proper', often used to describe Jewish food laws about the right things to eat

Lord's Prayer – the prayer that Jesus taught, which begins 'Our Father'

Mass – the Roman Catholic name for a service of Holy Communion, sometimes called the Eucharist, where Christians remember the sacrifice of Jesus' death

Prayer – talking and listening to God

Pulpit – a raised platform used by a preacher in church, so that everyone can see and hear

Worship – giving something great worth and a central place in your life

The end of life: Christianity

Body and soul

This section will help you understand Christian ideas about the soul.

What is the soul?

While the word 'body' refers to the physical part of a person, '**soul**' means the non-physical part of a person. It is often used to refer to someone's mind, personality, or emotional being.

As the soul is unseen it is something of a mystery and is often the subject of fictional stories. In the Harry Potter series, for example, the character or Lord Voldemort resists going to the afterlife even when his body dies, by breaking his soul into seven parts. In the TV series *Buffy the Vampire Slayer*, the concept of 'soul' is identified with a person's moral conscience, which vampires do not have.

> *Justice, courage, self-control, magnanimity, magnificence, and all other similar states of mind, for they are virtues of the soul.*
> **(Aristotle)**

What do Christians believe about the body and soul?

Christians believe that humans, unlike other animals, have souls as well as bodies. They believe that the body and soul are not separate, but are different aspects of each human person, created and designed by God. The soul is the part of a person which can develop a relationship with God. The body will eventually die, but this is not the end of the person's life. Christians believe that after the death of the body, the soul continues to live eternally (for ever).

> *The Lord God formed the man from the dust of the ground and breathed into his nostrils the breath of life and the man became a living being.*
> **(Genesis 2:7)**

> *So it is written: 'The first man Adam became a living being', the last Adam a life-giving spirit.*
> **(1 Corinthians 15:45)**

Activity 1

Explain in your notes what Christians believe about the soul.

For Discussion

What is life after death?

Death means the end of all physical and mental life.

Life after death means that when we have died we still exist in some way.

Do you think people can live on in some way after their deaths? Talk about your views and explain your reasons.

Life after death

This section will help you understand Christian ideas about life after death.

What is 'life after death'?

In today's world, there is a wide variety of beliefs about the issue of life after death. Some people believe there is no life after death – when a person dies, that is completely the end of their existence physically and spiritually. Others believe that there is life after death – when a person dies, they still exist in some way.

Exam Practice

Practise your **evaluation** skills.

'There is no life after death – when we die, we just stop.'

Discuss this statement. You should include different, supported points of view and a personal viewpoint. You must refer to Christianity in your answer.

For this answer, you need to consider different beliefs about life after death. Start by showing you understand a Christian point of view, and explain why Christian beliefs disagree with the statement. Then give a different point of view; it could be the view of someone who agrees with the statement, or perhaps from someone who thinks it is impossible to know what happens after death. Finally, give your own opinion. Perhaps you agree with one of the views you have already outlined, or perhaps you have a different belief. Support your view with reasons.

This will help you in the exam when you answer part (e) questions.

For Discussion

Why might life after death be an important issue for some people?

Although there are immortal characters in books, films and television, such as superheroes or vampires, most people believe that they will have a physical death themselves. It is natural to think about what will happen after this death. Other people believe there is no life after death, because there is no scientific proof to confirm it.

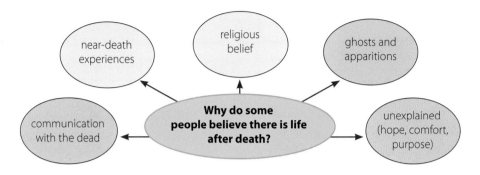

What do Christians believe about life after death?

Christians believe that when we die, that is not the end. Although a person's earthly body dies, their soul is still alive. Christians believe that God judges our lives on earth, and decides what happens to us in the afterlife. Some people will go to heaven, while others will go to hell.

Christians believe that by sending Jesus to earth to die on the cross, God made life after death possible.

Christians' beliefs about life after death come from:

- the Bible (including Jesus' teachings)
- the Church's teachings
- their own relationship with God.

Resurrection

Christians believe that after death, they will be resurrected, just as Jesus was resurrected. This means that they believe they will be given a new body. They will not be born back into this world, and will not just be a kind of spirit, but will become a perfect version of themselves, and able to continue living in heaven with others.

Christian teaching about life after death

Jesus' death and resurrection

> Jesus said to her, 'I am the resurrection and the life. He who believes in me will live, even though he dies; and whoever lives and believes in me will never die.'
>
> **(John 11:25-26)**

Jesus died and rose again so that believers might have eternal life.

> I want to know Christ and the power of his resurrection and the fellowship of sharing in his sufferings, becoming like him in his death, and so, somehow, to attain to the resurrection from the dead.
>
> **(Philippians 3:10-11)**

Eternal life

Eternal life means that their soul will never ever die.

> For God so loved the world that he gave his one and only Son, that whoever believes in him shall not perish but have eternal life.
>
> **(John 3:16)**

Judgement

God decides who is worthy of eternal life. The Nicene Creed says of Jesus:

> He will come again in glory to judge the living and the dead, and his kingdom will have no end.

Heaven and hell

Some people will go to heaven after they die, others will go to hell.

> Then they will go away to eternal punishment, but the righteous to eternal life.
>
> **(Matthew 25:46)**

Gustave Dore's illustration of Milton's Paradise Lost *shows a view from heaven.* ▼

Heaven and hell

What is heaven?

'Heaven' has many meanings, such as the sky or something really good. In religious terms, it usually means the ultimate holy place, which people aim to reach through faith, goodness or other means. Heaven is also the place where God lives.

Heaven is often associated with paradise, and it means different things to different people, depending upon their beliefs. For many people, heaven is not an other-worldly place, but rather a term used to refer to the ultimate happiness on earth. It is commonly used to describe everything that can be considered good in life: holidays, food, shops or relationships. For others, heaven brings up images of fluffy white clouds and halos, even if they have no religious beliefs about its existence. Heaven is often portrayed in this way in the media, which reflects and reinforces the stereotype.

Some atheists think that the idea of heaven is just something that people have made up so that they have a hope, something distant to look forward to instead of focusing on their lives. Others believe it is something that authorities have invented to give people an incentive to live morally good lives.

What do Christians believe heaven is like?

Most Christians believe that heaven exists in some form. Heaven is mentioned many times in the Bible, but although there are some passages which seem to describe heaven, there is not a complete description.

Some Christians believe that heaven is an actual *physical place*; others believe that heaven is a *situation* or *state*.

 At once I was in the Spirit, and there before me was a throne in heaven with someone sitting on it. And the one who sat there had the appearance of jasper and carnelian. A rainbow, resembling an emerald, encircled the throne. **(Revelation 4:2-3)**

Activity 2

Make a poster entitled 'What 'heaven' means to me', using your own beliefs or ideas. These can be religious or non-religious, and you should try to include at least ten points to describe your idea. You can include pictures if you like.

Some Christians take the Bible's descriptions literally; others take them as metaphors (symbols) of what heaven is like.

> Then I looked and heard the voice of many angels, numbering thousands upon thousands, and ten thousand times ten thousand.
>
> **(Revelation 5:11)**

Many Christians believe that:

God is in heaven

This belief is supported by the Bible, and it is often referred to in Christian prayers. Whether heaven is a physical place or a state, the belief can still stand.

Jesus called heaven 'God's throne':

> But I tell you, Do not swear at all: either by heaven, for it is God's throne; or by the earth, for it is his footstool. **(Matthew 5:34)**

The Lord's Prayer begins with these words:

> Our Father who is in heaven, hallowed be your name...

Jesus is in heaven with God

After Jesus died, he was resurrected and appeared to his disciples. He then ascended into heaven, according to the Bible.

The Bible tells of Jesus going to heaven:

> After the Lord Jesus had spoken to them, he was taken up into heaven and he sat at the right hand of God. **(Mark 16:19)**

Heaven is paradise (happy and amazing)

Jesus referred to heaven as paradise:

> I tell you the truth, today you will be with me in paradise. **(Luke 23:43)**

The Bible says there will be no unhappiness in heaven:

> There will be no more death or mourning or crying or pain for the old order of things has passed away. **(Revelation 21:4)**

The Bible does not describe exactly what heaven is like, so many Christians have different beliefs about this. Also, Christians interpret what the Bible says in different ways, with some Christians believing that everything the Bible says about heaven is fact, while others believe that it needs to be interpreted.

Heaven is to be in the presence of God

Most Christians agree that whether heaven is an actual physical place or not, heaven means to be in the presence of God.

Exam Practice

Practise your skills in **demonstrating knowledge and understanding**.

What do Christians mean by 'heaven'?

Try to keep your answer clear and to the point.

This will help in exam when you answer part (a) questions

◀ This vision of hell comes from Hortus deliciarum *by Herrad von Landsberg, dated in the late twelfth century.*

What is hell?

In today's world, many people use the word 'hell' to describe a bad situation, unhappiness, suffering or pain. In religious terms, hell usually means a place or state of punishment for sins after death.

Hell is often associated with suffering and punishment, and it means different things to different people, depending upon their beliefs. For many people, hell is not an other-worldly place, but rather a term used to refer to the ultimate misery or pain on earth. It is commonly used to describe everything that can be considered bad in life: illness, pain or problems. For others, hell brings up images of fire, darkness and pitchforks – even if they have no religious beliefs about its existence. Hell is often portrayed in this way in the media, which reflects and reinforces the stereotype.

Some atheists think that the idea of hell is just something that people have made up to scare people, something to warn people that their actions could have bad consequences in order to make them toe the line. Others believe it is something that authorities have invented to give people an incentive to live morally good lives and thus avoid hell.

What do Christians believe hell is like?

Some Christians believe that hell is an actual *physical place*; others believe that hell is a *situation* or *state*.

The Bible does give some descriptions of hell, which some Christians take literally while others believe that it gives an idea of what hell is like but needs to be interpreted.

Here are four examples of how the Bible refers to hell:

1 Fire

> *If anyone's name was not found written in the book of life, he was thrown into the lake of fire.*

> **(Revelation 20:15)**

Activity 3

Draw a mind map entitled 'Ideas about 'hell'' and fill it with as many ideas as you can about things associated with hell, including your own beliefs (religious or otherwise) about what 'hell' means. You should try to include at least six points on your mind map.

> *And if your eye causes you to sin, gouge it out and throw it away. It is better for you to enter life with one eye than to have two eyes and be thrown into the fire of hell.* **(Matthew 18:9)**

2 Darkness

> *For if God did not spare angels when they sinned, but sent them to hell, putting them into gloomy dungeons to be held for judgement.*
> **(2 Peter 2:4)**

Some Christians believe that this verse tells us that hell is literally 'gloomy dungeons'. Other Christians believe that the darkness represents the fact that they are away from the light of God.

3 Suffering

> *And they will go out and look upon the dead bodies of those who rebelled against me; their worm will not die, nor will their fire be quenched, and they will be loathsome to all mankind.* **(Isaiah 66:24)**

> *They will throw them into the fiery furnace, where there will be weeping and gnashing of teeth.* **(Matthew 13:42)**

4 Eternal

> *And the smoke of their torment rises for ever and ever. There is no rest day or night …*
> **(Revelation 14:11)**

The Bible does not describe exactly what hell is like; so many Christians have different beliefs about what hell is. Also, Christians understand what the Bible says in different ways, with some believing that everything the Bible says about hell is fact, while others believe that some of it needs to be interpreted.

Hell is to be away from the presence of God

Whatever their beliefs about whether hell is an actual place or not, most Christians agree that hell means to be without God.

Purgatory

Many Roman Catholics believe in **purgatory**, which is:

- preparation for heaven

- a purification process

- for most Catholics whose faith means they will not go to hell, but whose sins mean that they are not perfect enough to go straight to heaven.

Exam Practice

Practise your skills in **demonstrating knowledge and understanding**.

What do Christians mean by 'hell'?

Try to give a short, clear and concise explanation.

This will help in exam when you answer part (a) questions

Who do Christians believe will go to heaven or hell?

Christians do not always agree about who will go to heaven and who will go to hell. These beliefs are often determined by:

- what the Bible says
- their experience of God
- their church background.

Here are some examples of different Christian ideas about who goes to heaven or hell:

I believe that anyone who is born again – baptized as a believer in water and baptized in the Holy Spirit – will go to heaven. Anyone who has not been reborn in Jesus, even if they are a Christian, will go to hell.

All Christians will go to heaven, and all non-Christians will go to hell.

Good people will go to heaven, whatever their beliefs. Evil people will go to hell.

When I worship God, I get a great sense of how loving and kind He is. I can't imagine him condemning anyone to an eternal punishment.

No one will go to hell. In the afterlife, everyone will have the chance to learn from things they have done wrong and move up through the heavens until they reach God.

- Some Christians believe that whether you go to heaven or hell depends on faith (whether or not someone is a Christian and believes in God and Jesus).

- Other Christians believe that it is a matter of works (whether or not someone does good or evil things in their life).

- Some Christians believe that no-one will go to hell, because God is loving and would not punish anyone eternally.

- Roman Catholics believe in heaven for the really righteous, hell for the really unrighteous and purgatory (to work towards heaven) for others.

Although different Christians have different beliefs about who will go to heaven and who will go to hell, most Christians agree that God makes the decision based on what people have done in their lives.

What does the Bible say about who will go to heaven and hell?

Here are some examples of passages from the Bible about who will go to heaven or hell. Remember that some Christians take everything the Bible says as true fact, whereas others interpret it in different ways.

> *Whoever believes and is baptized will be saved, but whoever does not believe will be condemned.* **(Mark 16:16)**

> *Then the righteous will shine like the sun in the kingdom of their Father.* **(Matthew 13:43)**

> *In reply Jesus declared, 'I tell you the truth, no-one can see the kingdom of God unless he is born again.'*
>
> *'How can a man be born when he is old?' Nicodemus asked. 'Surely he cannot enter a second time into his mother's womb to be born!'*
>
> *Jesus answered, 'I tell you the truth, no-one can enter the kingdom of God unless he is born of water and the Spirit.* **(John 3:3-6)**

One of the criminals who were crucified next to Jesus talked to him about heaven:

> *Then he said, 'Jesus, remember me when you come into your kingdom.' Jesus answered him, 'I tell you the truth, today you will be with me in paradise.'* **(Luke 23:42-3)**

Activity 4

Outline different Christian beliefs about who will go to heaven and hell.

1 Suffering – Jesus was bullied and tortured.

2 Death – Jesus was crucified, which means nailed to a cross to die.

3 Resurrection – After his death, Jesus rose again and went to heaven.

Salvation and redemption

What do Christians believe about Jesus the saviour and redeemer?

The suffering of Christ

> *But he was pierced for our transgressions, he was crushed for our iniquities; the punishment that brought us peace was upon him, and by his wounds we are healed. We all, like sheep, have gone astray, each of us has turned to his own way; And the Lord has laid on him the iniquity of us all.* **(Isaiah 53:5-6)**

(Note: iniquity means sin)

According to the Bible, after Jesus was arrested he was brought before the chief priests and elders. People testified falsely against him, and they were trying to find evidence to put him to death, although there was none. Then he was physically assaulted:

> *Then some began to spit at him; they blindfolded him, struck him with their fists and said, 'Prophesy!' And the guards took him and beat him.*   (Mark 14:65)

Once it was decided that Jesus should be crucified, despite having committed no crime, he was tortured again:

> *They stripped him and put a scarlet robe on him, and then twisted together a crown of thorns and set it on his head.*
> (Matthew 27:28-29)

Jesus was made to carry his own cross to a place called Golgotha, where he was then crucified (nailed to a cross to die).

Saviour and redeemer

Christians believe that Jesus is the Son of God. God sent Jesus to earth as the **saviour** of humans, to save them from sin and its punishment. Jesus is also called the **Redeemer**, because his death paid the price for human sin and allows people to be free from the consequences of that sin.

Human nature means that even the nicest, most respectable people sometimes commit sin. Sin deserves punishment, but instead of punishing people with eternal damnation, Jesus took the punishment for human sin and that punishment was his suffering and death. Because Jesus paid the price for humans, Christians believe that he made it possible for them to go to heaven to be with God when they die.

> *... our great God and Saviour, Jesus Christ, who gave himself for us to redeem us from all wickedness and to purify for himself a people that are his very own, eager to do what is good.*
> (Titus 2:13-14)

Activity 5

(a) Read the following descriptions. Which do you think is an example of a saviour, and which is an example of a redeemer?

Leo had worked for the Armando family as a cleaner since he was a little boy. He never received any pay for his work and he had no freedom to come and go as he wanted, because Mr Armando said he owned Leo. Leo was a slave. One day, a wealthy lady paid a large sum of money to the Armandos so that they would let Leo leave their house and be free to go wherever he wanted. Then Leo was no longer a slave.

'Dithering dingbats, Flying-Tights-Man, those trains are going to crash head on. You've got to stop them!' This was no problem for Flying-Tights-Man, who used his stretchy tights to pull one of the trains onto a different track. 'Wow, Flying-Tights-Man, you've saved all those people. You're the best superhero ever!'

(b) 'Jesus is the saviour'. What do Christians mean by this idea? Explain it in your own words.

Judgement

What do Christians believe about God the judge?

God sees everything

Christians believe that God is the ultimate judge of all things on earth. They believe that he sees and knows everything, not just things that people say and do outwardly, but even their innermost thoughts and the feelings within their hearts.

What does it mean for God to judge?

As a judge, Christians believe that God assesses all people and decides what will happen to them after they die.

Christian responses to God the judge

Some Christians are fearful of God the judge, because of the extent of God's power, examples of God's anger in the Bible, or the idea of hell and punishment. This fear is not necessarily a bad thing – some Christians believe that it is important to realize the full extent and implications of God's power.

Some Christians believe that God is a fair judge, and that he makes judgements justly, based on the truth. Therefore, his position as the ultimate judge deserves respect.

> *Now we know that God's judgement against those who do such things is based on truth.*
> **(Romans 2:2)**

What impact does it have on Christians' lives?

Because Christians believe that God is watching and judging their lives on earth, this has a big impact on the way they live. It can shape their thoughts and actions, for example:

- **Moral and ethical principles**

  Many Christians have certain moral and ethical principles because of teachings of the Bible and the Church. Because they believe that God watches and judges their lives, they try to uphold these principles. For example in their social beliefs and actions, by trying to be stewards for the earth, or by opposing abortion.

- **Money**

  Christians' decisions about how to spend money, or whether money is important to them, may be affected by their belief that God is watching. For example the Christian principle of tithing (giving a percentage of their income to church), by giving money to charity or the poor and needy, or by being less materialistic.

- ### Actions towards others

   Christians may try to treat others as God wants them to because they believe he is watching (for example, loving their neighbour, helping people out, treating people kindly).

- ### Family decisions

   Many Christians base family decisions on what they believe God wants them to do, often based on biblical teachings (for example, getting married, having children).

- ### Developing faith

   Christians believe that God wants them to respect and worship Him (for example, praise and worship, prayer, Bible reading).

For Christians who believe that God bases his judgement about who deserves **salvation** on whether people live good lives, there is an element of both hope and fear involved – their belief that God the judge is watching means that they may be trying to show him that they are worthy of salvation by their actions.

For Christians who believe that the requirement for salvation is to be a Christian (faith) it may be more a matter of wanting to please God, who they know is watching.

> For he has set a day when he will judge the world with justice by the man he has appointed. He has given proof of this to all men by raising him from the dead.
>
> **(Acts 17:31)**

> ... if this is so, then the Lord knows how to rescue godly men from trials and to hold the unrighteous for the day of judgement, while continuing their punishment. This is especially true for those who follow the corrupt desire of the sinful nature and despise authority.
>
> **(2 Peter 2:9-10)**

> By the same word the present heavens and earth are reserved for fire, being kept for the day of judgement and destruction of ungodly men. **(2 Peter 3:7)**

Exam Practice

Practise your skills in **demonstrating knowledge and understanding**.

Explain Christian beliefs about life after death.

In your answer, try to explain key ideas such as resurrection, heaven, hell and judgement. Show that you understand Christian beliefs about Jesus as the Saviour.

This will help you in the exam when you answer part (d) questions.

Funeral rites

This section will help you understand what happens at a Christian funeral service.

EXAM FOCUS

Church ceremony. ▲
Christian burial. ▼

When someone dies, it is a sad time for Christians just as it is sad for people with different beliefs. However, because Christians believe in the possibility of eternal life in heaven with God, they try to make sure that funeral services emphasize hope as well as paying respect to the person who died. Christian funeral services usually have two parts: a church ceremony and the burial.

Some Christians are buried in coffins, others are cremated.

These acts reflect the Christian belief that the body is no longer needed; it is the soul that lives on. Some Christians believe in the resurrection of the body on Judgement Day, but most believe that this is not the same body they had on earth, but rather a heavenly body.

> *There are also heavenly bodies and there are earthly bodies; ...And just as we have borne the likeness of the earthly man, so shall we bear the likeness of the man from heaven.*
> **(1 Corinthians 15:40, 49)**

Christian funeral ceremonies:

- pay respect to the person who has died
- remember, celebrate and thank God for the life of the person who has died
- provide comfort and support to the bereaved
- reflect Christian beliefs.

How do funeral rites reflect Christian beliefs?

The belief in life after death is reflected in many ways throughout Christian funerals:

Through readings from the Bible

Christian funerals often begin with Jesus' words:

> *I am the resurrection and the life. He who believes in me will live, even though he dies; and whoever lives and believes in me will never die.* **(John 11:25-26)**

The following passage is frequently read out during funeral services:

> *Listen, I tell you a mystery: We will not all sleep, but we will all be changed – in a flash, in the twinkling of an eye, at the last trumpet. For the trumpet will sound, and the dead will be raised imperishable, and we will be changed. For the perishable must clothe itself with the imperishable, and the mortal with immortality. When the perishable has been clothed with the imperishable, and the mortal with immortality, then the saying that is written will come true: 'Death has been swallowed up in victory.*
> *Where, O death, is your victory?*
> *Where, O death, is your sting?'*
> **(1 Corinthians 15:51-55)**

These remind Christians of their belief that death is not the end because Jesus has given the opportunity for eternal life with God.

Through prayers

A Christian funeral service often includes prayers of thanks to God for Jesus' sacrifice, which allows the person who has died to have eternal life. There are prayers asking for God's comfort for the people left behind.

Through hymns

Christian hymns remind people of their beliefs. Singing together can help the people at the funeral feel united and supportive of each other.

Through the sermon

There is often a short sermon by the priest or vicar, which usually focuses on belief in life after death. It might help people to remember the good things about the person who died and remind them to thank God for that person's life.

Through the burial or cremation

Some Christians are buried in coffins, others are cremated. These acts reflect the Christian belief that the body is no longer needed; it is the soul that lives on.

At a burial (committal), the priest or vicar usually says these words:

> *We commit this body to the ground, earth to earth, ashes to ashes, dust to dust.*

These words reflect the belief that God created Adam from the earth, as the Bible says:

 The Lord God formed the man from the dust of the ground and breathed into his nostrils the breath of life, and the man became a living being.

(Genesis 2:7)

Flowers are traditionally sent to Christian funerals, to pay respect to the deceased. They are also said to represent the splendour of heaven. Candles are traditionally lit representing Jesus as the light and saviour of the world.

Roman Catholic funerals

A Roman Catholic funeral includes:

- Holy Communion (a requiem mass)

- prayers for the soul of the person who has died (which reflects the Roman Catholic belief in purgatory)

- the sprinkling of holy water on the coffin, and use of incense

- the Priest's words: 'In the waters of Baptism (name) died with Christ, and rose with him to new life. May he/she now share with him in eternal glory.'

Paying respect

Although Christians believe that the person's body is no longer needed, the funeral service shows respect to the person who has died:

- the body is respectfully buried or cremated

- flowers and wreaths are often sent

- wearing dark clothes as a traditional mark of respect (although at some funerals people wear celebratory bright colours instead)

- there may be a gravestone or commemorative plaque.

Exam Practice

Practise your skills in **demonstrating knowledge and understanding**.

How do Christian funeral rites reflect Christian beliefs about life after death?

In your answer, show that you know about different features of a Christian funeral service. Try to use key terms such as resurrection.

This will help you in the exam when you answer part (d) questions.

The importance of Christian funerals for the bereaved

An important function of funerals is to allow family and friends the chance to remember, pay respect to, and say goodbye to the person who has died. They are also an opportunity to grieve and mourn formally, and offer each other comfort, hope and support.

1 Reflect and remember
The eulogy (a talk about the deceased) allows the bereaved to remember their qualities and reflect on their shared memories.

2 Goodbye
The funeral allows the friends and family to say goodbye to the deceased's earthly existence.

3 Look forward to being reunited
Through the Christian belief in life after death, the bereaved are encouraged to look forward to one day being reunited with the person who has died in heaven.

How do Christian funeral rites aim to support the bereaved?

4 Encouraged to be happy for the deceased
The bereaved are encouraged to be happy for the person who has died, because they have gone to 'a better place' – to heaven to be with God.

5 Comfort and support
During and after the funeral service, family and friends are there to support the bereaved, providing comfort and encouragement, and allowing them to talk about their grief.

6 Work through grief
Funerals provide a way for some people to work through feelings of grief and mourn formally.

Exam Practice

Practise your **evaluation** skills.

'Christian funerals help believers to cope with death.'

Discuss this statement. You should include different, supported points of view and a personal viewpoint. You must refer to Christianity in your answer.

To help you:

Look at the mind map above, which shows some ways in which Christian funerals aim to support the bereaved. Think about how effective each of these ways is in supporting the bereaved. What would a Christians think? Is the idea of funerals supporting the bereaved really helpful in practice? What are the helpful points? Are there any problems, flaws or ways in which support could be more helpful?

You might not be a Christian, so you might believe that the funeral rites of a different religion are more helpful to the bereaved. What do you conclude – do you agree with the statement? Remember to give different points of view, and as well as your opinion.

This will help you in the exam when you answer part (e) questions.

Glossary

Heaven – a place or state of perfect happiness in the presence of God

Hell – a place or state of eternal punishment, away from the presence of God

Purgatory – a place or state of suffering where souls are purified before going to heaven

Redeemer – someone who pays the price to buy something back, like paying a ransom

Redemption – being saved from sin

Resurrection – restoring to life, Christ rising from the dead

Salvation – saving from sin through faith in Christ

Saviour – someone who rescues somone else from danger

Soul – the spiritual, non-physical, eternal part of a person

PHILOSOPHY 1

Body and soul

This section introduces you to the main Hindu beliefs about the body and soul. A person's soul plays an important part in Hinduism. Hindus believe that the way a person lives determines what happens to their soul when their physical body dies.

What is the soul?

The word '**atman**' is used by Hindus to describe the self, or the soul. There is no difference between the soul of a plant, an animal, or a human. The term 'atman' literally means 'true self'. Hindus have the belief that the atman never dies and goes through all the experiences of your life. Hindus believe that **Brahman**, the one Supreme God or Great Power, has always existed and that part of him exists in all things. They believe that Brahman is the true self, or atman and nothing would exist without him existing everywhere. So in essence, atman is our true self or soul, but also God living in us.

As all living creatures contain the eternal spirit of Brahman, many Hindus believe that all life is holy and worthy of respect. This is where the Hindu concept of ahimsa (non-violence) originates. Hindus are taught to respect creatures, humans, and nature alike. This concept is behind the vegetarian beliefs of many Hindus.

We are taught that God is in everything including us! This is atman.

Kumbh Mela is the world's largest religious gathering. The myth of the Kumbh Mela tells how the gods and demons fought over a pot containing the elixir of immortality; during the struggle drops of the elixir fell to earth on the four sites of the Mela pilgrimage. The sites' sacred rivers give worshippers the chance to bathe in the essence of purity, auspiciousness and immortality. The faithful believe bathing will absolve sins and bring blessings on their lives. ▶

> *The Self cannot be pierced or burned, made wet or dry. It is everlasting and infinite, standing on the motionless foundations of eternity.*
>
> **(Bhagavad Gita 2:24)**

Exam Practice

Practise your skills in **demonstrating knowledge and understanding**.

Explain what is meant by the word 'atman'.

Try to make your answer clear, short and to the point.

This will help you in the exam when you answer part (a) questions.

For Discussion

What does the word 'soul' mean to you?

What do you think about the concept of the soul being reborn in 'new clothes'?

What is the relationship between the body and atman?

Hindus believe in **transmigration** of the soul. They believe that the atman and body are separate from one another and the atman resides inside the body whilst it is alive. After the body dies, the atman leaves the body and either enters a new one or it is reunited with Brahman. One way to compare the relationship between the body and atman is like a person and their clothes. A person wears their clothes but this is not the same as the person. When a person's clothes get worn out, they are removed and replaced with new ones.

> *As one abandons worn-out clothes and aquires new ones, so when the body is worn out a new one is acquired by the Self, who lives within.*
> **(Bhagavad Gita 2:22)**

What have we learned?

1 The soul is called atman.

2 The atman is separate from the body.

3 The atman is also part of Brahman, the one Supreme God.

4 The atman transmigrates from body to body at the end of life.

Life after death

This section introduces the main Hindu beliefs about life after death.

EXAM FOCUS

What do Hindus believe about life after death?

Hindus have very specific beliefs about life after death which influences their attitudes towards death. Hindus believe that life begins and ends, but that a person's soul (atman) exists forever. They believe in punishment and rewards for a person after they have died, but this is not in the form of heaven and hell that is common to other religions.

Hindus believe that death is an important step in the process of leaving the cycle of rebirth (**samsara**). They believe that a person's good and bad actions (**karma**) have a direct consequence to what happens to their soul (atman) when their body dies. They believe that everyone is trapped in the cycle of rebirth and it is the ultimate aim to be set free and be reunited with the one supreme god (Brahman).

As a Hindu, I believe that the atman is eternal and that my actions in this life will have a direct consequence on my future existence when I die.

◀ *Hindu scriptures contain stories about karma and life after death.*

For **Discussion**

How do Hindu beliefs about the afterlife compare with that of another religion you have studied, or your own beliefs?

What is samsara?

Samsara is a very important part of Hinduism. It is the Hindu term for the cycle of death and rebirth. Hindus believe that the atman and the body are separate, and when a person dies, their soul (atman) will be reborn into a new body. This death and rebirth can happen many times according to the samsara law. It is the ultimate aim of Hinduism for a person to be freed from the endless cycle of samsara.

When a human dies, most Hindus believe that their soul is most likely to be reborn in another human. Some Hindus believe that it is possible for a person with really bad karma to be reborn as an animal or a creature. Most Hindus consider samsara painful, and that it is a cycle of four problems: birth, disease, old-age, and death. It is therefore desirable to be free from suffering and samsara.

Hindus believe that the samsara cycle is painful. ▶

What is karma? How do our actions affect our future?

Karma literally means 'action', the law of cause and effect. During a lifetime, a person collects both good and bad karma according to their actions. If a person does something good, they will collect good karma, and if they do something bad, they will collect bad karma. The karma a person builds up in their lifetime will have a direct impact on their future existence and the possibility of achieving **moksha**.

Earl, from the TV show My Name is Earl, *has devoted his life to doing good deeds to reverse the bad karma he has previously acquired in his life.* ▶

An easy analogy to describe the importance of karma is a set of kitchen weighing scales: after a person dies, their good deeds (good karma), are weighed against their bad deeds (bad karma) This has an impact on whether they achieve liberation from the rebirth cycle, or the level of rebirth on earth. If a person has lived a good life and completed all of their religious duties, then they may be reborn into a better life than they have now. If a person lives an evil life, then they will be reborn into a life (or incarnation) that is not as good as the current one. Hindus believe that wicked actions of the past can cause suffering. The purpose of karma is to make people take responsibility for their actions even if this is done in their next life.

Many Hindus believe that there is no point in complaining about your life, or being proud about what you have, because it is a reflection of the karma from your previous life. Some Hindus believe that really wicked people's souls can be reborn as an animal. Also, some Hindus believe that doing something really good may give a person's soul a rest from the suffering of being reborn straight away.

For **Discussion**

Do you think that some bad deeds are worse than others? How do you decide what actually makes one bad deed worse than another?

In some ways Hinduism is similar to other mainstream religions in the sense that we are judged on the good and bad things that we all do. But, for Hindus, this is something we believe will affect us continuously, and how we exist.

Activity **1**

Draw a diagram to show the process of reincarnation and how moksha leads to Brahman.

Activity **2**

Explain in your own words what 'karma' means to a Hindu.

In your answer, you should give a brief definition of what karma means. You could also give some examples of both good and bad karma, and the impact of these on the atman's future existence.

Suicide is not encouraged in Hinduism as it is felt that everyone has to live with the consequences of karma, both good and bad. Therefore, it is against God's law to try and escape the punishments that we bring upon ourselves by ending our own lives. It is taught in the scriptures that if a person tries to escape the suffering in their life by committing suicide, they will suffer even more in their next life (Yajur Veda 40-43). This could mean that they come back as a lower form of human, or possibly even as an animal.

What is moksha? How is this a Hindu's ultimate goal?

Moksha literally means 'release'. It refers to the soul (atman) being freed from the samsara cycle and this is the fourth and ultimate goal (artha) for Hindus. When an atman achieves moksha, they no longer have to go through the death, rebirth, pain and suffering of the samsara cycle. They will exist in perfect happiness when the atman rejoins Brahman, where it began. They will also be free from the collection of bad karma that perhaps has been gathering over a series of lifetimes. A common illustration used to describe moksha is a river re-entering the sea.

Only a completely pure atman can rejoin Brahman. To achieve this, you must see beyond yourself, and recognize the true self (atman). This means that people need to overcome their own desires and ignorance. The irony of this is that a person must overcome the need for all desires including the desire to achieve moksha itself. Hindus are taught by their religious leader, the guru. They believe that the guru has the power to help break the chain of samsara and achieve moksha and so it would be wise to follow their teachings.

> *One who shirks action does not attain freedom; no one can gain perfection by abstaining from work.*
> **(Lord Krishna, Bhagavad Gita 3:4)**

According to the Bhagavad Gita, there are four paths that lead to moksha: knowledge, meditation, devotion, and action. Hindus believe that anyone can follow any of the paths to moksha and they are all of equal importance. All the paths lead to moksha but each journey may be different.

- **Knowledge (Jnana-yoga)** – this refers to spiritual knowledge, to understand the relationship between the soul (atman) and Brahman.

- **Meditation (Raja-yoga)** – requires a person to concentrate so hard that they forget about themself and are able to reach the true self within. This path is not ideal for people with lots of worries and responsibilities as it may be hard to clear your mind. This meditation has special positions and breathing exercises, and is the kind of yoga with which Western people are most familiar.

- **Devotion (Bhakti-yoga)** – involves devoting your life to the worship of a particular god/goddess, and making sure everything you do is an offering to them.

- **Good works (Karma-yoga)** – this is doing good deeds in your life. Many Hindus believe that this is the easiest path to follow as it involves doing your own religious duty to the best of your ability. This is sometimes referred to as 'the path of disinterested action'.

> *Great souls make their lives perfect and discover me; they are freed from mortality and the suffering of this seperate existence. Every creature in the universe is subject to rebirth, except the one who is united with me.*
> **(Bhagavad Gita 8:15)**

Exam Practice

Practise your skills in **demonstrating knowledge and understanding**.

What do Hindus believe about life after death?

In your answer, show that you understand Hindus believe in rebirth into this world as a new person or animal. For high marks, show that you understand and can use key terms such as karma, samsara and moksha.

This will help you in the exam when you answer part (c) questions.

For Discussion

How difficult do you think it is for a person to give up life's pleasures?

Hindus are taught that they can achieve moksha after their life if they follow the concept of the ashramas, although very few people have the willpower to complete it all. Hindus are taught that life is divided into four stages (or ashramas):

- **Student** (aged between eight and 20) when a person learns about their religion.

- **Grihastha** (until about the age of 50) meaning householder, where a person earns a living and has a family.

- **Vanaprastha** preparing to die. When a person enters the vanaprastha stage, they are supposed to give up pleasurable things in their life. Few people achieve this third stage.

- **Sannyasin** (the last stage) meaning holy man. This stage is achieved by very few people as they are now expected to have no fixed home, and have very few possessions. It is in this final stage that a person will be best judge about life and can make the decision to give it up or not.

What is dharma?

The term **dharma** is challenging to explain because there is no exact equivalent word in English. Dharma is sometimes understood to mean religion, but the term really means a mixture of truth, law, duty and obligation. Dharma is a duty that is unique to the individual. The harmony of the world must be maintained, and an individual's dharma must be fulfilled.

The concept of dharma is used to describe a person's social and religious duty. For many people dharma describes what it means to be human. Therefore, Hindus believe that there is nothing in life which can be separated from a person's dharma. Dharma is something connected to both moral and religious behaviour.

Each person has a different dharma depending on their birth and life circumstances such as doing your job properly. Dharma is for many Hindus the first aim of a person's life. As a result, Hindus believe that their religion is a way of life rather than a religion. In fact, many Hindus prefer to call their religion Sanatana Dharma, meaning eternal truths. Hindus are considered to be true to their dharma if they carry out their religious and moral duties effectively. This might involve being a good wife, following a vegetarian diet, doing their job well, avoiding violence, and taking time to meditate and practise devotion to God.

◀ *Carrying out one's religious duties is of great importance to Hindus.*

What is varnashrama?

Varnashrama concerns itself with society. Varna, which means class, plays an important part in Hindu society and determines a person's dharma. Many Hindus today believe that this system belongs in the past and that everyone should be treated equally.

Hindus believe that all people have been given special gifts or talents in this life and that they should make the most of them. These gifts or talents vary from person to person depending upon which varna they are part of. A person's varna depends on the way they have behaved in their previous lives.

Varnashrama is a very old way of dividing Hindu people into different groups. Each group, or varna, has a different kind of role to play in society. According to a very old hymn in the Hindu scriptures, the different groups are like the different parts of a human body:

The mouth is represented by a varna called Brahmins. These people are priests and can give advice and teach the scriptures.

The arms are represented by a varna of warriors, called the Kshatriya. These people defend the community.

The thighs are a varna of people such as shopkeepers and businessmen, called the Vaishya. These people support society.

The feet are people called the Shudras. These people do manual work, for example in the fields as farmers or in the city as servants to members of higher varnas.

There is another group that is beneath the four main varnas in traditional Hindu society. These people are called the 'untouchables' because they did the work that no one else would do, such as working with leather. The untouchables were often forced to live outside villages. The practice was outlawed in the 1950s although this continues to be a problem in India.

Over time, these main categories of people have been divided further into smaller categories depending on the jobs that a person does. Traditionally in India, a son would normally take the same job as his father. Some strict Hindus even today refuse to eat food prepared by someone in a lower caste, and also would never consider marrying someone beneath them. Other Hindus are less strict when it comes to their category and do jobs not in their varna. These Hindus tend to be members of the middle two varnas.

The varnas were organized according to their importance. The first three classes were labelled 'twice-born', and boys are given a special thread in an initiation ceremony called upanayana. Only 'twice-born' males were permitted to hear the Veda scriptures being read.

Generally speaking, the higher the varnashrama level, the more pure a person is considered. If a person leads a good life, then hopefully they will be reincarnated into someone belonging to a higher level in the next life.

Activity 3

Write one or two sentences to explain what each of the following words mean:

- atman
- karma
- samsara
- moksha.

For Discussion

What do you think happens when you die? Do you think you might live on after death, in some way? Or do you just stop?

Different views about life after death

Mark

I'm a humanist and I do not believe in God. I believe that when a person dies, they are no more. The only hope of an afterlife is the memories that are left behind in others.

Claire

I'm an atheist and I also do not believe in God. In my opinion, when a person dies there is nothing. The body is either cremated or buried but there is no hope of any further existence.

Ryan

I disagree, as a Christian I believe when a person dies God will decide whether the person's soul goes to heaven or hell.

Nilima

As a Hindu, I believe that death is part of the cycle of rebirth. I believe that everyone dies, but that this is not the end of existence as the atman will move on to a new existence, wherever that may be.

For Discussion

Mark, Claire, Ryan, and Nilima have different viewpoints about what happens when a person dies. Some people believe that there is another part to our existence after we die, but others disagree. What do you think?

Exam Practice

Practise your **evaluation** skills.

'When people die there is no further existence.'

Discuss this statement. You should include different, supported points of view and a personal viewpoint. You must refer to Hinduism in your answer.

1 In the first paragraph give one point of view about the statement. You could perhaps write about Hindu belief about the samsara cycle, and the atman. You will receive marks for discussing the statement so make sure you support the viewpoint fully.

2 In the next paragraph you should choose a contrasting viewpoint. You could write about an atheist's point of view as they agree with the statement. Whichever point of view you select, make sure you explain your points fully. If you have time, you could mention some further viewpoints but only do this if you have enough time to finish.

3 To conclude, you should give your opinion on the statement. You could agree with either of the viewpoints that you have already written about. If you are unsure, you can write this as long as you give reasons for you answer.

This will help you in the exam when you answer part (e) questions.

What have we learned?

1 Hindu beliefs about life after death affect the way in which Hindus live their lives.

2 Every atman is trapped in the samsara cycle, the continuous cycle of rebirth.

3 A person's actions are counted and the good and bad deeds are weighed against each other to determine what the atman's next existence will be. This is called karma.

4 It is possible to be freed from the samsara cycle by certain paths.

5 Everyone has to live by his or her dharma, which means people should do their religious and moral duties.

6 Traditional Hindu society has an organized hierarchy so it functions correctly. This is called varnashrama.

Funeral rites

This section will help you to understand and think about what happens at a Hindu funeral.

What happens at a Hindu funeral?

Hindus believe death is more than just the end of life. It is an important stage because it is the time when the atman (soul) leaves the body and is ready for rebirth as another human life.

 As the same person inhabits the body through childhood, youth, and old age, so too at the time of death he attains another body.
(Bhagavad Gita 2:13)

Many Hindus believe that it is more desirable for the dying to die in their own home. It is also important for affairs to be sorted out before death, including resolving any conflicts and ensuring that unmarried daughters are married. Usually, a Hindu would be cremated when they die, and if possible this would be carried out on the same day as their death.

▲ *Hindu funeral procession.*

Due to the complexity of the Hindu faith, Hindu **funeral rites** vary around the world. However, most commonly they follow this procedure. Firstly, the body is washed and wrapped in a large white cloth and put onto a stretcher. If the deceased is male it is normal for their hair to be shaven. It is common for a lit candle to be placed by the head of the deceased and a garland of flowers placed on the body. Next, there is a procession to the cremation ground led by the eldest son or male relative who would normally carry a jar of water. At the cremation place, the stretcher is placed on the funeral pyre and the son or male relative sprinkle water on the floor as he circles the pyre three times and then smashes the jar onto the floor near the deceased's head. This is symbolic of the atman being released from the body and transmigrating. Scripture readings and prayers take place, and sweet smelling spices are added to the cremation to burn. After the cremation, it is common for the ashes to be scattered into water.

> *Oh, Thou, Supporter of Beings, Womb of the World, Nourisher of Creatures. This one belonging to the changing world is dead; lead Thou him to heaven!*
> *Thou art born from him; may he be born again from you. He is an offering to the heaven.*
> **(Prayers from the Garuda Purana translated by Ernest Wood and S.V. Subrahmanyam (1911))**

India

It is common practice in India for the mourners to stay and witness the entire cremation. When the cremation is in the latter stages, the chief mourner carries out a ritual called 'kapol kriya', which is when the skull is broken with a long pole. This enables the atman to leave the body and transmigrate (move on to its next human body for a new life).

Mourning for the dead relative normally lasts for around ten days and the family living room is usually transformed into a mourning room.

In India, there are a number of different superstitions about the place a person dies and how this affects the afterlife. For example, many Hindus wish to die in Varanasi (also known as Benares) in India and have their ashes from their cremation scattered in the sacred river, the Ganges. It is believed that rivers are a symbol of God who gives life and that bathing in holy water will wash away bad karma. Many Hindus believe that Shiva, the god of destruction, once lived in Varanasi by the river Ganges and that if a person dies in this place and has their ashes scattered into the river, Brahman will save them from samsara.

United Kingdom

Hindus that die in the UK normally use modern crematoriums as used by other citizens living here. Some Hindus have their ashes scattered in a memorial garden, but many request that their ashes are scattered into one of the sacred rivers in India such as the River Ganges. This may take some time as relatives will have to save money for the journey.

Possibly due to the traditionally hot climate in India, it is customary for the cremation to happen on the day of a person's death. This is not possible in the UK due to legal formalities, and the cremation of the body may not take place until several days pass.

Activity 1

What reasons can you think of for the differences in how the funeral rites are carried out in the UK compared to in India?

Activity 2

Write one or two sentences to explain what each of the following words mean:

- Brahman
- dharma
- varnashrama
- funeral rites
- transmigration.

Final preparations at a Hindu cremation. ▶

How do Hindu funeral rites reflect belief?

Belief	Funeral rite
1. The soul transmigrates	a. The eldest son or male relative smashes a jar of water near the deceased's head.
	b. The skull is broken to help let the atman leave the body.
	c. The burning of the body is symbolic of the atman moving on.
2. God will wash away bad karma	Bathing in holy water.
3. Brahman will save the atman from samsara	Many cremations take place by rivers, especially by the River Ganges where the God Shiva used to live.
4. Possible pollution of death	The last sacrifice ceremony controls the pollution of death and reintroduces the bereaved family into 'normal' life.
5. Thanking God for the life of the deceased	Offerings of rice and milk are given.
6. The eldest son takes on the role of head of the family from his father	The eldest son leads many parts of the funeral including those that are connected with the releasing of the atman.

How do funeral rites support the bereaved?

In Hinduism, funeral rites are more for the benefit of the deceased rather than for the bereaved. These are essential to enable a smoother transmigration of the atman to its next existence. However, there is a period of mourning after the funeral and cremation to allow bereavement.

Death in the family is always a distressing experience. Hindus believe that a person who has been near a dead body is unclean and so relatives tend to avoid meeting other people until the entire funeral rites are completed. The last ceremony, called the kriya ceremony, takes place around ten days after the cremation of the body. Rice and milk are prepared into offerings for all family members that have died in the past. For Hindus, rice is an important food and milk comes from the sacred cow. After this ceremony, most Hindus believe that the person's atman has transmigrated into a new body and that the family can get back to their normal lives.

Hindus believe in good and bad deaths. A good death occurs at old age in the right place, hopefully the home. A bad death is premature and uncontrolled. By preparing for a good death, the family will be helped in their bereavement because they know that there is a much better chance of the deceased person reaching moksha after death.

There are some Hindu rituals at the funeral that can help bereavement. Hindus living in India believe that breaking the deceased's skull towards the end of the cremation allows the atman to leave the body and move on to its next existence. This practice will help the bereaved family to a degree because they believe this is best for the deceased.

At the funeral, the family are reminded of the importance of death in the process of reaching moksha. The Bhagavad Gita is explicit that the atman and body are separate entities: the body may have died but the real person, the atman, remains alive. The bereaved relatives would probably find this concept comforting because there is hope for the future.

Many Hindus hold annual events to help with the bereavement of a dead relative. Shradh is usually practised one year after the death of a relative. For some this becomes an annual event but the purpose is to give food to the poor in memory of the deceased. At Shradh, a priest will say prayers for the deceased, and the family will not buy any new clothes or attend parties as a sign of respect.

Exam Practice

Practise your skills in **demonstrating knowledge and understanding**.

How do the Hindu funeral rites reflect beliefs about the afterlife?

This type of question requires you to demonstrate your knowledge of Hindu funeral rites. It is not concerned with viewpoints and does not want you to discuss these. When approaching this type of question, it is best to make a rough list of what you know and expand upon three or four of these ideas.

In this question, you should choose three or four parts of the Hindu funeral that you know about, and describe what happens, and then explain how the rites reflect beliefs about the afterlife (for example, the skull is broken to reflect beliefs in transmigration of the soul).

This will help you in the exam when you answer part (d) questions.

What have we learned?
Hindu funeral rites reflect their beliefs about the afterlife and the transmigration of the soul.

- Most Hindus prefer to die in their own home.

- Hindus prefer to have their bodies cremated.

- It is encouraged by Hindus to have their ashes scattered in water, preferably a river.

- The eldest son or male relative plays an important part in the funeral of the deceased.

Activity 3

Create a storyboard outlining the rites traditionally found at a Hindu funeral.

Glossary

Atman – the soul in everything, part of the one Supreme God

Brahman – this refers to the one Supreme God or Great Power

Dharma – this is one's religious duty

Funeral rites – this refers to the events that take place at the funeral

Karma – this is a person's actions. Karma can be both good and bad and affects a person's future existence including their rebirth

Moksha – this is the achievement of bringing the samsara cycle to an end

Samsara – this is the cycle of death and rebirth, or reincarnation

Transmigration – this refers to the soul leaving one body and being reincarnated into another form

Varnashrama – duty as a member of a particular class in Hindu society

PHILOSOPHY 1

Public and private worship

This section will help you understand and consider what worshipping Allah means to Muslims.

EXAM FOCUS

For religious people, it is important to believe the right things and to behave in the right way, but it is also important to worship God. To 'worship' means to give something or someone great worth; to give that person or thing a central part in your life and to recognize its importance.

The concept of worship in Islam

The word 'Islam' means 'the way of peace' or 'the way of submission'. In order to worship Allah properly Muslims must submit their whole lives to him. For Muslims worship is not just about performing the right rituals in the right way at the right times. Worshipping Allah is about giving one's whole life to Allah in every way. Worship involves everything that a Muslim does during each day, and all the thoughts that go through a Muslim's head. Muslims believe that Allah created people so that they could worship him; so worship ought to be each Muslim's focus in everything that he or she does.

As a Muslim, I believe that my whole life should be devoted to worshipping Allah. I try to worship Allah with everything I say, and with the way I treat other people, and in all the decisions I make.

Why do Muslims worship together?

Muslims worship Allah in private, at home and at work, but they also gather in the **mosque** to worship together (communal worship). Men visit the mosque for worship, but it is more common for women to worship at home. If women do go to the mosque, there is a separate area for them to sit and to pray, so that they can be more private and are not a distraction to the men.

- Worshipping together gives Muslims a sense of unity with their own community and with other Muslims around the world.

- It gives them a feeling of tradition, when they worship in the same way as Muslims from the past.

- It helps them to get along with each other and to find peaceful ways of resolving disagreements.

- It gives them the opportunity to learn from each other and look at Islam in new ways.

- Members of a Muslim community can support each other in times of difficulty.

Exam Practice

Practise your skills in **demonstrating knowledge and understanding**.

What is meant by 'worship'?

This is a short answer, so you can be quite brief. You need to give a definition of the word 'worship' and you might show that you understand it by giving an example.

This will help you in the exam when you answer part (a) questions.

▲ *The Ka'bah is the most sacred place for Muslim worship.*

The Dome of the Rock in Jerusalem is one of Islam's most important mosques. ▼

The Ka'bah

The Ka'bah is the most holy site of worship in Islam. It is a cube-shaped building near to the holy city of Makkah. The Ka'bah was built about 2000 years ago on a site which Muslims believe was the same place where Adam, the first man, built a shrine to worship God, and where Ibrahim (Abraham) was commanded by Allah to make a house. All Muslims around the world face the direction of the Ka'bah when they pray, and all Muslims hope to visit it on pilgrimage at some time in their lives.

Worship in the mosque

The place in each community where Muslims meet for worship is called a mosque (which means a place for bowing down in worship) or a *masjid*. Muslims do not need to have a specially-designed place of worship as they believe that Allah can be worshipped anywhere, as long as that place is clean. There are many Muslims who worship in houses, in public halls and in the open air. Even so, Muslims like to have special buildings for worship so that they have somewhere comfortable where they can join together with other worshippers for prayer, for education and for community life. These buildings can often be recognized by a dome, a tower called a minaret, and sometimes a star and crescent symbol.

Activity 1

(a) Explain in your own words the main features of a mosque.

(b) Why might Muslims prefer to have a mosque rather than meeting in a school hall or in someone's house?

Purpose-built mosques usually have special features which remind Muslims of their faith and which help them to worship Allah. These include:

- **A place to leave shoes:** it is important for Muslims that people take off their shoes when they enter the mosque, as a sign of respect.

- **A place for washing:** Muslims prepare for prayer by washing in a special way, so a mosque will provide the facilities for doing this. It might be a washbasin, or a fountain, or separate bathrooms for men and women.

- **A prayer hall:** this does not have furniture in it, because the floor space is needed for prayer. It is a large open space, often with a pattern on the floor to help people to stand in straight lines. There will be no pictures or statues.

- **The *qibla* wall and *mihrab*:** when Muslims worship Allah, wherever they are in the world, they face in the direction of a special building in Makkah known as the Ka'bah. The *qibla* (meaning 'direction') wall of the mosque shows people which way to face for prayer. In this wall, there is an alcove called a *mihrab*.

- **The *minbar*:** the set of steps and a platform in the prayer hall, where the **imam** (the leader) stands when he teaches believers about the Muslim faith.

The mihrab *is an alcove in the wall showing the direction of Makkah.* ▶

The minbar *provides a platform for the imam when he speaks.* ▼

- **A minaret (tower):** in Muslim countries, people are called to prayer five times a day. The muezzin is a man who calls from the minaret to let people know that they should stop what they are doing and come to prayer. The tower of the minaret allows his voice to carry further.

- **The dome:** in hot countries, the dome of the mosque has practical uses. It helps air to circulate and keeps the inside of the building cool. The acoustics of the dome help everyone to hear the voice of the imam. The dome also has a symbolic meaning for Muslims as it represents the universe, created by Allah. The square shape of the prayer hall represents the earth, and the dome above reminds Muslims that Allah is in control of everything and that they should worship him.

Why don't Muslims use symbols in their worship?

Islam is a religion which is strictly **monotheistic**. This means that Muslims believe there is only one God, whom they call Allah. They believe that Allah is unique and that nothing can compare with him. This belief is known as **tawhid**.

Muslims believe that there is nothing to equal Allah and that Allah is beyond the understanding of the human mind. Because of this belief Muslims think it is wrong to use symbols in worship. Symbols and religious pictures might mislead people into thinking that Allah is easy to understand, or people might believe that they can create things which are just as good as Allah. (The sin of comparing anything to Allah is called **shirk**.) Using symbols is seen by Muslims to be similar to making idols, because people might start worshipping the symbols instead of worshipping Allah.

When Islam first began the Prophet Muhammad wanted to make it clear that Islam was different from other religions and that followers of Allah were not going to worship any idols. At the time of the Prophet, the people of Makkah worshipped many idols made of wood and clay which they kept in the Ka'bah. This caused Muhammad a great deal of concern, and one of the key points of the Prophet's life was the moment when he was able to lead an army into Makkah and destroy all these idols, returning to Ka'bah to the worship of Allah alone.

Although Muslims have no pictures or statues in the mosque, it is often a very beautiful building. Sometimes the mosque is decorated with **calligraphy** – the word means 'beautiful writing'. Words from the Qur'an, words of prayer or words describing Allah are written in a beautifully decorative way, so that when believers look at them they are reminded of their faith.

▲ *Calligraphy (beautiful writing) is a popular form of Islamic art.*

Mosques can also be decorated with geometric patterns, which might appear on the walls and ceilings using mosaic tiles, or might be carved on pillars and woven into carpets. The patterns sometimes use plant forms, but they are never realistic. When a repeating pattern is used, a 'deliberate mistake' is often introduced to show that although human creativity can be beautiful, it can never match the perfection of Allah's creation.

▲ *Islamic art uses beautiful geometric patterns instead of pictures of living things, to show that only Allah can create life.*

Practise your skills in **demonstrating knowledge and understanding**.

Explain Muslim ideas about using art in worship.

For this question, you need to show that you understand Muslim views about the sorts of art which are acceptable, and the sorts which are unacceptable. Describe the kinds of art a Muslim would not want to see, and also the kinds which might be used to make a mosque more beautiful. Explain the reasons for these Muslim beliefs.

This will help you in the exam when you answer part (d) questions.

Worship at home

Muslims worship Allah at home and at work, as well as at the mosque. Muslims are required to pray at least five times a day and, for many people, it would not be practical to go to the mosque at every prayer time. Men go to the mosque more often than women, who usually worship at home. The direction of Makkah is shown in the house so that family and visitors know which way to face when they pray.

I go to the mosque sometimes, but usually I do my prayers at home with the children. When it's time for prayer, we stop whatever we were doing and get out our prayer mats so that we have a clean place to pray, out of respect for Allah. In our house, we have a framed photo of the holy city on the wall in the sitting room; it shows us which way to face. But we don't just worship Allah at prayer times. We want to worship Allah in everything we do. As a Muslim mother, I try to worship Allah in the way I bring up the children, and in the way I prepare food, and in my relationships with my husband and family and friends. We try to think about Allah all the time, even when we are doing ordinary household jobs.

Exam Practice

Practise your **evaluation** skills.

'People should be able to worship wherever they want to. There is no need for special religious buildings.'

Discuss this statement. You should include different, supported points of view and a personal viewpoint. You must refer to Islam in your answer.

For this answer, you need to consider different points of view. What might a Muslim think? Perhaps they would agree that Allah can be worshipped anywhere, but they might also think that special buildings are needed – how would they support this view?

You also need to think about another point of view. It could be the point of view of someone from a different religion, or from no religious belief. What might their opinion be, and what reasons might they give to support it?

You also need to give your own view, and explain your own reasons for it. It does not have to be a third opinion – you might want to agree with one of the ideas you have already explained.

This will help you in the exam when you answer part (e) questions.

Prayer and meditation

This section helps you to understand why prayer is so important to Muslims.

The concept of prayer

Prayer is a very important part of life for Muslims. It involves talking to Allah and also trying to listen to him. When Muslims pray, they think about Allah and remember that they are created by him. They remember their duties towards Allah and towards each other, and they think about how they can put their faith into practice in everyday life.

Prayer is important to me because it's part of my duty as a Muslim. When I pray, I'm aware of being part of a worldwide community of Muslims. It's a chance for me to stop whatever I'm doing and think about my relationship with God. It makes me feel peaceful because it reminds me that God is in charge of the universe.

Prayer and its role as a Pillar of Islam

Islamic life has as its centre 'Five Pillars'. These are five different aspects of faith which all work together to support the Muslim community, in the same way that pillars support buildings.

The Pillars are:

1 Belief

2 Prayer

3 Giving money

4 Pilgrimage

5 Fasting

Prayer is the second of the Five Pillars of Islam. Muslims can pray whenever they want to, but the Prophet Muhammad taught followers of Islam that they must pray a minimum of five times a day, at set prayer times.

The five times for prayer are:

1 Fajr – between the first light of dawn and the sun rising in the sky

2 Zuhr – after midday

3 Asr – between late afternoon and sunset

4 Maghrib – between sunset and darkness

5 Isha – night

Praying five times a day might seem like a lot if you're not a Muslim, but the rule is there to help us. When I was little, my father explained it to me like this: if you had to see the head teacher once a term to talk about your work and behaviour, you would start working much harder the week before, wouldn't you? But the rest of the time you might get a bit lazy. If you had to see the head teacher once a week, every Friday, you'd probably work hard on Thursdays, but maybe not so much on Mondays. But if you saw the head teacher every day, then you'd do your best all the time. And it's like that for us, with Allah. We come to Allah five times every day, so we never forget that we are Muslims, and never forget that when we die, we will have to explain our behaviour and Allah will judge us.

Muslims try hard to pray at the right times of day, but this is not always possible; for example, they might have an exam. If they have a good reason to miss a prayer time, they can catch up with their prayers in the evening when they get home. They are not allowed to say their prayers in advance of the right time, because this would seem as though they were keen to get the prayers out of the way rather than appreciating them as a privilege.

Why do Muslims pray?

Muslims pray for several reasons. They pray because:

- **Prayer is a religious duty** – Muslims believe that Allah has commanded them to pray at least five times a day. They believe that this life is a test and that they will be judged by Allah when they die, so it is important for them to perform all their religious duties.

- **God listens** – Muslims believe that because Allah is all-powerful and all-knowing, he listens to every prayer and responds to it.

- **It gives them a chance to express their concerns** – many Muslims find that praying helps them to cope with daily life. They can talk to Allah about anything that is worrying them, and this helps them to tackle the difficulties they meet in everyday life.

- **Prayer reminds them of important beliefs** – when Muslims pray, they remind themselves of their belief that Allah is in charge of the world and cares for them.

- **Prayer helps them with moral decisions** – when Muslims are not sure what to do when they have an important decision to make, they pray about it and ask Allah to show them what they should do.

- **Prayer unites them** – when Muslims pray together, they feel united in their belief. They have a sense of belonging to the community of Muslims all around the world, and a sense of tradition.

- **Prayer gives support** – Muslims believe that they can support other people with their prayers. They believe that when they pray for people who are ill or hungry or in danger, Allah will listen to their prayers.

Exam Practice

Practise your skills in **demonstrating knowledge and understanding**.

What is meant by 'prayer'?

This is a short answer, so you do not need to write at great length. Try to make your answer clear, concise and accurate.

This will help you in the exam when you answer part (a) questions.

How do Muslims prepare for prayer?

Muslims believe that it is important to prepare for prayer with a ritual known as **wudu** which means 'washing'. The worshipper puts his or her mind and body into a clean state, to show respect for Allah and to separate the time of prayer from other more ordinary times of day. They take off their shoes and make sure they are decently dressed.

First, the believer says the words 'In the name of Allah, the Compassionate, the Merciful'. These words remind him or her that the prayers are not just being said for the sake of it, but are being addressed to almighty God; they are called 'making your intention'. Muslims believe that if they are not in the right frame of mind to pray, then they might as well not bother; if they are thinking about what to cook for dinner, or keep going over an argument in their heads while saying the words of the prayer, or if they are only praying so that other people admire them, then the prayer is a waste of time.

> *So woe to the worshippers who are neglectful of their Prayers, those who (want but) to be seen (of men).*
>
> **(Qur'an 107:4-6)**

After Muslims have made their intentions, they wash themselves in a special way, to make themselves clean before Allah. This washing is known as wudu, and it follows a special sequence:

1 The hands are washed thoroughly, first the right and then the left.

2 The mouth is rinsed three times.

3 The nostrils are washed three times.

4 The face is washed from the top of the forehead down to the chin and to the ears.

5 The arms are washed to the elbows three times, first the right and then the left.

6 Wet hands are wiped over the hair.

7 The ears are wiped with wet hands.

8 The feet are washed up to the ankle three times, first the right and then the left.

◄ *Muslims wash in a special way known as wudu, to prepare themselves for prayer.*

Activity 1

You can probably think of plenty of symbolic gestures that people use when they want to insult someone, but can you think of gestures people use when they want to show respect? For example:

What symbolic gesture might a soldier perform if he or she met a commanding officer?

How might people stand to show respect at a funeral?

What might people do if they were being introduced to the King or Queen?

See how many 'respectful gestures' you can think of.

At the end of the wudu, the Muslim says:

> *I bear witness that there is no god but Allah, and Muhammad is his Prophet.*

In the mosque, there are special facilities for performing wudu, and these are usually separate for men and women.

What do Muslims say and do during prayer?

Formal Muslim prayers are known as **salah**. There are also other kinds of prayers that Muslims want to say, such as prayers in their own words at any time of day. Salah uses a set of memorized words, and when Muslims say them, they also perform a set of symbolic actions known as a **rak'ah**.

The first thing a Muslim needs to do before beginning salah is to face the direction of Makkah and stand in a clean place. Many Muslims use special prayer mats to stand on, so that they know they are on a clean surface. They might take the prayer mats with them when they go to school or work.

The prayer sequence (rak'ah) begins by putting the hands up to the ears, and saying the words 'Allahuh Akbar', which means 'God is the greatest'. This gesture shows that the worshipper is cutting out all the rest of the day's distractions and just concentrating on Allah. Then the worshipper says words from the Qur'an, before bowing down with the hands on the knees, to show that he or she is waiting for Allah's orders.

The next movement, which is done three times, involves bowing right down and touching the forehead and nose to the ground, while saying words of praise to Allah. This is called prostration, and it shows that the worshipper is completely submitting to whatever Allah wants.

When the right number of rak'ahs have been completed, the worshipper sits with his or her feet tucked under the body, and says words of blessing for other Muslims, as a reminder that they are all one community worshipping together.

During prayer, Muslims perform symbolic actions to show that they submit to Allah and are willing to do whatever he wants. ▼

I don't understand why Muslims want to use set words for their prayers. I'm a Christian, not a Muslim, and when I pray I talk to God about whatever I want. I think this is much more personal, using my own thoughts and ideas rather than just reciting words from other people.

I like using set words for prayer, because it gives me a sense of unity with other Muslims around the world who are saying the same words. I know I am talking to Allah in the right way, with the right amount of respect. I say prayers in my own words too, but the set prayers make me feel confident that I am doing it right.

Exam Practice

Practise your **evaluation** skills.

'Prayer should be in your own words, not just repeating words that come from someone else.'

Discuss this statement. You should include different, supported points of view and a personal viewpoint. You must refer to Islam in your answer.

For this answer, you need to write several short paragraphs, outlining different points of view.

Start by saying what a Muslim might think about this. Remember that Muslims use prayers with set words, and also use prayers in their own words. Why might they want both sorts of prayer, rather than just praying in their own way?

Then try to think of a point of view which might disagree with this. Perhaps some people might think that using set words is not personal enough. Try and support this second point of view with reasons.

Finally give your own point of view. You might think prayer is a waste of time, whatever people say when they do it; you might agree with one of the views you have already outlined; or you might have a different opinion.

This will help you in the exam when you answer part (e) questions.

Food and fasting

This section will help you understand Muslim beliefs about food and fasting.

EXAM FOCUS

Why do Muslims fast during Ramadan?

Fasting is an essential part of religious life for Muslims. Every year, Muslims have a whole month which is set aside for religious purposes. It is the ninth month of the Muslim year – this holy month is known as **Ramadan**. It is more holy than other times of year because it was the month when, according to Islam, the Prophet Muhammad was given the words of the Qur'an directly from Allah. During the month of Ramadan, Muslims are meant to make special efforts to devote themselves to Allah even more than they do the rest of the year. They should be careful to keep their thoughts pure, to be kind to others, to avoid selfishness and to give extra to people in need. They also fast during the hours of daylight, for a whole month.

Fasting means going without food, and Muslims call it **sawm**. Like prayer, it is one of the Five Pillars of Islam – it is one of the aspects of religion that keeps the Muslim faith alive and supports it. Muslims do not just fast if they feel like joining in; they believe that have a religious duty to do it.

> *O ye who believe! Fasting is prescribed to you, as it was prescribed to those before you, that ye may (learn) self-restraint.*
>
> **(Qur'an 2:183)**

When Muslims fast during Ramadan, they eat and drink nothing at all during daylight hours. They get up very early to have their breakfast before it gets light, and then eat and drink nothing until it is dark again. Breakfast is usually food that will give them energy during the day, and nothing too spicy or salty, because this would make them thirsty and uncomfortable during daylight. When they can at last have something to eat and drink again after nightfall, they usually begin with a glass of water and something sweet, such as dates or apricots, to give themselves an energy boost. They will then have a proper meal, shared with all the family.

The evening meal during Ramadan is a happy time for Muslim families. They get together and encourage each other to continue with the fast. ▶

Fasting can be very difficult for Muslims. The months of the Muslim year are not the same as the traditional calendar months, so Ramadan does not always happen in the same season. Sometimes it falls in the winter and, in a country like the UK, this can be easier because daylight begins later and it gets dark early. However, it can still be hard for Muslims to fast if special celebrations such as Christmas are happening and everyone else at school or work is having special food and treats. In the summer, Ramadan is especially hard because daylight hours can be very long. People might have to go for 18 hours without food or drink, and the warm weather might make this more difficult so that they feel unwell.

Not everyone has to fast during Ramadan, these are some exceptions:

- Women who are pregnant or breastfeeding should carry on eating as normal, and all women are allowed to break the fast while they have their period.

- Elderly people, young children and anyone else whose health might be damaged by fasting, such as people with diabetes, do not have to fast.

- People who are working in occupations where they really need to keep up their strength and concentration are exempt from fasting.

- People with learning difficulties who might not understand why they were hungry and thirsty do not have to fast.

- People who have to travel long distances are also exempt from fasting.

Muslim families usually teach their children about fasting by getting them used to it gradually as they grow older. When they are small, they might just go without sweets or snacks. Once they reach the age of about 12, they are expected to keep Ramadan in the same way as adults.

What are the positives in fasting?

Muslims view fasting as being a positive part of their religion and follow the example set by the Prophet Muhammad. For Muslims, there a number of benefits to fasting:

- Fasting encourages a sense of community – as all Muslims are expected to fast at the same time regardless of their circumstances, fasting can be seen as an exercise in team bonding.

- By being reminded about Allah – as Muslims fast to follow God's instructions, every time they feel hungry they focus more on Him.

- To gain an understanding of being poor and appreciate good things – it is easy to forget the problems of being poor when we become engrossed with our own lives. Fasting enables a time of empathy for the poor and appreciation of the things we have.

- To learn self control – living a life of luxury such as overeating and drinking makes us get into bad habits.

Why do Muslims give to the poor during Ramadan?

The third Pillar of Islam, Zakah, giving money to the poor, is carried out by many Muslims towards the end of the holy month of Ramadan during the festival Eid ul-Fitr. This festival that marks the end of Ramadan is often known as the festival of charity and Muslims ensure that the needy are able to celebrate with things such as good food. By giving to the poor Muslims believe they will be helped to purify their desires such as greed and selfishness. Many Muslims give about 2.5% of their wealth to the poor which is considered by most to be a duty rather than a gift and is regarded as an act of worship in itself.

> **❝** *But it is righteous – To believe in Allah … to spend of your substance, out of love for Him, … for the needy.* **❞**
>
> **(Qur'an 2:177)**

Food for festivals

Food plays an important part in Islamic festivals. We have already read about how Muslims are taught to fast during the holy month of Ramadan and the reasons behind this. To celebrate festivals, many Muslims have special food they share with their families and friends as it is a time to spend together as a family.

The second biggest Muslim festival called Eid ul-Adha, has a big emphasis on food. The festival takes place at the end of Hajj to remember that the prophet Abraham was willing to sacrifice his own son Ishmael when God commanded it. Each year, Muslims follow in the tradition that the Prophet Muhammad started and sacrifice a sheep to show symbolically that they are willing to devote themselves to God the way Abraham did. As this sacrifice is only symbolic, the meat is then shared out with friends, relatives and the poor.

Haram and halal as they relate to food

Muslims are taught that they should live holy lives in a way that is pleasing to God. When it comes to behaviour, Islam offers two concepts that list the things we can (**halal**) and cannot (**haram**) do. When it comes to the things we eat, these two concepts can also be applied – halal describes the food that Muslims can eat and haram describes those they cannot. Both haram and halal are concepts based in the Qur'an. There are special shops and restaurants that Muslims can go to buy halal food.

Haram: firstly, Muslims must never consume alcohol nor should they be in the company of people who are drinking alcohol as this may affect the way they behave. Muslims are not allowed to eat carnivorous animals (those that eat other animals) or pigs. The Qur'an makes it clear how to kill animals for food correctly (see halal, page 81). If this is not followed, then the meat becomes haram. This can include products from animals such as cheese. As the cow is not killed when the farmer collects its milk to make cheese, it is classed as haram.

" *Forbidden to you (for food) are: dead meat, blood, the flesh of swine and that on which hath been invoked the name of other than Allah; that which hath been killed by strangling, or by a violent blow, or by a headlong fall, or by being gored to death; that which hath been (partly) eaten by a wild animal; unless ye are able to slaughter it (in due form); that which is sacrificed on stone (altars); (forbidden) also is the division (of meat) by raffling with arrows: that is impiety. This day have those who reject Faith given up all hope of your religion: yet fear them not but fear Me. This day have I perfected your religion for you, completed my favour upon you, and have chosen for you Islam as your religion. But if any is forced by hunger, with no inclination to transgression, Allah is indeed Oft-Forgiving Most Merciful.* "

(Qur'an 5:3)

Halal: many animals are permitted to be eaten as long as they are slaughtered by a Muslim in a way that follows certain rules (ritual slaughter). These include slaughtering the animal by slitting its throat and draining its blood. This is considered the most humane method of killing an animal, more so than electrocution which is often carried out by non-Muslims. The name of Allah must also be repeated to show that the food is taken with His permission. Other foods such as fish, fruit, grain and vegetables are all permitted to be eaten by Muslims.

Haram (Forbidden)	Halal (Allowed)
Pig and its by-products	Milk
Carnivorous animals	Honey
Reptiles and insects	Fish
Animals not killed following halal procedures	Plants which are non-toxic
Alcohol	Vegetables
	Various nuts
	Grains such as wheat and barley
	Permitted animals which have been killed in the right way

Exam Practice

Practise your skills in **demonstrating knowledge and understanding.**

What is meant by 'haram'?

This is just a short answer, so you do not need to write at great length. Try to make your answer clear, concise and accurate.

This will help you in the exam when you answer part (a) questions.

Glossary

Calligraphy – a special form of writing often found inside the mosque

Fasting – going without food usually during daylight hours during the month of Ramadan

Halal – 'permitted' and refers to behaviour that is permitted including the consumption of certain foods

Haram – 'forbidden or sacred' and usually refers to behaviour that is forbidden

Imam – means 'in the front' and refers to the leader of prayers who stands at the front of the mosque to lead prayers

Mihrab – an alcove in the wall inside the mosque to show the direction for prayer

Minbar – the platform inside the mosque

Monotheism – the belief that there is only one God

Mosque – where Muslims meet for worship

Qibla – the direction Muslims should face (towards the Ka'bah) when praying

Rak'ah – symbolic actions during prayer

Ramadan – the ninth month of the Islamic calendar when Muslims fast and go on Hajj

Salah – the special prayer carried out five times daily

Sawm – fasting

Shirk – sharing or associating, is the sin of comparing things to Allah or associating Allah with objects or images

Tawhid – the doctrine that there is only one God

Wudu – ritual washing in preparation for prayer or worship

PHILOSOPHY 2

Good and evil

This section will help you understand Christian beliefs about good and evil.

How do Christians understand good and evil?

Christians believe that God is perfectly good, and that all good things come from God. They believe that when the world was created God made everything 'very good':

> *God saw all that he had made, and it was very good.*
>
> **(Genesis 1:31)**

One of the ways in which Christians think that God shows his goodness to humanity is through the giving of moral laws. The Bible sets out clear rules for people to follow, and Christians believe that these rules come from God. God sets the standard of goodness, showing humanity what is right and wrong:

> *You shall not murder. You shall not commit adultery. You shall not steal.*
>
> **(Exodus 20:13-15)**

Christians believe that they should be good because God is good. They believe they should try and become closer to God through behaving morally and following God's commandments. Christians say that it is impossible to love God unless you are doing the things that God wants, so living a good life and keeping the commandments of the Bible is very important in the life of a Christian.

According to Christians, Jesus came to the world as the Son of God, and gave people the perfect example of human goodness. He showed them how to worship God, to think of others before themselves, to look after the poor and the weak, and to be prepared to sacrifice themselves for other people. Christians believe that when they read stories of Jesus, they gain a better understanding of the goodness of God.

Christians understand evil as the opposite of good. They believe that when people break the commandments God has given, they are committing sins and doing evil. Evil includes all the things that keep people away from God and prevent them from having a relationship with him.

Exam Practice

Practise your skills in **demonstrating knowledge and understanding**.

Explain how Christians understand good and evil.

In this answer to achieve high marks you should try to make several points. If possible, support the points you make with examples.

This will help you in the exam when you answer part (d) questions.

God and the Devil

What do Christians believe about the Devil?

Christians have differing views about the **Devil**, and Christian beliefs about the Devil have changed over the centuries. In the Bible, the Devil is seen in the form of temptation, and the Tempter is another name used to mean the Devil. In the book of Job in the Old Testament, the Devil tried to tempt a good man called Job away from God by sending him all kinds of suffering in the hope that Job would turn against God and lose his faith.

In the New Testament, the Devil tried to tempt Jesus. Jesus was about to begin his ministry of teaching and healing and wanted to prepare himself by going into the wilderness for a time of quiet prayer and thought. In the story, the Devil knew that Jesus was the Son of God, and tried to persuade him to use God's power for selfish reasons or to show off, rather than for the good of the world.

Other names for the Devil are Lucifer and Satan. The name Lucifer means 'bringer of light', although Christians do not believe that the Devil brings light. The name comes from a story where an angel of light in heaven tried to challenge God and to set himself up as a rival power. He was expelled from heaven and is called a 'fallen angel'. The name Satan might come from a Hebrew word meaning 'to wander', showing that the Devil wanders the earth looking to cause trouble.

Symbolism and the Devil

In Christian art, the Devil is often shown as similar to a male human figure, but with wings, hooves, horns and a forked tail. This symbolizes the way in which temptation can often take different forms, and people can be tempted to do wrong without always realizing it. The Devil is also often painted red, the colour of passion and anger, to show that people are more likely to do wrong when they are in the grip of strong emotions. He can be shown with tongues of fire, to represent the fires of Hell. Traditionally, the Devil is believed to be in charge of Hell, a place where people go if they live a life of sin and do not accept the forgiveness of God.

Some Christians believe that the Devil is a supernatural person, who can make plans, do deliberate acts of wrong, and who aims to overthrow God. Others believe that the Devil is not a person with feelings and a mind, but is a poetic way of describing human struggles to choose between right and wrong. They believe that there can be no power to rival God, so the Devil cannot be a personal power but represents sin and the absence of God.

Traditionally the Devil is shown as a semi-human person who can appear in different forms. ▼

The Fall

The **Fall** is the name given to the story in Genesis of the first man and woman, Adam and Eve, and how they disobeyed God and brought an end to human life in Paradise. According to the story, God made Adam and Eve to be partners for one another, and gave them a beautiful garden in which to live – the Garden of Eden. This garden provided the couple with all the food they needed, and God put them in charge of looking after the other species of animals and plants. God gave Adam and Eve some rules: he told them to be good stewards of the earth, to produce children, and that they could eat from any tree in the garden except for the one in the middle, which was forbidden, and that they would die if they ate it:

> *And the Lord God commanded the man, 'You are free to eat from any tree in the garden; but you must not eat from the tree of the knowledge of good and evil, for when you eat of it you will surely die'.*
>
> **(Genesis 2:16-17)**

However, one of the creatures in the garden, the serpent, decided to tempt Adam and Eve to disobey God. He told them that God was not telling them the truth about death, and that eating the fruit would give them special knowledge:

> *'You will surely not die,' the serpent said to the woman. 'For God knows that when you eat of it your eyes will be opened, and you will be like God, knowing good and evil.'*
>
> **(Genesis 3:4)**

The woman, Eve, was tempted into eating the fruit and she gave some to Adam, who ate it too. The act of disobedience is known as 'the Fall' because humanity 'fell from grace'. Instead of being in a perfect relationship with God, they did wrong and challenged God's authority.

Once the people had disobeyed God, everything started to go wrong. They began to be ashamed of their own bodies, and covered themselves with clothes. They stopped accepting responsibility for their own actions and started blaming each other for doing wrong; Adam blamed God for giving him Eve in the first place. The people had changed from being perfect to being sinful. **Sin** means an action which breaks a rule made by God; Christians believe that people sin every time they disobey God or fail to do the things God wants.

Good and evil: Christianity

God punished Adam and Eve because of their disobedience. He made it difficult for Adam to grow his own food, so that he would have to work hard, and he gave Eve pain in childbirth. The people were no longer allowed to live in the beautiful garden but had to go out into the world and make their own way.

▲ *The story of the fall – where Adam and Eve are sent out of the Garden of Eden is one of the most well known of all Bible stories. Different Christians have different views about what it means.*

For **Discussion**

Do you think that the story of the Fall is literally true? Or do you think it is a myth? Or do you think it has no truth in it at all? Try to support your answer with reasons.

Some Christians believe that the story of the Fall is literally true; they believe that all the details are historically accurate and that Adam and Eve were real people. Others believe that the story is a myth, which is a story given to express truths which might be difficult to understand in another way. People who think the story is a myth say that it symbolizes the ways in which all people separate themselves from God through sin.

Original sin and redemption

Exam Practice

Practise your skills in **demonstrating knowledge and understanding**.

Explain what is meant by 'original sin'.

In your answer, you need to give a short but clear explanation, showing that you understand what Christians mean by the term 'original sin'. You should include an explanation of what 'sin' means.

This will help you in the exam when you answer part (b) questions.

For Discussion

Do you think that someone could do something morally wrong without realizing it? Or is an action only wrong if it is deliberate?

Some Christians believe that because Adam and Eve disobeyed God, all people in the world are born in a state of original sin. This means that even when they are newly born, they are not innocent and do not have a perfect relationship with God, because the sin of Adam and Eve has been passed on down the generations throughout the whole of humanity. Christians who believe in original sin think that everyone needs the forgiveness of God, right from the moment they are born.

Some Christian Churches baptize babies as a symbol to show that they are being washed from original sin by the forgiveness of God, even though the babies seem too young to have done anything wrong and are too young to understand the idea of obeying or disobeying God. This is because of the belief in original sin.

Not all Christians share this belief. Some think that a sin has to be a deliberate act of doing wrong, so they would argue that although everyone does sin, people are not born sinful but become sinful through the choices they make once they are old enough to know right from wrong.

One of the most important beliefs in Christianity is that Jesus died to save people from their sins. Christians believe that Jesus' death on the cross was an act of redemption. This means paying the price for something, in order to get it back. Christians call Jesus 'the Redeemer' or the 'Saviour'. They believe that because all people sin, everyone deserves to die and no one earns the right to live with God in heaven after death. They believe that Jesus came to earth as the Son of God, and that he was the only human being ever to be totally free from sin. Although he was tempted by the Devil in the wilderness, Jesus did not give in to temptation but used God's power to do good for humanity. The Bible teaches that although Jesus did nothing wrong, he was put to death by crucifixion, and his death paid the price for human sin, because he gave his life as a sacrifice for others.

> *For the wages of sin is death, but the gift of God is eternal life in Christ Jesus our Lord.*
> **(Romans 6:23)**

When Christians talk about people being 'saved from their sins', they mean that although everyone fails to meet the standards of goodness set by God, this does not mean that they have to be separated from God for ever. Christians believe that everyone who faces up to the wrong they have done and who accepts Jesus as the Redeemer will be saved from sin, and will be able to have eternal life after death with God in heaven.

Exam Practice

Practise your skills in **demonstrating knowledge and understanding**.

Explain in your own words what Christians mean by the word 'redemption'.

Try to make your answer clear, short and to the point.

This will help you in the exam when you answer part (b) questions.

The problem of evil

This section explores Christian responses to the problem why a good God allows suffering.

What is meant by 'natural' and 'moral' evil?

One of the big problems for religious believers is trying to understand why God allows evil and suffering in the world. Sometimes, as a way of helping to understand this problem and find ways of answering it, thinkers talk about two different kinds of evil: natural evil and moral evil.

- **Natural evil** refers to the suffering and pain caused by experiences which are beyond human control. For example, an event such as a hurricane, earthquake or tsunami might be considered natural evil, because they cause suffering but were not deliberate human actions.

▲ *The devastating tsunami of 2004 was caused by an earthquake under the Indian Ocean: a natural evil.*

- **Moral evil** refers to the suffering and pain caused by human wrong. It is known by religious believers as 'sin'. Some examples of moral evil might be theft, bullying, violence and terrorism.

Exam Practice

Practise your skills in **demonstrating knowledge and understanding**.

Explain what is meant by 'natural evil' and 'moral evil'.

In your answer, try to give some examples to make your explanation clearer.

This will help you in the exam when you answer part (c) questions.

Why is there evil and suffering in the world?

When my child died, I found it very difficult to accept. I wanted to understand, why did an innocent child have to die so young? I still don't have any answers to this.

Many people find it difficult to understand why bad things happen. When people are the victims of a crime, for example, they might wonder why it happened to them, particularly if they don't commit crimes themselves. Of course, bad things don't always happen to bad people; sometimes the kindest and most loving people suffer terrible disasters or illnesses or die young.

The question of why bad things happen is a very difficult one for Christians to answer, because they believe that God is perfectly good and loving, and also **omnipotent** (all-powerful). People ask themselves, if there is a God, why does he allow pain? If God is **omnibenevolent**, surely he would not want any of his creation to suffer, and if he is all-powerful, surely he can stop suffering when it happens. But the world contains a lot of pain, and God does not always seem to do anything about it.

Some people respond to this problem by coming to the conclusion that there can't be a God after all; or, if there is a God, he can't be all-loving and all-powerful. But Christians give different responses.

Christian responses

One response given by Christians is that evil and suffering came into the world as the result of the Fall. God made the world perfectly good, but Adam and Eve spoiled it with their disobedience, and the consequences of this were so great that it even spoiled the natural world, so that earthquakes and hurricanes sometimes happen. People can be blamed for the existence of all evil and suffering, whether it is moral evil or natural evil.

Other people might argue against this view. They might argue that the Fall was not a real historical event. Or they might argue that, even if people did disobey God in this way, God is meant to be all-loving and all-powerful, so he could have stopped sin spoiling the world.

Another possible Christian response is that evil and suffering provide people with a way to grow in faith and develop as human beings. An early Christian thinker called Irenaeus taught that God never intended that people should live in a comfortable paradise with no challenges. He thought that God gives us difficulties to face so that we can learn to overcome them. He believed that we would not have important qualities such as bravery, compassion and generosity, if we never had any fear or if no one ever needed any help.

People might argue against this view by saying that people do not always learn from the bad things that happen. Sometimes they become worse people, not better ones, because of their suffering. They might also argue that terrible events such as terrorism, bereavement and painful illnesses might teach us things, but what we learn is not worth the amount of pain.

Sometimes Christians say that we need suffering in order to develop as human beings. But other people argue that we suffer too much and don't always become better people because of it. ▶

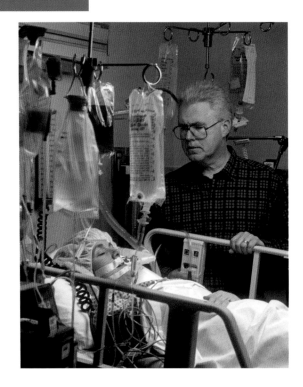

Christians often argue that we have evil and suffering in the world because we need them in order to make free choices. They say that we would not be fully human unless we were able to make real choices between right and wrong and these would not be *free* choices if we were only able to choose the right thing to do and were not capable of sin. They would also not be free choices if God set right the wrong things we do, rather than making us live with the consequences.

People might disagree with this by saying that our freedom of choice is not worth the amount of pain we suffer and that the world might have been a better place if God did not give people the freedom to choose cruelty and murder. Or they might argue that if God is all-powerful, he should be able to give us free choice without evil, because God is supposed to be able to do anything.

The story of Job in the Bible considers the questions raised by innocent suffering. It tells the story of a good and innocent man who suffers great pain because the Devil was testing him to see if he would turn against God. In the end, Job asks God for an explanation, as he wants to understand why he has suffered so much. God tells Job that there are many things that humans cannot understand. God has great powers, but humans are very limited, and therefore they should not question God. Some Christians might interpret this story to mean that we cannot always expect to have answers to our questions. When we suffer, we can't always understand the reason for it, and maybe we never will.

Exam Practice

Practise your skills in **demonstrating knowledge and understanding**.

Explain how Christians might answer the problem of why there is evil and suffering in the world.

In this answer, you could give several different responses, to show that you realize there are different ways of approaching the problem of evil.

This will help you in the exam when you answer part (d) questions.

When I suffer with depression, I keep asking God, why does this happen? For a long time I couldn't understand it and I needed to have an answer. But after talking with Christian friends, I realized that there are some things people just can't understand. We have to trust that God loves us and doesn't make mistakes. Perhaps one day in heaven I will understand.

Activity 1

Practise your **evaluation** skills.

Do you think that we need to have suffering and challenges in the world? Or would the world be better if nothing ever went wrong?

Think carefully about your answer. Try to give at least one reason to explain your point of view. When you write your answer, make sure you have included the word 'because'.

I think there is so much wrong with the world that there can't possibly be a loving and powerful God. A good God would get rid of things like cancer and wouldn't let good people die young. I think that when bad things happen, it is just chance, and some people are unluckier than others.

Does the problem of evil prove that there is no God?

Many people argue that there is so much evil and suffering in the world that there can't possibly be an all-loving and all-powerful God. Although Christians have tried to provide some answers to the problem of evil, perhaps none of the answers can completely satisfy someone who wants to understand why life can be so painful.

I'm a Christian, and I know that evil and suffering can be very hard to understand. But I don't think the problem of evil proves that there can't be a God. There are so many wonderful things in the world, so many beautiful things, and there is a lot of happiness and love. I think God leaves it up to us to choose whether or not to believe in him, and sometimes we need a lot of faith.

Exam practice

Practise your **evaluation** skills.

'The problem of evil makes it impossible to believe in God'

Discuss this statement. You should use different, supported points of view and a personal viewpoint. You must refer to Christianity in your answer.

Think about your opinion – does the suffering in the world prove that the God of Christianity can't possibly exist? Or could there still be a loving God even if people do suffer pain? Try to support your answer with reasons. In this answer, show why Christians and non-Christians might disagree. Try to use examples to support your answer.

This will help you in the exam when you answer part (e) questions.

Coping with suffering

EXAM FOCUS

This section will help you understand how Christians cope with evil and suffering.

Coping through prayer

Prayer is an important part of life for Christians. They believe that they can communicate with God by talking and listening, and that God will answer their prayers, even though he might not always give them what they want. One of the ways that Christians cope when they suffer pain is by praying about it, either on their own or with other Christians. They might talk to God about their feelings, and pray that they will be given strength to deal with the difficulty. They might ask God for healing if someone is ill, or they might ask for comfort. In some Christian churches there are boxes or noticeboards for people to write their prayer requests on pieces of paper, so that others will pray for them and support them.

▲ *One of the ways that Christians cope with suffering is through prayer.*

Remembering the suffering of Jesus

Some Christian churches emphasize stories of the suffering of Jesus. Roman Catholic churches often have statues or pictures of the Stations of the Cross, showing scenes from the story of the trial of Jesus to the crucifixion. These help believers to remember that Jesus suffered, and it can make them feel that they are not alone when they are in pain, because they believe that God suffers too and knows what humans are going through. Christians might try to follow the example of Jesus when they are suffering, by being patient and not complaining.

Reading the Bible

Christians often turn to the Bible for help when they face times of suffering. They might read stories of Biblical characters who suffered but put their trust in God. They might choose to read passages which give a message of comfort and hope for the future, for example this one from John's Gospel:

> *Peace I leave with you; my peace I give you. I do not give to you as the world gives. Do not let your hearts be troubled and do not be afraid.*
> **(John 14:27)**

Talking to other Christians

Christians, like other people, often find it helpful to talk about their problems with others who share their beliefs. Leaders in the church set aside special times in the week where people can go and see them to talk about their worries. Christians try to support each other with advice, and give each other time and comfort.

Helping others who suffer

Another way Christians might cope with suffering is by using their time to help others and support those who are in pain. Christians try to help other members of their community at times of difficulty, because they believe that it is important to treat others the way that you would like to be treated yourself and they believe that everyone is important to God. They also try to help people who suffer in other parts of the world, by giving some of their money to aid agencies such as Christian Aid and CAFOD.

There are many ways Christians could help people who are suffering, for example they could:

- visit the elderly, people who are ill or people who have been bereaved

- spend time with people who are lonely

- raise funds to help people or animals who are suffering

- use their vote carefully and try and choose leaders who care about people with problems

- offer childcare when families are struggling

- volunteer for a local scheme such as reading to people with visual difficulties.

When I had a bad fall, I was so glad that I belonged to a church. Other Christians came to visit me when I was in hospital, and someone came to give me a lift home when I was ready. The vicar came to see if I was all right, and lots of people sent me cards. All of this support helped me to cope and cheered me up. ▶

Exam Practice

Practise your skills in showing **knowledge and understanding**.

How might Christians help others who are suffering?

You could use some of the ideas here, and you could add some of your own ideas about how a Christian might help others who are suffering. Try to show in your answer that you understand Christian beliefs about the need to help others.

This will help you in the exam when you answer part (d) questions.

Sources and reasons for moral behaviour

This section explores ideas about how people make moral decisions.

Most people want to lead good lives and to choose to do the right thing. However, people don't always share the same opinions about right and wrong and they have different views on many moral issues. They might argue about whether it is right or wrong to eat meat, or go to war, or have an abortion. When people have different opinions, it can be difficult or impossible to know which of them is right. Some people think that with a lot of issues there isn't one 'right answer', but different actions could be right for different people.

Christians believe that standards of right behaviour come from God, so when there is a moral issue, there will be a 'right answer'. But how might they find out what these answers are? For Christians, there are several different ways of understanding what God wants:

- **Prayer** – talking to God is always important for Christians. When they have a difficult moral decision to make, Christians will pray and ask God to guide them by showing them what to do. They might feel that their prayers are answered by a strong inner sense of the right choice, or they might believe that God answers them by directing them to a special passage in the Bible of through the words of the preacher in church.

▲ *Christians might believe that God teaches them the right way to behave through the words of the preacher in church.*

When you have a difficult moral decision to make, how do you come to a decision about it? Whose opinions do you value most?

Do you think that the conscience is a good guide for morality?

The Bible – most Christians use the Bible for help when they are thinking about issues of right and wrong. The Bible gives rules and stories to illustrate moral behaviour, and Christians believe that God speaks to them when they read it. However, there can be problems with using the Bible to settle moral questions. Sometimes it gives rules which can seem to contradict each other, such as rules about divorce.

In Matthew's Gospel, Jesus teaches that divorce should not be allowed unless the woman has been unfaithful to her husband, but Mark's Gospel teaches that divorce is not allowed under any circumstances. Also, the Bible does not have answers to every question; some people think that because the Bible was written so long ago, it can be difficult to apply its teachings to modern society.

- **The example of Jesus** – Because Christians believe that Jesus lived a life without sin, they often use Jesus' behaviour as an example when they are trying to make a moral decision. They try to imagine what Jesus would do in the same circumstances, and they use this as a pattern for their own behaviour. This can be useful, but it can be difficult to know how Jesus might behave if he lived in the modern world.

Practise your skills in **demonstrating knowledge and understanding**.

Explain how Christians might know what to do when they have a moral decision to make.

In your answer, you could give several different ideas. For high marks, try to think of examples to support and illustrate the points you make.

This will help you in the exam when you answer part (d) questions.

The teaching of the Church
– the Christian Churches give teachings about moral issues, and many Christians use these teachings when they are making decisions in their personal lives. Sometimes churches make official statements about a moral issue, setting out their views of the right Christian response on questions such as abortion and climate change.

In church services, the person giving the sermon (talk) will often explain Christian beliefs about morality in a way that will help people to apply church teaching to their own lives.

Ways of understanding what God wants

The conscience – many people, whether they are Christian or not, think that humans have a special sense of right and wrong, which they call the conscience. It is sometimes described as an 'inner voice', which lets people know whether their behaviour is right or wrong. Some people argue that this voice is just a reflection of the way they were brought up, and has nothing to do with God.

But many Christians think that the conscience is one way of hearing the voice of God. Someone's conscience might make them feel guilty about what they have done, so that they know it was wrong, or they might have a strong sense that they ought to behave in a certain way. Christianity teaches that people can train their consciences to be guided by the Holy Spirit, so that when they think about a moral question and wonder what to do, God can give them an inner sense of what is right.

This can sometimes cause problems for Christians, however, if the Church or the Bible teaches one thing but their conscience seems to be telling them something else. It can be difficult in these circumstances to know which decision to make.

Glossary

Conscience – an 'inner voice' letting people know right from wrong

Devil – the Tempter, a force of evil

Fall – the Biblical story in which Adam and Eve disobey God by eating forbidden fruit

Moral evil – evil and suffering caused by human choice to do wrong

Natural evil – suffering that happens because of the natural world and not because of human fault

Omnibenevolent – perfectly good and perfectly loving

Omnipotent – all-powerful

Original sin – the sin that people are born with, inherited from the sin of Adam and Eve

Redemption – paying the price to buy something back

Sin – something morally wrong which goes against the teachings of God

PHILOSOPHY 2

Form and nature of revelation

This section concentrates on providing an understanding of the importance of revelation in Christianity, for through revelation God reveals himself to mankind.

Revelation is when something is revealed to humanity by God. Christians believe that God reveals himself in a variety of ways, such as through religious experience, through nature, through Jesus, and through the Bible. Revelation can help to prove God's existence, and also to reveal things about God's nature.

General revelation – revelation through things available to everyone

(for example, the Bible, nature, religious leaders).

Special revelation – a direct, personal experience of God by a person or group

(for example, dreams and visions).

Exam Practice

Practise your skills in **demonstrating knowledge and understanding**.

Explain in your own words what is meant by the word 'revelation'.

Try to make your answer clear, concise and to the point.

This will help you in the exam when you answer part (a) questions.

Mystical and religious experience

How do Christians believe God reveals himself through miracles?

A **miracle** is a special event which is believed to have a supernatural or divine cause. Many Christians believe that God has the power to perform miracles. There are examples of miracles in the Bible and throughout history, and some Christians claim that miracles still occur today.

One type of miracle is the healing of a physical or mental illness. Sometimes healings cannot be explained medically or scientifically, and Christians may say that they are miracles of God.

Miracles reveal God's power because God has the ability to do things which humans are unable to do, and which may not seem scientifically or naturally possible.

Through miracles, Christians believe that God's presence is revealed. Miracles show that God is active in the world.

◀ *Healings at Lourdes*
Many people make pilgrimages to Lourdes in France. Lots of people, especially Roman Catholics, believe it is a sacred place because the Virgin Mary is believed to have appeared there, and many people claim to have been healed in the spring waters nearby.

God has shown Pharaoh what he is about to do…The reason the dream was given to Pharaoh in two forms is that the matter has been firmly decided by God, and God will do it soon.
(Genesis 41:28, 32) ▶
Ronaldo in action. ▼

Some Christians believe God has revealed himself to them in a vision or dream.

- Sometimes Christians may believe that they have actually physically seen something with their eyes. In this case they believe the vision is of an actual spiritual form. At Lourdes in France, a French teenager Bernadette is believed to have seen the Virgin Mary numerous times.

- Lorna Byrne, author of *Angels in my Hair*, claims to have seen angels all her life and believes she has had a vision of the nativity.

- Other Christians believe that they have visions in their mind, because they have connected with God. One example of such visions is when some Christians see a mental picture that they believe is a prophecy (prediction of the future) from God.

- Some Christians believe God has revealed himself to them in a dream. This might mean that they wake up with the awareness that they have had contact with God. Other Christians may feel 'changed' in some way, or believe that they have been given instructions from God through a dream.

Christians believe God reveals things through dreams in the Bible, such as in this story (see left) about Joseph interpreting Pharaoh's dreams.

How do Christians believe God reveals himself through prayer?

Prayer is a way for Christians to communicate with God. They believe that God listens to their prayers and answers them (although not always in the way they expect). Christians pray in a variety of ways, both in public and in private.

For example:

- a group of people may pray together in a Christian church, led by a priest or minister, with their hands joined in prayer

- a Catholic may pray alone, using their rosary beads

- a sportsman such as Cristiano Ronaldo may hold their hands in prayer during a football game.

Sometimes prayer gives Christians a strong sense of God's presence. They believe that prayer can bring people closer to God, and can allow Christians to share a deeper relationship with God.

Prayer allows Christians to speak to God, who listens to them. Prayer is also an opportunity for Christians to hear what God is saying. Through prayer, many Christians believe that God gives them instructions about what to do – not just about religious matters but about every area of their lives.

Prayer allows Christians to share their problems with God, and also to give thanks for things they are grateful for. Through prayer, Christians may be filled with a sense of wonder or deep inner peace, which reveals something of the greatness of God.

When Christians pray to God, they believe they are relating to God as a person in the wholeness of his character, and therefore prayer can reveal different aspects of God's nature (for example, forgiving, powerful, kind).

The Bible often says that prayer changes the way God acts:

 You do not have, because you do not ask God.
(James 4:2)

This implies that if you fail to ask God for something, you may be deprived of receiving what he would have given. Christians believe that when they ask, God responds. Therefore prayer is very important to Christians, and God wants Christians to pray. Not only that, but God may even change the way he acts because of prayer.

How do Christians believe God reveals himself through worship?

Worship is the act of paying divine honour to God, showing devotion, respect and admiration for God above all other things.

Christians worship God in a variety of ways.

- The sacraments (religious rites) are an example of worship in some Christian denominations, although not all Christians follow them. The sacrament of Holy Communion, for example, allows Christians to honour Jesus, as it is followed to remember the Last Supper.

- Some Christians may show outward signs of respect for God, such as making the sign of the cross.

- Christians may worship God through music. This can be done in a variety of ways, such as singing in church on a Sunday, or playing an instrument alone. When Christians worship through music, their music is devoted to God and their focus may be on pleasing and connecting with God.

- For many Christians, worship is a way of life. They pay honour to God throughout their everyday lives, not just at set times. Their whole attitude is focused on praising and respecting God in everything they do.

Some Christians (including Roman Catholics) believe that through the sacraments, God can directly reveal his grace. In the sacrament of confession, for example, the priest forgives the sinner in God's name. Some Christians believe that this reveals God's kind and forgiving nature.

For Christians, worship can help them to be close to God, and allow them to have a personal relationship with God. God welcomes and accepts their worship, and God gives things in return – peace, strength, clarity or forgiveness, for example. Through worship, God may give Christians grace and help in their lives. Christian worship is a two-way activity between the worshipper and God.

How do Christians believe God reveals himself through the Holy Spirit?

Christians believe in the Trinity. This means one God who has three different 'forms' – The Father, Son and Holy Spirit. So, the Holy Spirit is one of God's 'natures'.

The Holy Spirit is the living presence of God in a person or situation. Christians believe that God is immanent (in the world with us). For Christians, the Holy Spirit is God's active, invisible power in people's lives.

Examples of the Holy Spirit in the Bible

The Holy Spirit is mentioned in the Genesis account of God's creation:

> *…and the Spirit of God was hovering over the waters.*
>
> **(Genesis 1:2)**

> *And I will ask the Father, and he will give you another Counsellor to be with you for ever – the Spirit of truth.*
>
> **(John 14:16-17)**

In the Bible, the disciples were filled with the Holy Spirit a few days after Jesus' resurrection:

> *Suddenly a sound like the blowing of a violent wind came from heaven and filled the whole house where they were sitting. They saw what seemed to be tongues of fire that separated and came to rest on each of them. All of them were filled with the Holy Spirit and began to speak in other tongues as the Spirit enabled them.*
>
> **(Acts 2:2-4)**

People speaking in tongues believe they are experiencing some aspect of God's nature, and are filled with the Holy Spirit. ▼

Some Christians believe that they can be filled with the Holy Spirit. This can bring an increased sense of emotions such as peace or joy, and even lead to reactions such as singing dancing, shaking or crying. Some people may 'speak in tongues' (unknown languages), or have visions or prophesy (predict the future).

The Holy Spirit is part of God, so Christians who think they have been filled with the Holy Spirit believe that they have experienced God, and that God has revealed something of himself to them.

Conversion

Some people have a conversion experience. They may believe God has come into their lives and decide to 'give their lives to Jesus'.

Conversion means 'change', and for Christians conversion can change their lives dramatically.

Christians who have had a conversion experience may say they have been 'saved' or 'born again'.

Mysticism is an advanced form of religious experience. A mystical experience gives a strong awareness of the unseen, or things beyond. For Christians, a mystical experience is an example of revelation of God. It can bring illumination and be life-changing.

How might Christians believe God reveals himself through the world?

Many Christians believe that God is revealed through the world. God created the world, so nature reveals a part of God. Some Christians believe that the wonder of the world reveals something of the wonder of God, since he created it.

For some Christians, nature is so wonderful and complex that it provokes a sense of awe, a feeling of the presence of God. They may be filled with the awareness of something greater than themselves. This is sometimes referred to as 'numinous'.

Sights such as these can make people feel a sense of awe at nature:

- a beautiful autumn day with trees in coloured leaf

- a newborn baby

- waves crashing on a rock

- a bird weaving a nest from twigs.

▲ *Many Christians believe that the wonders of nature act as a reminder of God's meaning and purpose in our lives, or simply give a sense of 'otherness' or holiness.*

Revelation of God through the person of Jesus

Christians believe that Jesus is the Son of God:

> *So the holy one to be born will be called the Son of God.*
>
> **(Luke 1:35)**

and that Jesus is God incarnate, which means God in human form:

> *I and the Father are one.*
>
> **(John 10:30)**

Christians believe that God sent Jesus to earth to bring salvation. They believe that sin is part of human nature, and separates us from God, who is perfect. Through his death and resurrection, Jesus paid the price for our sins, so that Christians can be reunited with God in heaven.

Christians believe that although Jesus was the Son of God, he took on human form and became a man.

> *...Christ Jesus: Who, being in very nature God, did not consider equality with God something to be grasped, but made himself nothing, taking the very nature of a servant, being made in human likeness. And being found in appearance as a man, he humbled himself and became obedient to death – even death on a cross!*
>
> **(Philippians 2:5-8)**

The fact that God took on human form in this way is really important in revealing God's character, because Jesus is a role model for how Christians should act in real human situations.

Christians believe that Jesus reveals the nature and intentions of God through his actions, words and teachings.

Look at these examples of how God's nature is revealed through Jesus:

LOVE

Christians believe that Jesus' death on the cross is the ultimate demonstration of God's love for humans.

For God so loved the world that he gave his one and only Son, that whoever believes in him shall not perish but have eternal life.

(John 3:16)

POWER

Jesus calms the storm and shows power over the natural world.

Then he got up and rebuked the winds and the waves, and it was completely calm. The men were amazed and asked, 'What kind of man is this? Even the winds and the waves obey him!'

(Matthew 8:26-27)

RIGHTEOUS ANGER

Jesus clears the temple, showing that God cares about human behaviour.

When it was almost time for the Jewish Passover, Jesus went up to Jerusalem. In the temple courts he found men selling cattle, sheep and doves, and others sitting at tables exchanging money. So he made a whip out of cords, and drove all from the temple area, both sheep and cattle; he scattered the coins of the money-changers and overturned their tables. To those who sold doves he said, 'Get these out of here! How dare you turn my Father's house into a market!'

(John 2:13-16)

FORGIVENESS

Jesus heals a paralysed man, showing God's compassion and forgiveness

When Jesus saw their faith, he said to the paralytic, 'Son, your sins are forgiven.'

Now some teachers of the law were sitting there, thinking to themselves, 'Why does this fellow talk like that? He's blaspheming! Who can forgive sins but God alone?'

Immediately Jesus knew in his spirit that this was what they were thinking in their hearts, and he said to them, 'Why are you thinking these things?...

...But you may know that the Son of Man has authority on earth to forgive sins...'

(Mark 2:5-10)

How is the revelation of God through Jesus relevant for modern Christians?

Many issues addressed by Jesus are still very relevant today. One example is what Jesus says about the issue of divorce:

> *It has been said, 'Anyone who divorces his wife must give her a certificate of divorce.' But I tell you that anyone who divorces his wife, except for marital unfaithfulness, causes her to become an adulteress, and anyone who marries the divorced woman commits adultery.*
>
> **(Matthew 5:31-32)**

Jesus said:

> *Come to me, all you who are weary and burdened, and I will give you rest.*
>
> **(Matthew 11:28)**

Christians today may be encouraged by these words, which tell them that God will give them relief when they have problems – they can turn to God in times of need.

Contemporary Christians can learn a lot from Jesus' attitude towards people. He talked to people who others disregarded because of their race, social status or morality, such as a promiscuous Samaritan woman (see John 4:1-26).

Jesus demonstrated forgiveness, even towards those who crucified him:

> *Jesus said, 'Father, forgive them, for they do not know what they are doing.'*
>
> **(Luke 23:34)**

Many modern Christians try to follow Jesus' example of forgiving others. Look at this powerful contemporary example:

"I forgive you", mother tells racist thugs who killed her son

The mother of Anthony Walker drew on her Christian faith yesterday to find forgiveness for the two thugs who murdered him with a mountaineering axe because he was black.

Outside the court, Mrs Walker, with her daughter Dominique, who had gone to school with Taylor, said: 'Do I forgive them? At the point of death Jesus said "I forgive them because they don't know what they did".

'I've got to forgive them. I still forgive them. My family and I still stand by what we believe: forgiveness.' She said that she had never been in doubt about the verdict.

(*Daily Telegraph* 2 December 2005)

Authority and importance of sacred texts

This section will help you understand why the Bible is so important for Christians.

EXAM FOCUS

Most religions have sacred texts to help them understand about God. Sacred texts can also be called scriptures or holy books. For Christians, the most important sacred text is the Bible.

The Bible

The Bible is a collection of many books written over a very long period of time – about 1000 years. It is written in different styles and languages and has two sections – the Old Testament and the New Testament. The Old Testament was mainly written before Jesus was born. As well as being part of the Christian Bible, the Old Testament is also the Jewish Bible. Christians believe that the Old Testament tells how people prepared for Jesus coming to Earth. The New Testament is written by early Christians, and teaches about Jesus' life and death and about Christianity.

Authority of the Bible

When Christians say that the Bible has **authority**, they may be referring to its power and influence, or to its legitimacy and right to put its power into effect.

Christians believe God is the ultimate authority, greater than any human authority or wisdom. Christians believe that the Bible is the 'Word of God', which was revealed to people by God. Therefore the Bible, as the 'Word of God', is entitled to great power.

So, why do so many Christians believe that the Bible is definitely the 'Word of God'? There are four main reasons:

The Bible claims itself the 'Word of God'

- It has direct quotes from God, such as the hundreds of passages in the Old Testament that begin 'The Lord says …'

> *All scripture is God-breathed and is useful for teaching, rebuking, correcting and training in righteousness.*
>
> **(2 Timothy 3:16)**

- Jesus, Son of God, says things about scripture being correct.
- Several passages in the New Testament assert the authority of the Bible:

> *I warn everyone who hears the words of the prophecy of this book: If anyone adds anything to them, God will add to him the plagues described in this book. And if anyone takes words away from this book of prophecy, God will take away from him his share in the tree of life and in the holy city, which are described in this book.*
>
> **(Revelation 22:18-19)**

- When Christians read the Bible, they may have a spiritual awareness that it is the 'Word of God'. This gives Christians faith in the authority of the Bible.

◀ *Another reason for the authority of the Bible is that it is has the approval of the Christian community and Churches as the most important sacred text.*

◀ *Christians believe that the Bible has the power to change lives. It contains instructions, commands and eye-opening stories. Many Christians have changed the way they live to follow its teachings.*

The meaning of the Bible

Christians believe the Bible reveals:

- God's purpose for humans
- God's nature
- the story of God's son, Jesus.

Fundamentalists are Christians who take everything in the Bible literally, believing everything happened just as it describes, because it came directly from God.

Some Christians have a more liberal view of the Bible, believing that not everything in the Bible is literally true, but that it contains truth in its interpretation. It is not the direct 'Word of God', but it contains the 'Word of God' within it.

How do Christians use the Bible?

Christians read and study the Bible

Many Christians read parts of the Bible every day. They believe that because it is a sacred text, it is important to know and understand it.

Christians may study the Bible. This can involve looking for significant themes (for example, love, money, church) or interpreting it.

Christians may learn passages of the Bible off by heart, so that they can easily remember them when they are in different situations.

Activity 1

Think about the account of creation in Genesis. How might fundamentalists view this story? How might some Christians take a more liberal view?

For Christians Jesus is a role model for knowing scripture off by heart. He uses scripture in response when the Devil tempts him, such as in the following passage which quotes from the Old Testament book Deuteronomy.

 It is written: 'Man does not live on bread alone, but on every word that comes from the mouth of God.'

(Matthew 4:4)

Some Christians study the Bible together

The Bible is read in churches. Sometimes this is in formal 'readings' where a set passage is read at a specific time in a service. Other churches may allow members to read passages out in the middle of worship, unplanned, because God has told them that it is appropriate.

In Christian churches, the leader will often give a sermon (which means speech or message) to explain how to understand parts of the Bible.

Christians try to follow the teachings of the Bible

Christians believe that the Bible contains teachings that are relevant today. They try to understand these teachings, and work out how they can apply them to their lives, and to the modern world.

 The Ten Commandments
You shall have no other gods before me.
You shall not make yourself an idol in the form of anything in heaven above or on the earth beneath or in the waters below.
You shall not misuse the name of the Lord your God.
Remember the Sabbath day by keeping it holy.
Honour your father and your mother.
You shall not murder.
You shall not commit adultery.
You shall not steal.
You shall not give false testimony against your neighbour.
You shall not covet your neighbour's house …
or anything that belongs to your neighbour.

(Exodus 20:3-17)

People who want to get rich fall into temptation and a trap and into many foolish and harmful desires that plunge men into ruin and destruction.

(1 Timothy 6:9)

How might Christians say that this teaching is relevant to the credit crunch?

Dear friends, let us love one another, for love comes from God.

(1 John 4:7)

Christians believe that the teachings of the Bible are still very relevant today, because:

- Many of the issues in the Bible are the same as modern issues, for example, forgiveness, love, money, violence, sex, religion.

- Even if an issue is not directly addressed, many Christians believe that the teachings of the Bible can be interpreted to address it.

Exam Practice

Practise your skills in **demonstrating knowledge and understanding**.

Explain the importance of the Bible to Christians.

In your answer, show how Christians might use the Bible in different situations, and how they might be helped by it. Explain why Christians think the Bible is more important than other books, and try to give some examples of situations where a Christian might turn to the Bible. For high marks, try to use key vocabulary such as 'authority'

This will help you in the exam when you answer part (d) questions.

Christians believe that the Bible reveals the nature of God

Christians believe that the Bible reveals the nature of God. Look at these examples:

> *If you believe, you will receive whatever you ask for in prayer.*
>
> **(Matthew 21:22)**

Christians believe this reveals that God wants people to pray, and also that God will answer prayers as long as they have faith.

> *With man this is impossible, but with God all things are possible.*
>
> **(Matthew 19:26)**

Christians believe this reveals that God is all powerful.

Glossary

Authority – the right to make rules; an accepted source of truth

Conversion – changing; in Christianity, conversion means changing beliefs and becoming a Christian

Miracle – a special event, believed to have been caused by God which breaks the laws of nature

Prayer – talking and listening to God

Revelation – when God reveals something to humanity

Trinity – three in one: Father, Son and Holy Spirit

Origins of the world and life: scientific theories

Exam Practice

Practise your skills in **demonstrating knowledge and understanding**.

Explain in your own words what is meant by the word 'cosmology'.

For this answer, you need to be quite concise. Notice that you are being asked for an explanation here, and not for your own opinions or beliefs.

This will help you in the exam when you answer part (a) questions.

This section will help you to understand how scientific ideas about the origins of the world compare with Christian ideas.

The Big Bang theory says that at the beginning of time about 14 billion years ago there was a huge explosion of a small volume of matter at very high density and temperature, and from this all the stars and planets evolved.

Although the Big Bang theory is a theory, rather than a proven *fact*, it does have:

- significance: it is the most important scientific theory about how the world began

- acceptance: the theory is widely accepted by most scientists and many people

- evidence: it is supported by some scientific evidence.

Evidence

There is some scientific evidence for this theory. For example:

- the universe seems to still be expanding today, just as the theory says it began to do after the Big Bang (when matter was thrown out in all directions)

- in the 1960s, it was accidentally discovered that the universe is filled in all directions with radiation, thought to be an after-effect of the Big Bang.

Limitations

The Big Bang theory does have its limitations, which is understandable since it tries to explain events that happened millions of years ago, outside any human experience or memory. For example:

- it does not explain how intelligent life was formed, just how the world in which it survives might have originated

- it fails to explain where most of the elements (parts of substances) came from

- there is no ultimate proof, so no one can say that it is definitely true.

Scientists are continuing to work on filling in the gaps of the Big Bang theory.

Darwin: evolution and natural selection

Charles Darwin wrote a book called *On the Origin of Species*, published in 1859. He had noticed that birds in the Galapagos Islands varied from island to island, for example, their beaks differed depending on the food available to them. This led him to believe that the birds had originally all had the same kind of beak but as they moved to different environments they had each adapted for survival within that environment. These findings were the start of his theory about evolution.

Darwin's theory of **evolution** was that simple cells evolved (developed) over millions of years into all the different types of living things, including humans. He said that this evolution happened through **natural selection**.

Exam Practice

Practise your skills in **demonstrating knowledge and understanding**.

Describe a scientific theory concerning the origins of the Earth.

For this answer, you need to be quite concise. Notice that you are being asked for an explanation here, and not for your own opinions or beliefs.

This will help you when you answer part (c) questions.

Darwin's theory explains how humanity and apes could have shared common ancestors.

Natural selection
Darwin's theory of evolution by natural selection stated that animals which were best adapted to survive and reproduce in their environment survived, while those less adapted tended to die out. Therefore the species gradually evolved and took on characteristics of the survivors.

There is some scientific evidence of evolution by natural selection, for example:

- changes that scientists have seen in microorganisms like bacteria
- fossils, bones and other archaeological finds.

Origins of the world and life: Bible teachings

EXAM FOCUS

This section will help you understand what the Bible teaches about the beginnings of the universe and of human life.

> *Now the earth was formless and empty... and the Spirit of God was hovering over the waters.*
>
> **(Genesis 1:2)**

Activity 1

Read Genesis from the beginning up to the end of Chapter 3, as a story.

The book of Genesis describes how God was in control of creating the universe and everything in it. It describes how God made all the elements of the universe carefully and in order. According to the Bible, the universe was planned and designed; there is no suggestion that it came into being through a random explosion or accident.

The Bible presents a story of how God created the first man and woman, Adam and Eve. Adam was made out of dust, and Eve was made from one of Adam's ribs. God made the people 'in his own image', and they seem to have been perfectly formed as humans right from the start of Creation, rather than developing gradually. In the story all the other animals were also designed by God as complete creatures. There is no suggestion that they gradually evolved.

> *The Lord God formed the man from the dust of the ground and breathed into his nostrils the breath of life, and the man became a living being.*
>
> **(Genesis 2:7)**

Activity 2

Do you think a Christian may have any questions about origins of the universe after reading the account in Genesis?

Some Christians believe that the Bible stories are literally true, so that if you could go back in time, you would see things happening exactly as the Bible says. Others believe that the stories are myths, which are a special way of giving important and true messages through telling vivid stories.

The relationship between scientific and religious understandings of the origins of the world and humanity

Different people have different understandings of, and beliefs about, the origins of the world and humanity. Here are three different views:

1 **God created the heavens and earth and everything on it, exactly as it says in the Bible.**
Historically, Christians generally believed that the Genesis account of Creation is literally and completely true. There are still Christians today who believe that this is the case, because they believe that the Bible is the Word of God and therefore contains the truth.

For those who believe that the Genesis account of the beginning of the world is literally true, there is conflict with the most widely accepted scientific theories.

For example:

- On the sixth day God created humans and animals as we know them, which suggests they did not evolve from earlier living things by natural selection.

- God created Adam and Eve and the human race has descended from them, which would mean that humans did not descend from apes as the theory of natural selection suggests.

- Some Christians believe that God created humans as a distinctly separate species. This means that they may disagree with the Darwin's theory because it implies that humans are the same as animals, except for some superiorities.

- Scientific research claims to have found evidence that the earth has existed for thousands of millions of years longer than human life. This does not fit in with the biblical account of the earth and humans being created just days apart.

Christians who reject Darwin's theory of evolution may dismiss scientific evidence saying that scientists could have misinterpreted what it is or when it is from. They could also argue that science has been wrong in the past (for example, when people believed that the earth was flat). Also they could say that working within human experience is limiting – we may believe that we know something through evidence, but without the full picture we cannot be sure.

2 **God created the heavens and earth, but the account in Genesis is symbolic and the Big Bang theory and evolutionary theory of natural selection are also true.**
Many modern Christians believe that the Creation account in Genesis is symbolic. This means it is a story that contains truth but every detail is not a literal fact.

This interpretation allows people to believe in both the Bible and science.

- They may believe that the Big Bang did start the universe, but that it was God who caused the Big Bang.

- The order in which God created the world in the Genesis account is very similar to the order in which scientific theory says that things evolved. Therefore some Christians believe that the Genesis account is compatible with Darwin's theory of evolution, but the timescale in Genesis is symbolic of the much longer scientific timescale.

- Human capacity for love and empathy (thinking about others) is compatible with Darwin's theory.

- '… I have stretched out the heavens …' (Isaiah 45:12) Some Christians believe this describes the same expansion of the universe as the Big Bang theory.

The Bible focuses on *why* God created the earth, whereas scientific theories focus on *how* the earth began. Many Christians believe that the two explanations are compatible, because they explain different aspects of God's creation.

In 2008 the Church of England apologized for its original negative reaction against Darwin's theories on evolution, claiming to have reacted emotionally due to a misunderstanding of his idea of natural selection. The apology article, written by Rev Dr Malcolm Brown, Director of Mission and Public Affairs for the Church of England, warns against misuse of Darwinism as a social theory, rather than a biological one – meaning 'weaker' people would be allowed to die out, an idea which can lead to discrimination and selfishness. The Church of England emphasizes that science and religion are compatible: 'Good religion needs good science'. It says that science can be seen as a way of revealing further truths about God and the wonder of his creation. (www.cofe.anglican.org)

There are many scientists who are also Christians. These Christians believe that science can glorify God, because it is a way of celebrating his creation and science can lead to the revelation of God the creator.

The Church of England website (www.cofe.anglican.org) says:

'Jesus himself warned his disciples that there was more that he could say to them and that the Spirit of truth would lead them into truth' (John 16: 12-13). There is no reason to doubt that Christ still draws people towards truth through the work of scientists as well as others, and many scientists are motivated in their work by a perception of the deep beauty of the created world.

3 The earth was created by the Big Bang and life evolved by natural selection. The earth was not created by God.

Many scientists believe that there is no truth in the Biblical account of the creation of the world – it is just a story. They believe that while there is some evidence for the scientific theories, there is no compelling evidence to support the idea of a creator God. Some people also think that the idea of God creating humans as they are today does not fit in with the idea that humans evolved from apes through natural selection, for which there is scientific evidence. Basically, they think that scientific evidence has seriously undermined religious belief, and so they reject Christianity.

Exam Practice

Practise your **evaluation** skills.

'Science is right about the origin of the world, and religion is wrong.'

Discuss this statement. You should include different, supported points of view and a personal viewpoint. You must refer to Christianity in your answer.

This will help you in the exam when you answer part (e) questions.

People and animals

This section will help you understand Christian views about the relationship between humans and other animals.

Although some animals are left to live naturally in the wild, in many situations humans are in control of their actions and behaviour. There are animals that are bigger and stronger than humans, animals who can run much faster, and those which have specialist skills which humans do not have. In spite of this, in general humans are in charge of animals and we use them in a variety of ways to fulfil our needs and desires, making decisions about the environments in which they live.

Activity 1

Practise your **evaluation** skills.

Look at the following list of words. What issues do they raise about the relation between humans and other animals? What is your own opinion about each of these issues?'

- Pets
- Meat
- Milk
- Eggs
- Fishing
- Hunting
- Zoo
- Circus
- Medical research
- Rainforest

Although there are many similarities between humans and animals, we are also very different to other animals:

- superior intelligence: humans have superior intelligence to animals.

- rationality: humans have the ability to rationalize in a way that animals do not. We can reason, question things in a more complex way, work out answers, and look at the past and future in order to plan.

- inherited knowledge: humans progress at a faster rate through the generations, because we are superior at passing on what each generation has learnt and developed to the next generation, and then building on this.

- emotions: humans have a greater capacity for emotions than animals do. For example, humans are capable of love in a way that other animals are not.

Some people think that some of the ways in which humans use or treat animals are wrong and opinions on the subject of how we should treat animals are extremely varied. Some people believe that we can treat animals in any way we want because humans are superior. Other people believe that we should use animals as necessary, but that we should not cause them any unnecessary suffering. Others again believe that we should not use animals for our own purposes at all and that they should be free to live 'by their natures'.

Animal rights and animal welfare

Animal rights	Animal welfare
The idea that animals should have rights in the same way as humans, and should be treated as members of our community, not as property.	The idea of avoiding cruelty and unnecessary suffering of animals, although it may be morally acceptable for humans to use animals.
Animal rights supporters believe that animals should not be used for food, clothing, medical research or entertainment.	Animal welfare supporters believe that animals can be used for food, clothing, medical research and entertainment, as long as there is no unnecessary suffering.
Criticism Animals do not have the same intelligence or capacity for social contracts as humans, and cannot have duties or make moral choices, so how can they have rights?	Criticism Animal rights supporters say that the principle of animal welfare is not logical, because it only considers animals in a way that fits in around human desires. Some animal welfare supporters have been criticized as prejudiced and hypocritical by showing preference for 'cute' animals, such as pets.

PETA (People for the Ethical Treatment of Animals) (www.peta.org)

Why should animals have rights? Philosopher Jeremy Bentham argued that when deciding on a being's rights, 'the question is not, Can they *reason*? nor, Can they *talk*? but, Can they *suffer*?' Leading animal rights group People for the Ethical Treatment of Animals (PETA) contends that animals have an inherent worth – a value completely separate from their abilities, relative intelligence or usefulness to humans. PETA believes that every creature with a will to live has a right to live free from pain and suffering, and that only prejudice allows us to deny others the rights that we expect to have for ourselves.

PETA US formed in 1980 in the United States and has more than 2 million members and supporters, making it the largest animal rights organization in the world.

PETA US and PETA Europe are dedicated to establishing and protecting the rights of all animals. Like humans, animals are capable of suffering and have interests in leading their own lives; therefore, they are not ours to use – for food, clothing, entertainment, experimentation or any other reason.

PETA-named affiliates around the world educate policymakers and the public about cruelty to animals and promote an understanding of the right of all animals to be treated with respect.

PETA US and PETA Europe work through public education, research, legislation, special events, celebrity involvement and protest campaigns.

Animal welfare laws are designed for the protection of animals. ▶

The Animal Welfare Act of 2006

This Act marks the biggest change in UK law concerning animal welfare in almost 100 years.

- The Act makes animal cruelty against the law.

- It also makes owners and keepers responsible for ensuring that the welfare needs of their animals are met.

These needs include:

1. Suitable environment (place to live)
2. Suitable diet
3. To exhibit normal behaviour patterns
4. To be housed with, or apart from, other animals (if applicable)
5. To be protected from pain, injury, suffering and disease.

Penalties for breaking this law are:

- A ban from owning animals
- A fine of up to £20,000
- A prison sentence.

◀ *In 2008, celebrity chefs Jamie Oliver and Hugh Fearnley-Whittingstall launched a highly publicized campaign to raise awareness of the welfare of chickens in the poultry industry.*

Christian beliefs about humans and animals

> *Rule over the fish of the sea and the birds of the air and over every living creature that moves on the ground.*
>
> **(Genesis 1:28)**

> *You made him ruler over the works of your hands;*
> *you put everything under his feet:*
> *all flocks and herds,*
> *and the beasts of the field,*
> *the birds of the air,*
> *and the fish of the sea,*
> *all that swim the paths of the seas.*
>
> **(Psalm 8:6-8)**

Within Christianity there are differing beliefs about the relationship between humans and animals. Most Christians agree that the Bible says that God put humans in charge of animals.

Different Christians interpret this in different ways: some believe it means that people have the right to use and treat animals however they want, most believe it means that people have a duty to look after animals.

Generally, Christians do not believe that animals have 'rights', but rather that humans have a duty to be caring and respectful towards them. This duty of care and respect towards animals is because God created animals, and also because God made humans the **stewards** of his creation.

Because of this sense of responsibility, many Christians are supporters of the animal welfare movement, and believe that animals should not undergo unnecessary suffering, cruelty or neglect.

Christians believe that humans have rights which other animals do not have because:

- Humans were made in the image of God

> *Then God said, 'Let us make man in our image, in our likeness…*
>
> **(Genesis 1:26)**

- God gave humans a soul

> *God… breathed into his nostrils the breath of life, and the man became a living being.*
>
> **(Genesis 2:7)**

- Humans can have a personal relationship with God, while other animals cannot.

- God put humans in charge of the other animals

> *…let them rule over the fish of the sea and the birds of the air, over the livestock, over all the earth, and over all the creatures that move along the ground.*
>
> **(Genesis 1:26)**

Further Bible references about animals

> Do not muzzle an ox while it is treading out the grain.
>
> **(Deuteronomy 25:4)**

> A righteous man cares for the needs of his animal, but the kindest acts of the wicked are cruel.
>
> **(Proverbs 12:10)**

I do not believe that animals should be used for food or medical research by humans at all. We do not need to eat meat, therefore it is unnecessary to slaughter animals for food. With medical research, we should use any alternatives other than testing on animals. Animals were created by God, and their lives are as valuable as human lives, as the Bible says: Are not two sparrows sold for a penny? Yet not one of them will fall to the ground apart from the will of your Father. (Matthew 10:29)

Most Christians believe that the Bible values human life as more important than animal life. Therefore, a balanced approach to the issue of animal rights and welfare is common among Christians: it is acceptable to use animals, but the animals should not suffer or die needlessly because as well as having the right to be in charge of them, we have a responsibility to look after them.

Here are two examples of different Christian views about the use of animals:

I eat meat, but I try to only buy meat that has a higher welfare standard mark on the packaging. I believe that it is acceptable to use animals for food, but they should be slaughtered without pain, and farmers should care for their livestock as best they can. It is okay for animals to be used for medical research, but only when absolutely necessary.

Animal testing

Animal research refers to scientific experimentation on animals. This has been happening for a very long time – animal testing even took place in Ancient Greece in the third and fourth century BCE! It is possible to find evidence of Aristotle and Erasistratus performing experiments on living animals.

There are many reasons for animal testing in the UK and around the world.

- Many new products are tested on animals such as pesticides, paint, and industrial chemicals. Some cosmetic products are tested on animals, but this is no longer legal in the UK. Many people believe that it is better to see what the effects of a new product will be on animals before they are used on humans.

- New medicines are tested on animals in the UK as the law states that any new medicine must be tested on at least two varieties of mammal before it is used by humans. Animal testing has led to important advancements in the treatment of HIV, cancer, measles and mumps.

It is believed that tens of millions of animals are used in animal experiments globally each year (three million in the UK alone in 2004); many die during the experiments and others are put down afterwards (euthanized) to prevent further suffering. In the UK, there are laws preventing animal cruelty during testing and the RSPCA keep records of companies that carry out such experiments.

Weighing up arguments for and against animal research

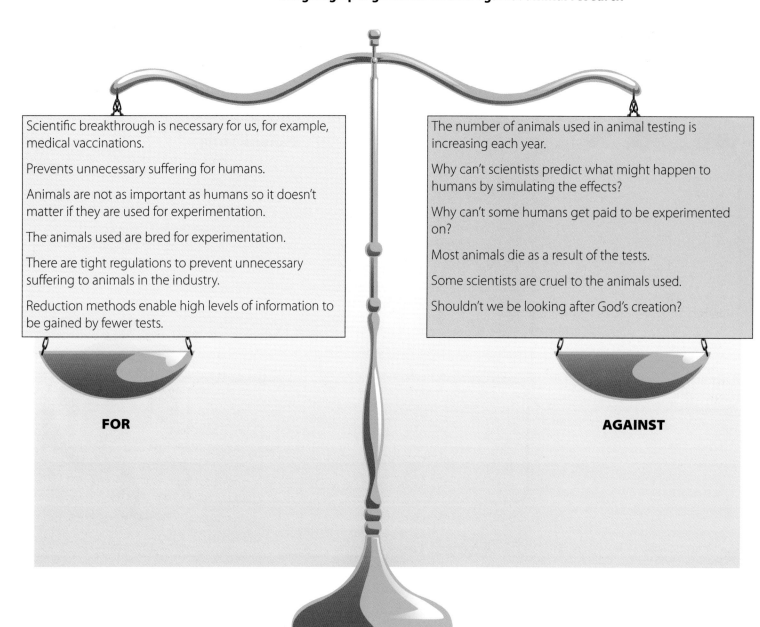

FOR	AGAINST
Scientific breakthrough is necessary for us, for example, medical vaccinations.	The number of animals used in animal testing is increasing each year.
Prevents unnecessary suffering for humans.	Why can't scientists predict what might happen to humans by simulating the effects?
Animals are not as important as humans so it doesn't matter if they are used for experimentation.	Why can't some humans get paid to be experimented on?
The animals used are bred for experimentation.	Most animals die as a result of the tests.
There are tight regulations to prevent unnecessary suffering to animals in the industry.	Some scientists are cruel to the animals used.
Reduction methods enable high levels of information to be gained by fewer tests.	Shouldn't we be looking after God's creation?

Christian responses

Animal testing is a thought-provoking topic for all people, whether they belong to a Christian community or not, and everyone has their own opinion on whether they agree or disagree with the practice.

The Catholic Church and Church of England teach that animal testing is permitted as long as it is a benefit to us, such as the development of medicines or vaccines. The Church of England also teaches that animal testing should be closely monitored and cruelty reflects badly on humans.

For **Discussion**

Do you think that animal testing is necessary?

Why might some people have such strong opinions about animal testing?

Vegetarianism

A vegetarian is someone who has a plant-based diet and does not eat meat.

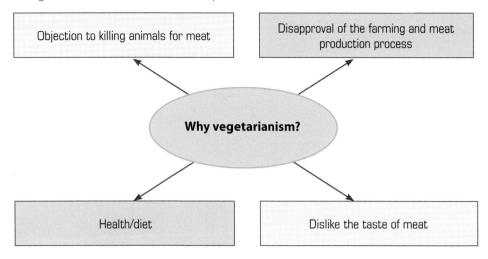

Many people believe that it is acceptable for humans to eat meat, because:

- it is natural (other animals eat meat)
- our bodies were intended to eat meat, for example, we have carnivorous (meat-eating) teeth
- humans have traditionally eaten meat for a very long time
- it is sometimes necessary for survival.

Vegetarians may argue that we can survive without eating meat, therefore it is unnecessary. They may think that animals should be allowed to live by their natures, not bred for the selfish needs of humans. They question: How can processes such as intensive farming be natural or fair to animals?

> Then God blessed Noah and his sons, saying to them, '…The fear and dread of you will fall upon all the beasts of the earth and all the birds of the air, upon every creature that moves along the ground, and upon all the fish of the sea; they are given into your hands. Everything that lives and moves will be food for you. Just as I gave you the green plants, now I give you everything.'
>
> **(Genesis 9:1-3)**

Although eating meat does not go against most Christians' religious beliefs, as long as the animals do not undergo unnecessary suffering or cruelty, there are some Christians who believe that vegetarianism plays a part in good stewardship. For example, the aims of the organization The Christian Vegetarian Association are: Environment and health, Animal rights and welfare and Discipleship. Its mission is to: support and encourage Christian vegetarians in the UK; to share with other Christians how a vegetarian diet can add meaning to their faith; to show that a plant-based way of life represents good Christian stewardship for all of God's creation.

Practise your **evaluation** skills.

'Animal testing is essential for humans to have a higher quality of living.'

Discuss this statement. You should include different, supported points of view and a personal viewpoint. You must refer to Christianity in your answer.

In your answer, you need to show that you understand a Christian point of view, and also that you understand other points of view. What do you think Christians might say about animal testing – would they be in favour of it, or against it? Then give a different opinion – it could be a different Christian view, or it could be from a different religious tradition or a non-religious view. Finally explain your own views about animal testing, and support them with reasons.

This will help you in the exam when you answer part (e) questions.

Activity 2

Look at the passage Acts 10:9–15 in the Bible and discuss its impact on the Christian attitude towards eating meat.

Environmental issues

This section will help you think about environmental issues and understand Christian views about them.

In recent years, the issue of the environment has become a hot topic. Many people are concerned about how much damage is being done to the environment by human behaviour and that this human impact is causing serious problems for the future. Behaviour such as cutting down forests, polluting the air, land and water, and putting lots of rubbish in landfill sites has a big impact. People are becoming more aware that this type of behaviour needs to change very quickly if we want to avoid serious damage to our environment.

The environment

Climate change
Climate change refers to changes in the environment and weather due to global warming. It will bring changes to weather patterns, causing rising sea levels, and more extreme weather.

Pollution
Pollution is when the natural environment such as air, water and land becomes contaminated or made dirty. This can affect the air we breathe, the water we drink and can harm people and animals, and play a part in global warming.

Deforestation
This is when trees in the rainforests are cut down. Humans have destroyed large areas of rainforest in order to use the wood, or to use or build on the land. Deforestation destroys all the plants and animals that live there; it also increases carbon dioxide (CO_2) and decreases oxygen (O_2) because trees use up CO_2 and release O_2.

Global warming
means the heating up of the earth, leading to climate change. It is caused by too much carbon dioxide (CO_2) produced by human behaviour.

What can we do to protect the environment?

We could	How?	More about it
Reduce food waste	Do not buy too much food. Use or freeze leftovers.	Each household in the UK throws away an average of £420 worth of edible goods a year, adding up to 4.1 million tonnes as a whole. (Figure based on the Cabinet Office review of food policy from 2008.)
Save energy	Switch off appliances when not in use. Use energy-saving light bulbs. Boil just enough water for a drink each time. Turn down the heating a few degrees. Wash clothes at lower temperatures.	The average television uses around £40 of electricity a year if left on standby.
Recycle	Use council recycling schemes. Recycle paper, glass, tins, plastic and so on, as much as possible.	It takes 95% less energy to make the average fizzy drink can from a recycled one than to make a brand new one.
Reuse	Reduce your rubbish by re-using things, for example, making a new skirt out of an old one, or using shoe boxes as storage. Pass on things you don't need to someone else, such as a charity shop, rather than throwing them away.	Cheaper imported goods mean we buy more and more items each.
Buy greener	Buy recycled products, second-hand items, or those made by a process that releases less CO_2 into the environment.	You can even buy pencils that are made from old CDs.
Travel greener	Don't use the car for short journeys: cycle or walk instead. Car-share or use public transport. Reduce air travel.	The planet will become congested if more vehicles are on the roads.
Look after nature	Plant trees and plants, which give off oxygen and use up CO_2. Encourage wildlife.	Maintain the natural environment to keep the planet healthy.
Support an organization	Support a 'green' organization or charity, which can have an impact on increasing awareness of the environment and making a bigger impact nationally and globally.	Find out about local branches of organizations such as Greenpeace and join in.

For **Discussion**

What three things could you change about your lifestyle to help save the environment?

◀ *Shoppers are encouraged to reuse carrier bags.*

Exam Practice

Practise your skills in **demonstrating knowledge and understanding**.

Explain in your own words what is meant by the word 'stewardship'.

Try to make your answer clear, short and to the point.

This will help you when you answer part (a) questions.

Christian stewardship

Christians believe that God made humans the stewards of the earth. This means they believe he put humans in charge of looking after the earth: but God still owns the earth.

> *The earth is the Lord's, and everything in it, the world and all who live in it; for he founded it upon the seas and established it upon the waters.*
>
> **(Psalms 24:1-2)**

> *Rule over the fish of the sea and the birds of the air and over every living creature that moves on the ground.*
>
> **(Genesis 1:28)**

God placed man in the Garden of Eden to cultivate and guard it. In giving man stewardship of God's earth came: rights; responsibilities; duty of care; the need to look after and protect.

How do Christians protect the environment?

Christians believe that God created the world and told humans to look after it so they understand that all living things, including humans, will suffer if the environment is damaged. Many Christians believe that in order to be good stewards of the earth, as God wants, it is very important to try to protect the environment.

This can involve:

- making a special effort to take care of the environment in their everyday lives
- encouraging and supporting others in caring for the environment
- supporting charities and organizations related to environmental protection, for example, by giving money or doing volunteer work
- prayer.

Prayer is very important for Christians, as it is a way of communicating with God. Christians might pray to God about the environment. For example, they may ask God for guidance about what they can do to protect the environment.

Ministers and church leaders can help to guide Christians in how to be good stewards, through:

- giving sermons about environmental stewardship

- showing a good example, for example, and so on by recycling, energy saving, running bus services to and from church, having second-hand sales and so on.

- raising awareness of environmental problems and solutions.

The Church of England also has a national environmental campaign called 'Shrinking the Footprint', aimed at reducing our carbon footprint (i.e. the amount of CO_2 produced by human behaviour). See www.shrinkingthefootprint.cofe.anglican.org.

Non-Christian stewardship

Of course, it is not just Christians who believe in stewardship of the earth. Many non-Christians also think that it is important to look after the environment so that the earth is kept in good condition for the future.

- Some people want to make sure that the earth is looked after for future generations. They might have children, and want to imagine that their grandchildren, great-grandchildren and so on will have a good life.

- Scientists have found evidence that the earth is billions of years old, but humans have not existed for as long. The average human today will live to be in their seventies or eighties. Each human is on the earth for such a short time, compared to how long the earth has existed. This makes some people feel like they do not 'own' the earth, and so do not have the right to abuse it.

Glossary

Cosmology – the study of the origin and development of the universe; considering theories about how the universe was created, including the Big Bang theory

Evolution – gradual change or development of living things over lots of generations

Natural selection – the process where some living things are best adapted to survive and reproduce, while others are less adapted and tend to die out, resulting in the survival of the fittest

Steward – someone who is responsible for looking after something that they do not own, to the best of their ability

Theory – an unproven explanation, usually backed up by some evidence

ETHICS 1

Roles of men and women in the family

Do men and women have different roles to play in the family? ▼

This section will encourage you to think about the roles of men and woman, and to compare your own views with Christian beliefs.

Christians have differing attitudes about the roles of men and women in the family. Different Christians have very different opinions, including:

- men and women's roles in the family are very different
- men and women's roles in the family are the same
- men and women's roles in the family are the same in some ways but different in others.

There are also different Christian attitudes about the importance and rights of men and women in the family. The main Christian beliefs about these are:

- men are more important than women in the family, and men are in charge
- men and women are equally important in the family, but men are in charge
- men and women are complete equals – they are equally important and have equal rights in the family.

The Bible makes many references to the roles of men and women and some of these might seem to contradict each other. Different Christians interpret the Bible's teachings on the roles of men and women in different ways.

Some Christians believe men and women have different roles …

Some Christians believe that the roles of men and women are very different, but equally important. This view is based on Biblical teachings, historical roles, and on the practical understanding that men are better at some things than women (in many cases, things requiring physical strength, for example) and women are better at some things than men.

Some Christians believe that the role of men is more important than the role of women, who are intended to be men's helpers. This view is supported by the Bible story of Eve being created by God as Adam's companion, and also by the fact that Jesus' disciples were all men.

Some Christians even believe that women are weaker and more likely to sin than men, because in the Bible Eve sinned first and tempted Adam to copy her.

> *Wives … be submissive to your husbands …*
> *Husbands, in the same way be considerate as*
> *you live with your wives, and treat them with*
> *respect as the weaker partner.*
>
> **(1 Peter 3:1,7)**

Some Christians believe the roles of men and women are very different and that the man is the leader, while the woman is his helper. ▼

▲ *The Temptation and Fall of Eve by William Blake, an illustration for Milton's* Paradise Lost *shows Eve in the Garden of Eden.*

Women should …

… run the home

… raise the children

… obey their husbands

Men should …

… be in charge

… provide for their family

… love their wives

> *Then the Lord God made a woman from the rib*
> *he had taken out of the man, and he brought*
> *her to the man.*
>
> **(Genesis 2:22)**

> *I do not permit a woman to teach or to have*
> *authority over a man; she must be silent. For*
> *Adam was formed first and then Eve.*
>
> **(1 Timothy 2:12-13)**

> *Wives, submit to your husbands as to the Lord.*
> *For the husband is the head of the wife as*
> *Christ is the head of the church.*
>
> **(Ephesians 5:22-23)**

Research is continually looking at differences between men and women and we read articles and news stories debating whether the sexes think in the same way or differently. An article entitled 'Scientists say genetic variations show that men think differently' published in *The Times* (20 June 2008) quoted research that indicated that men and women's brains may work in different ways. Some research seems to show that male and female brains work in different ways, and that this may be due to the structure of the brain rather than the ways in which boys and girls are brought up.

Different roles – relevant?

1 The different roles of men and women make use of the different skills God gave them. Men and women are different by nature – this is as true today as it ever was.

2 When men take on the role of provider, and women take on the role of carer, this helps families to get on well together and get everything done. If they both tried to take on the same role, some things would be missing and the family would suffer.

3 To obey your husband is not an old-fashioned idea – women can still share their views and decide lots of things jointly, and as long as the man loves and respects his wife it is a good thing. He is in charge, but today this usually means he is a leader – guiding his family and taking their wellbeing and opinions into account.

Different roles – outdated?

4 The Christian idea of men going out to work while women stay at home to bring up the children is sexist and outdated! Women have proved themselves in the workplace, and have as much right to work as men do.

5 Men and women are equally important human beings, and to say that men should be in charge of women is outright gender discrimination, which has no place in today's society.

6 Not all Christians believe that the roles of men and women should be so separate. Lots of Christian women go out to work, and lots of Christian men do housework and childcare.

... other Christians believe that men and women have the same roles

Some Christians believe that the roles of men and women in the family are the same. This view is held by many Protestant Churches, including Church of England and Methodist Churches. They think:

- men and women should share childcare and housework
- women can work outside the home if they want
- a husband and wife are equally in charge of the family.

They believe that God created men and women as equals. Although there are obvious biological differences, this does not change their role.

Biblical society was very different from modern society, and some Christians believe that the Bible only refers to men and women as having unequal roles because that was how society was at the time. They believe that such references in the Bible should be interpreted for modern society, where men and women have equal roles. They believe that this can be done while still living according to the teachings of the Bible. In fact, there are passages in the Bible which support the importance of women, and some Christians think that this means that women should have equal roles to men.

Here are some examples of how the importance of women is shown in the Bible:

- In Genesis 1, men and women were created at the same time and equally.
- Jesus treated women as important. He gave them important teachings and included them in his miracles and parables.
- In his letters to new churches, Paul taught that men and women were equal members of the Christian community and should not focus on their differences but on their shared faith.

For **Discussion**

Do you think that men and women should have the same roles?

Look at both sides of the argument, including Christian beliefs. What are the good points about having the same roles? What are the bad points? State your own opinion and reasons for it.

> A Catholic view
>
> The Catholic Church teaches that men and women are equal but different: God values them equally but they have different natures.
>
> 'Man and woman have been *created*, which is to say, *willed* by God: on the one hand, in perfect equality as human persons; on the other, in their respective beings as man and woman.'
>
> (*Catechism of the Catholic Church, 369*)

Roles of men and women in the Church

There is a variety of differing views about the roles of men and women in the Christian Church. Different Christian denominations have their own teachings and policies on the issue, and this can be based on historical background and interpretation of the Bible.

Unequal roles

Some Christians believe that men should have greater authority and standing in the Church than women. This can be supported by the fact that the Bible sometimes seems to suggest that women have less authority than men. Here are some examples:

- Genesis 2:18 recalls God saying

 It is not good for the man to be alone. I will make a helper suitable for him.

The language used describes how God viewed woman to be needed to *help* man rather than work as an equal with him.

- In the Old Testament women were often treated as the property of their husband. When Noah went onto his ark in Genesis 7 he took his wife and three sons and their wives. We are told the dimensions of the ark but the names of the wives are never revealed, which may suggest they were less important.

- All of Jesus' 12 disciples were men.

- There are some passages in the Bible which seem to teach that women should not be allowed to speak in church, or be teachers and leaders, such as this letter from Paul:

 A woman should learn in quietness and full submission. I do not permit a woman to teach or to have authority over a man; she must be silent. For Adam was formed first, then Eve. And Adam was not the one deceived; it was the woman who was deceived and became a sinner.

(1 Timothy 2:11-14)

Equal roles

Some Christians believe that the roles of men and women in the Church should be equal and the same. One of the reasons for this is because of passages in the Bible which show men and women as equals. Man and woman were created equally in the image of God and Jesus seems to treat women as equals. Here are some examples:

- Jesus treated a Samaritan woman as his equal (see John 4).

- Although his 12 disciples were men, he had female followers who were with him at his crucifixion unlike the men, who fled.

- Jesus appeared to women first after the resurrection.

- Paul taught that men and women are equal in Christ:

> *You are all sons of God through faith in Christ Jesus, for all of you who were baptized into Christ have clothed yourselves with Christ. There is neither Jew nor Greek, slave nor free, male nor female, for you are all one in Christ Jesus.*
>
> **(Galatians 3:26-28)**

The Catholic Church has very clear guidelines on the roles of men and women in the Church. Men and women are equal, and so women and men are equally allowed some positions of responsibility such as being Eucharistic ministers (distributing the bread and wine), religious leaders, or pastoral visitors.

The role of priests and bishops, however, are only for men. The Catholic Church teaches that this is not because of any inequality or weakness, but for the following reasons:

- The hierarchy of the Church reflects Jesus and his apostles.

- The priest represents Jesus, who was a man, and therefore the priest should be male.

- Bishops are descendants of Jesus' apostles, who were also male.

- The Pope (head of the Catholic Church) is always a man because he is the successor of Peter, the foundation of the Church (see Matthew 16:18).

The Church of England now permits female clergy. The roles of women in society have changed (women now have equal rights to work and vote), and following this development the Church of England decided in 1994 to allow female vicars. This was a controversial move, and while many Christians agreed with the decision, others were outraged. There are now many female vicars within the Church of England.

Other churches such as The Salvation Army are more liberal in the roles of men and women in their church family. Both male and female ministers (officers) are allowed to lead equally and have equal responsibility to run their church (corps). In this denomination, married couples are both allowed to train and become equal church leaders together at a church (corps) which is unlike most other denominations. In the 1990s, a female officer was promoted to the rank of General, the top position in The Salvation Army around the world (there is only one General at a time). She was allowed to make important decisions about the direction of the church globally and had male officers working for her, some of whom had voted to appoint her to the role.

The roles of men and women vary from church to church, and whether or not they are equal, Christians believe that men and women are both important and valuable.

For **Discussion**

Do you think men and women are treated equally in the Church? Do you think the roles of men and women in the Church are right?

Marriage and marriage ceremonies

This section will help you think about Christian beliefs about marriage and weddings, and help you form your own opinions.

EXAM FOCUS

Christian marriage

Marriage means a relationship between a husband and wife which is legally recognized, and established by a religious or civil marriage ceremony.

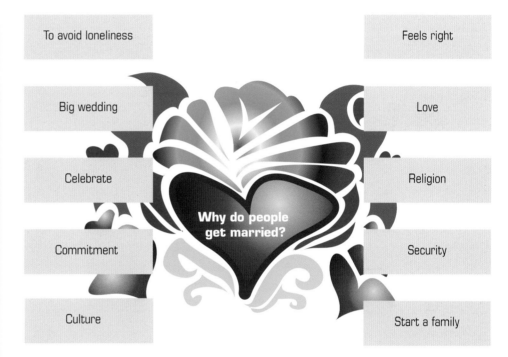

To avoid loneliness

Feels right

Big wedding

Love

Celebrate

Religion

Why do people get married?

Commitment

Security

Culture

Start a family

Activity 1

Use the ideas in the diagram on this page to write a paragraph explaining why people get married

Christians who are planning to get married

When couples are planning a wedding they become very involved in organizing their perfect day including the bride's dress, the reception or party, guests and the honeymoon. However, the wedding is just one day, as marriage is meant to be for life, couples should consider how they will face their future lives together too.

Christians are urged to consider the things they have in common and their expectations for marriage. Before their wedding they will meet with the minister to talk these things through. Sometimes marriage preparation sessions are also provided to give couples the opportunity to think through possible areas of difficulty and how they will handle them as a couple. Areas for consideration might include how well they communicate with each other, how they will cope with conflict as well as their attitudes to money, sex and having children.

Exam Practice

Practise your skills in **demonstrating knowledge and understanding**.

What is meant by marriage?

Try to give a short but clear definition.

This will help you in the exam when you answer part (a) and part (b) questions.

The Christian marriage ceremony

<u>Order of Service</u>

The marriage of Hannah and John

at Saint Michael's C of E Church

Reverend J. Byrne

....

Entrance - **Arrival of the Queen of Sheba**, Handel

Welcome

Hymn - In Christ Alone, my hope is found

The marriage ceremony

Reading - 1 John 4:7-12

Address

Hymn - Praise my soul, the King of heaven

Prayers

Hymn - Love divine, all loves excelling

Signing of the register

Wedding March from **A Midsummer's Night Dream** by Mendelssohn

A Church of England marriage service

- **The entrance**

The bride traditionally enters the church after the groom, on the arm of her father (or sometimes another relative or friend instead, or alone). This reflects the traditional Christian belief that the father 'gives' his daughter to the groom. Many modern Christians do not believe that this means the bride is 'owned' by her father or husband, but some do believe that the man is in charge of the household. Other Christians believe that men and women have equal roles, but still include this entrance out of tradition.

- **The welcome and introduction**

The minister welcomes the congregation, and may talk about the important role of the couple's family and friends as witnesses and supporters of their marriage. There is then an opening speech by the minister, who usually explains the Christian beliefs about marriage.

The minister may refer to passages from the Bible, such as:

> *God is love. Whoever lives in love lives in*
> *God, and God in him.*
>
> **(1 John 4:16)**

- **The marriage ceremony**

The marriage ceremony contains declarations and vows. A declaration is where someone declares (says) something, and a vow is a promise.

The declarations

Declarations are an important part of a Christian marriage ceremony.

- The couple and the congregation are asked to declare any reason why the couple may not lawfully marry.
  The couple are reminded that the vows they are about to take are to be made in the presence of God, *'who is judge of all and knows all the secrets of our hearts'*. This emphasizes Christian beliefs about God's presence in their lives, his all-knowing nature, and role as judge.

- The bride and groom declare their marriage promises before God, their friends and their families. They declare that they will love, comfort, honour and protect their partner and be faithful to them as long as they both shall live.
  The couple's friends and family are asked to declare that they will support and uphold the couple's marriage.

The declarations reflect Christian beliefs about:

- How long marriage should last: 'as long as we both shall live'.

- Some of the purposes or characteristics of a Christian marriage: 'love, comfort, honour and protect'.

- The importance of God in the marriage ceremony: 'The vows you are about to take are to be made in the presence of God, who is judge of all and knows all the secrets of our hearts'.

- The supporting role of friends and family: 'Will you, the families and friends of *(name)* and *(name)*, support and uphold them in their marriage now and in the years to come?'

Christian marriage vows

The couple now face each other and take each other's right hand while they make their vows:

> *I, (name), take you, (name),*
> *to be my wife/husband,*
> *to have and to hold*
> *from this day forward;*
> *for better, for worse,*
> *for richer, for poorer,*
> *in sickness and in health,*
> *to love and to cherish,*
> *till death us do part;*
> *according to God's holy law.*
> *In the presence of God I make this vow.*
>
> **(vows taken from Common Worship)**

The vows reflect Christian beliefs:

- That marriage should last a lifetime: 'till death do us part'.

- Emphasizing God's presence and importance in their marriage: '…according to God's holy law. In the presence of God I make this vow.'

- The characteristics of Christian marriage: 'to love and to cherish'.

- **The rings**

The groom places a ring on the bride's finger, and the bride may place a ring on the groom's finger. The ring is a symbol of their marriage and acts as a physical reminder of their commitment throughout their lives. The continuous, circular shape of the ring traditionally represents unbroken love, faithfulness and eternity.

There is now a reminder of the vows:

> *With my body I honour you,*
> *all that I am I give to you,*
> *and all that I have I share with you,*
> *within the love of God,*
> *Father, Son and Holy Spirit.*

This again reflects the important role of God, and characteristics of a Christian marriage: honouring each other's bodies through marital sex, sharing themselves entirely and becoming a unit.

- **The proclamation**

The minister announces that the couple are married: 'I now pronounce you husband and wife'.

- **Prayers**

Prayers are said for God's blessing and help in the marriage. The couple can discuss details of what prayers they would like with their minister beforehand, if they want prayers to God for specific blessings, such as the gift of children.

- **Bible readings and sermon (talk)**

Christian weddings usually have one or more readings from the Bible (some churches allow an additional reading that is not from the Bible). The Bible readings usually emphasize Christian beliefs about marriage and love, and because the Bible is believed to be the word of God, the readings demonstrate the importance of God in the marriage ceremony. The minister will generally give a talk or sermon.

- **Signing of the register**

It is a legal requirement that the bride, groom and two witnesses must sign the register. The couple receive a copy of the marriage certificate.

Exam Practice

Practise your skills in **demonstrating knowledge and understanding**.

How do Christian marriage ceremonies reflect Christian beliefs?

For this answer you need to show an accurate knowledge of what happens during a Christian marriage service. You also need to show that you understand why these features of the ceremony are important in the Christian faith.

This will help you in the exam when you answer part (d) questions.

A Catholic marriage ceremony

In the Catholic Church, marriage is a sacrament.

Marriage preparations (called pre-cana) where the couple talks to the priest about the meaning of marriage and their intentions for their married life are compulsory for Catholics who want to get married.

Sometimes Catholic marriage ceremonies have Mass and celebrate the Eucharist, but sometimes they do not. Either way, the ceremony includes hymns, Bible readings (including one from the Old Testament, one from the New Testament and one from the Gospels), a homily (practical sermon), questions about faithfulness and willingness to bring up children, vows, and exchange of rings.

Christian responses to same-sex civil partnerships

In 2005, same-sex civil partnerships became legal in the UK. There is a strong difference of opinion within Christianity on this issue. Some Christians believe that gay and lesbian couples should be free to commit to each other, because God made them just as they are and loves them. There are many Christian groups who actively work towards making Christianity inclusive of all relationships equally. Other Christians believe that **homosexuality** is a sin and that civil partnerships should not be allowed because they equate same-sex relationships with heterosexual marriage.

One reason for the great split in opinion on the matter is different interpretations of the Bible: some people say it condemns homosexuality, others interpret it differently or put it down to historical context (if everything were taken literally the Bible might be seen to promote polygamy or slavery too).

(For more on Christian responses to homosexuality, see page 143)

Divorce

This section will help you to understand Christian attitudes to divorce and remarriage.

EXAM FOCUS

Divorce means the legal and final end or separation of a marriage.

Why might marriages break down?

The road to divorce: why do marriages break down? ▶

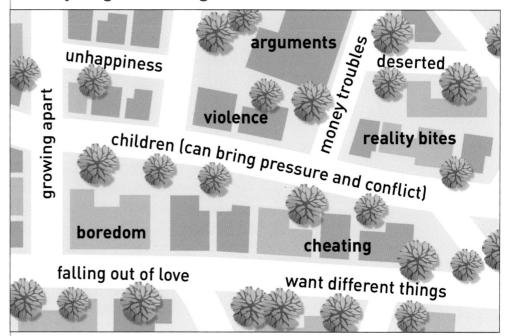

unhappiness
arguments
money troubles
deserted
growing apart
violence
reality bites
children (can bring pressure and conflict)
boredom
cheating
falling out of love
want different things

For Discussion

For each of the reasons why marriages break down, shown on the picture, discuss what alternatives there are to divorce. How could the problem be resolved? How could it have been avoided in the first place?

What do Christians believe about divorce?

There are differing beliefs about divorce within Christianity. Some Christians believe that divorce is always wrong, because the Bible seems to teach this, and it was the traditional view of the Christian Church. Other Christians believe that divorce is sometimes acceptable. Many modern Christians try to avoid divorce, but do not judge or think badly of people who get divorced. Biblical teachings on forgiveness and the importance of not judging others support their views.

Against divorce...

• **The Bible**
In the Bible, there are some direct teachings against divorce:

> 'Haven't you read,' he (Jesus) replied, 'that at the beginning the Creator 'made them male and female', and said, 'For this reason a man will leave his father and mother and be united to his wife, and the two will become one flesh'? So they are no longer two, but one. Therefore what God has joined together, let man not separate.'
>
> **(Matthew 19:4-6)**

> " If a man takes a wife and, after lying with her, dislikes her... She shall continue to be his wife; he must not divorce her as long as he lives. "
>
> **(Deuteronomy 22: 13,19)**

> " To the married I give this command (not I, but the Lord): A wife must not separate from her husband. But if she does, she must remain unmarried or else be reconciled to her husband. And a husband must not divorce his wife. "
>
> **(1 Corinthians 7:10-11)**

> " 'Why then,' they (the Pharisees) asked, 'did Moses command that a man give his wife a certificate of divorce and send her away?' Jesus replied, 'Moses permitted you to divorce your wives because your hearts were hard. But it was not this way from the beginning.' "
>
> **(Matthew 19:7-8)**

- **Sanctity of marriage**

Many Christians believe that when a couple get married they are joined together by God. Therefore, they do not believe that divorce has the power to destroy God's bond of marriage: 'What God has joined together… '.

Christian wedding vows are a promise before God, to stay with each other even if things are difficult ('For better or for worse…'). Many Christians believe that divorce is wrong because it breaks a promise made before God. Many of the reasons for divorce, such as arguments, wanting different things, or money problems are considered by many Christians to be things that should be worked through, as promised in the wedding vows. According to Christian wedding vows, only death can separate a married couple: '…till death do us part.'

- **Impact on people**

As well as going against biblical teachings and breaking the promises made in the wedding vows, some Christians believe that divorce can have negative impacts on people's lives and society as a whole. Here are some examples of Christian views:

Divorce can affect a couple's children, taking away the stability of a traditional family environment.

Making divorce more acceptable can make people give up on their marriage when there is still a chance to make it work.

Divorce can leave partners lonely and lacking the support of a life partner.

A society in which divorce is acceptable and common can lead to people becoming self-centred, selfish, pleasure-seeking, and unwilling to stand by loved ones through difficult times.

The acceptability of divorce can make partners less likely to put everything in to their marriage in case they get hurt if it fails, leading to unhappiness and making the marriage more likely to fail.

For divorce...

- **The Bible**

Although the Bible contains some direct teachings against divorce, some Christians believe that there other passages that are relevant, and might suggest that divorce should not be completely condemned.

> *But I tell you that anyone who divorces his wife, except for marital unfaithfulness, causes her to become an adulteress.*
>
> **(Matthew 5:32)**

> *... a man marries a woman who becomes displeasing to him because he finds something indecent about her, and he writes her a certificate of divorce, gives it to her and sends her from his house.*
>
> **(Deuteronomy 24:1-4)**

- **Impact on people**

Some Christians believe that divorce can have a positive impact on people. In the case of couples who are unhappy together, perhaps because of arguments or wanting different things, divorce can bring an end to their unhappiness. Some Christians believe that although divorce is not the ideal, and no one should go into marriage without intending a lifelong commitment, sometimes things go wrong and couples should not be made to stay together. Some Christians believe that since God is loving and kind, he would not want people to suffer by having to stay in an unhappy marriage.

Some Christians think that there are some cases when divorce is acceptable – in an abusive relationship, for example, or when one partner wants children but the other refuses.

The Bible teaches that we should forgive people's mistakes, and so some Christians believe that it is important to accept that sometimes people make mistakes either in marrying someone and later wanting a divorce, or in doing something wrong that leads to marriage breakdown (for example, cheating on a partner).

> *For if you forgive men when they sin against you, your heavenly Father will also forgive you.*
> **(Matthew 6:14)**

Many Christians believe that while divorce is not ideal, and should not be encouraged, it is not up to them to judge whether it is right or wrong for other people to get divorced.

> *Do not judge, or you too will be judged.*
> **(Matthew 7:1)**

Roman Catholic teaching on divorce

Catholics believe that divorce cannot separate a married couple, because they have been joined together by God. However if it is believed that the marriage was not a true marriage in the first place it can be annulled (cancelled).

Reasons for this might be:

- the man or the woman did not consent to the marriage

- the man or the woman did not understand what marriage is about

- the couple did not or could not have sex

- the man or the woman refused to have children.

Annulment is not easy to obtain; it is not just another way of getting a divorce.

Alternatives to divorce

Preparation before marriage

Many Christian churches run pre-marriage preparation courses, to help couples to understand what marriage is all about, and to resolve any issues (such as differences of opinion about having children) before marriage. Many Christians believe that thinking and talking things through beforehand can sometimes avoid problems later on.

Marriage guidance agencies

Marriage guidance agencies such as Relate (which is not associated with any religion) can help married couples to stay together by providing a confidential counselling service to help couples to resolve any problems.

How might divorce be avoided?

Belief in marriage as a life-long commitment

Some Christians believe that if couples go into marriage believing that it will not be for ever their marriage is more likely to end in divorce. If people believe that they are making a life-long commitment when they marry they are more likely to work positively to resolve any problems.

What do Christians believe about whether divorced people should remarry?

Some Christians believe that divorced people should be forgiven and allowed to remarry, because once a person is divorced they have no longer got any tie to their former partner and so nothing is stopping them from making a new commitment. In the Church of England, some vicars will allow divorced people to remarry in the church.

YES

Other Christians believe that divorce does not separate a couple – they are still married in God's eyes because he joined them together in marriage until they die. Therefore if they remarry, this new marriage is not valid and they are effectively cheating on their first husband or wife with their new partner. This is the teaching of the Roman Catholic Church.

NO

Should divorced people remarry?

Exam Practice

Practise your **evaluation** skills.

'Divorce is always wrong.'

Discuss this statement, including different, supported viewpoints and your own opinion. You must refer to Christianity in your answer.

In your answer, start by making it clear that you understand what divorce is. Then show why some people might agree that divorce is always wrong, using reference to Christianity (such as Roman Catholic teaching). Give a different point of view, to show why others might think divorce can sometimes be right. Lastly, give your own opinion and say why you hold this view.

This will help you in the exam when you answer part (e) questions.

The Bible seems to teach that divorced people should not remarry. However, some Christians interpret the Bible in different ways, and while many Christians believe that it gives direct instructions about the ethics of remarriage, other Christians believe that it has to be interpreted or applied to individual situations. Biblical teaching on forgiveness means that some Christians believe that divorced people should be forgiven and allowed a fresh start in a new marriage.

> *It has been said, 'Anyone who divorces his wife must give her a certificate of divorce.' But I tell you that anyone who divorces his wife, except for marital unfaithfulness, causes her to become an adulteress, and anyone who marries the divorced woman commits adultery.*
>
> **(Matthew 5:31-32)**

> *To the married I give this command (not I, but the Lord): A wife must not separate from her husband. But if she does, she must remain unmarried or else be reconciled to her husband. And a husband must not divorce his wife.*
>
> **(1 Corinthians 7:10-11)**

Sexual relationships and contraception

This section will help you understand Christian beliefs about sexual relationships and attitudes to contraception.

Christian beliefs about sexual relationships

There are differing beliefs and teachings within Christianity about sexual relationships.

 Male and female he (God) created them. God blessed them and said to them, 'Be fruitful and increase in number.'

(Genesis 1:27-28)

Traditionally, Christians believed that the purpose of sex was reproduction (having children). Nowadays, most Catholics still believe that reproduction is the main purpose of sex. The Catholic Church teaches that reproduction should be possible every time a couple have sex. However, many Christians today believe that as well as to produce children, sexual relationships are intended by God to bring pleasure and intimacy.

Many Christians believe that sex is an expression of love within a marriage. Traditionally, Christians believed that sexual relationships should only be within marriage, and many Christians still believe this. Their beliefs about this are based on the Bible, Christian teachings, their relationship with God, and their personal ethics.

Various studies have looked at the issue of sex within marriage and have concluded that as it can provide a couple with the opportunity to express the love and respect they have for each other, in a long-term relationship, it is very successful. Indeed, one study based on responses from 16,000 adults in the USA found that married people have much more sex than other groups.

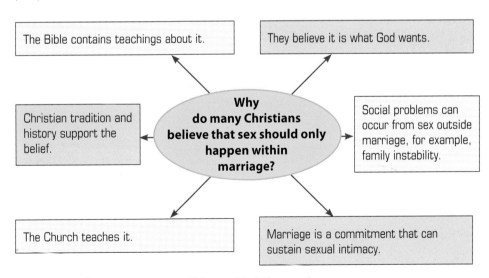

The Bible contains teachings about it.

They believe it is what God wants.

Christian tradition and history support the belief.

Why do many Christians believe that sex should only happen within marriage?

Social problems can occur from sex outside marriage, for example, family instability.

The Church teaches it.

Marriage is a commitment that can sustain sexual intimacy.

 For this reason a man will leave his father and mother and be united to his wife, and they will become one flesh. The man and his wife were both naked, and they felt no shame.

(Genesis 2:24-25)

Sex outside marriage

Although Christian teachings generally say that sex should happen within marriage, there are some Christians who believe that sex outside marriage is acceptable if it is in a committed relationship, for example, if a couple are engaged. Some Christians believe that the Bible's teachings about sex are set in the context of a very different society, and they need to be interpreted for people today.

Other Christians believe that the Bible clearly teaches that sex outside marriage is a sin, and this is still the case today, because the Bible is the Word of God and should be followed exactly.

> *For God did not call us to be impure, but to live a holy life. Therefore, he who rejects this instruction does not reject man, but God, who also gives you his Holy Spirit.*
> **(1 Thessalonians 4:7-8)**

Individual Christians have different responses to alternative types of sexual relationships such as same-gender sexual relationships, prostitution, casual sex and sex outside marriage.

Christian responses to alternative types of sexual relationships

Promiscuity: Christian teachings say that **promiscuity** (having many sexual partners) is wrong and dishonourable.

Sexual sin: The Bible refers to avoiding 'sexual sin', and Christians interpret this to mean either sex outside marriage, promiscuity, **adultery** or other sexual relationships which go against Church teachings.

> *It is God's will that you should be sanctified: that you should avoid sexual immorality; that each of you should learn to control his own body in a way that is holy and honourable, not in passionate lust like the heathen, who do not know God.*
> **(1 Thessalonians 4:3-5)**

Adultery: Christians generally believe that adultery (cheating on your wife or husband) is wrong. The Bible is quite clear on this issue, because it is one of the Ten Commandments, and also Jesus gave direct teachings on the matter:

> *You shall not commit adultery.*
> **(Deuteronomy 5:18)**

> *You have heard that it was said, 'Do not commit adultery.' But I tell you that anyone who looks at a woman lustfully has already committed adultery with her in his heart.*
> **(Matthew 5:27-28)**

Although many Christians believe that sex outside marriage, including adultery (cheating) is not ideal, many Christians believe it is important not to judge people on such things. In the Bible, there is an example of how Jesus responded to a woman who had committed adultery:

> *They made her stand before the group and said to Jesus, 'Teacher, this woman was caught in the act of adultery. In the Law Moses commanded us to stone such women. Now what do you say?' …(he) said to them, 'If any one of you is without sin, let him be the first to throw a stone at her.' …'Woman, where are they? Has no-one condemned you?' 'No-one, sir,' she said. 'Then neither do I condemn you,' Jesus declared. 'Go now and leave your life of sin.'*
>
> **(John 8:3-5,7, 10-11)**

Many Christians today use Jesus as an example of how to respond to people who do things which are against their Christian beliefs about sex. They may try not to condemn the person for their actions, but encourage them to change their ways.

Christian attitudes to homosexuality

There are differing Christian beliefs about whether or not homosexuality is acceptable:

Some Christians are completely against homosexuality

- Traditionally, Christians believed that homosexuality is wrong. The Bible contains passages that seem to support this.

- Today, many Christians believe this is still true. However, the Christian Church no longer condemns homosexuality, but rather teaches that it is not the ideal.

- The Catholic Church teaches that homosexual sex is a sin.

- The Bible contains direct references to homosexuality, which seem to say that it is wrong.

Some Christians are completely in favour of homosexuality

- Some Christians believe that homosexuality is a completely natural characteristic of some people, and that is the way God made them, so following these natural feelings and having homosexual relationships is good. God loves everybody just the way they are – including gay and lesbian people.

- Some Christians believe that when the Bible refers to homosexuality as a sin, it must be remembered that it was written in a very different time for a very different society. There are other teachings in the Bible that most Christians do not believe apply today (such as stoning people to death, or slavery). References to homosexuality in the Bible are simply details of what society was like then, not literal rules for today.

'In the middle' about homosexuality

- Some Christians accept there are natural homosexual desires and tendencies, but think homosexual sex is wrong. They believe that homosexuality is a natural tendency which some people have, through no fault of their own, and such feelings are acceptable. However, they believe that acting on this by having homosexual sex is wrong.

- Some Christians believe homosexual relationships and sex are sometimes acceptable. They believe that homosexuality is a natural tendency for some people, and therefore homosexual relationships (including sex) are acceptable as long as they are faithful and monogamous.
Some Christians interpret references about homosexuality in the Bible as saying that *some* homosexual relationships are wrong (for example, if they involve rape, adultery, or the people are not in love), not homosexuality itself.

For **Discussion**

Some Christians who are homosexual (gay) make a choice not to have sexual relationships at all. This is called **celibacy**.

Do you think this is a good choice, or not? Try to support your view with reasons.

Contraception

The term **contraception** means deliberate prevention of pregnancy. It is sometimes called 'birth-control' and this can be artificial or natural.

Artificial contraception

Different types of artificial contraception prevent pregnancy in different ways. Here are some examples of artificial contraception:

- the pill
- condoms
- intrauterine device (IUD) often called 'the coil'
- diaphragm or cap.

Natural contraception

- The rhythm method (limiting sex to less fertile times of the month)

  This method of contraception is unreliable, as it is based on predicting 'safe' days and a woman's cycle can be different every month.

- The withdrawal method (withdrawing the penis before ejaculation)

  This method of contraception is very unreliable, as some sperm are released at any time during sex, before ejaculation.

The main difference between artificial and natural forms of contraception from a religious point of view is that natural contraception still allows for the possibility of pregnancy.

Why do people use contraception?

Generally, people use contraception to prevent pregnancy, because they do not want a baby at that time. Also, people use condoms to protect themselves from catching sexually transmitted diseases and infections.

We don't want any children at all, so we use contraception.

I am in a casual relationship, and I don't want the long-term commitment of children yet.

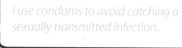

I use condoms to avoid catching a sexually transmitted infection.

We have got six-month-old twins, and we are not ready for another baby yet.

We are married, but are not ready for children yet – maybe in the future.

I have three children, and that's enough for me. I don't want any more.

What do Christians believe about contraception?

Different Christians have different beliefs about contraception.

Some Christians believe that artificial contraception is wrong because:

- it can interfere with God's intentions about a couple having a baby

- it goes against God's purpose for sex, which is reproduction.

Some Christians believe that artificial contraception is acceptable because it can:

- help prevent overcrowding and poverty

- help to maintain a better quality of family life

- help people to make responsible choices

- allow a couple to develop their relationship.

Many Christian churches, including the Church of England and the Methodist Church, teach that contraception is an acceptable method of avoiding unplanned pregnancy and restricting family size. But the Roman Catholic Church teaches that people should not interfere with 'natural law' and only natural methods of contraception are acceptable to the Catholic Church, but there should always be the possibility of pregnancy, in case God wants it to happen.

Some people believe that having control over whether or not they are at risk of getting pregnant is a human right – freedom of choice. Other Christians believe that only God has the right to choose whether or not someone has children.

Glossary

Adultery – being unfaithful to your husband or wife

Annulment – when a marriage is ended because it was not a true marriage in the first place

Celibacy – living without sexual relationships

Contraception – birth control, methods used to deliberately prevent pregnancy

Divorce – the legal ending of a marriage

Homosexuality – being emotionally and sexually attracted to members of the same sex

Marriage – a legally recognized relationship between husband and wife

Promiscuity – having a lot of casual sexual relationships

ETHICS 1

This section will help you understand Christian views about abortion, and will encourage you to think about your own views.

EXAM FOCUS

Exam Practice

Practise your skills in **demonstrating knowledge and understanding**.

Explain in your own words what is meant by the word 'abortion'.

Try to make your answer clear, short and to the point.

This will help you in the exam when you answer part (a) questions.

What is abortion?

The word **abortion** refers to the end of a pregnancy before the baby is able to survive outside the womb. When this happens naturally, it is often known as a **miscarriage**. A **procured abortion** is when the pregnancy is ended deliberately (this can also be called a **termination**). In everyday conversation, when people say that someone has had an abortion, they usually mean that a pregnancy was ended deliberately.

Making a decision to end a pregnancy is rarely easy for the people involved, but for many women faced with an unwanted pregnancy, it can seem the most sensible choice. In 2004, over 180,000 pregnancies were deliberately ended by abortion in England and Wales.

What does UK law say about abortion?

In the UK, there are laws about procured abortion. These laws are often debated by the government, because people have strong feelings about the issue. Some people want it to become much more difficult for pregnant women to choose to have abortions – but others want the law changed to make things easier for women who want abortions.

A pregnant woman cannot just make an appointment and then get an abortion in the same way that she might make an appointment to get a haircut. Instead, she has to explain her reasons to two doctors who agree that going through with the pregnancy and then the birth and parenting would put her at risk. It might put her mental or physical health at risk, or risk the well-being of her other children. Also, an abortion can only happen if the woman is less than 24 weeks pregnant. Doctors will only perform later abortions if continuing the pregnancy has very serious health risks.

I'm a nurse, and I disagree with abortion because of my religious beliefs. As a Roman Catholic, I think all human life is special to God, and I think it's wrong for a pregnant woman to choose abortion. Fortunately, the law says that I have the right to choose not to be involved with patients who want to terminate their pregnancies. ▶

For **Discussion**

Do you think British doctors and nurses should have to treat patients who want abortions, and keep their personal opinions to themselves? Or should they be allowed to choose to have nothing to do with abortions?

Think carefully about your answer. Try to give at least one reason to explain your point of view.

Activity 1

Look at the different reasons why a pregnant woman might think about having an abortion.

(a) Which, if any, do you think are good reasons for choosing abortion? Say why you think they are good reasons – support your opinion with explanation and examples.

(b) Which, if any, are bad reasons? Support your opinion again.

Why might a woman consider abortion?

There are many different reasons why a pregnant woman might consider having an abortion, for example:

- The pregnancy might not have been planned. It might have happened because the couple risked having unprotected sex, or they might have used contraception which failed to work.

- The woman might not be in a serious relationship with the father, or the relationship might break down after the woman becomes pregnant, and she might not want to bring up a baby on her own.

- The woman might be very young and not feel ready for a baby yet; or she might have older children and not want to go back to having a baby again.

- Tests during pregnancy might show that the baby is not developing normally and is likely to be born with some kind of disability.

- Circumstances might change during the pregnancy, for example the couple might get into financial difficulties.

- The pregnancy might be the result of sexual abuse.

- Tests during pregnancy might show that there is little chance of the baby being born alive.

- The woman might have wanted a baby, and then just changed her mind.

- Tests might reveal the sex of the baby, and the parents might not want a baby of that sex.

- Going through with the pregnancy might have serious mental or physical health risks for the woman.

What do Christians believe about abortion?

Within Christianity, there is a wide range of different attitudes towards abortion. Some Christians believe abortion should never be allowed. Other Christians think every woman has the right to choose abortion if she wants to. Many others think that abortion should only be allowed in some circumstances.

The Roman Catholic Church and some Evangelical churches teach that abortion should never be allowed. Roman Catholics believe that life begins at the moment of conception (when the sperm joins with the egg), so they think of a pregnancy as an unborn child, not just a lump of cells. Roman Catholics believe that abortion is always wrong because all human life comes from God, so to take away the life of an unborn child is a form of murder. Even if there are serious difficulties with the pregnancy, they argue that God would not have formed that life unless he wanted the child to be born. In some Roman Catholic countries, such as those in Latin America, abortion is completely forbidden by law and people who carry out abortions are punished with prison sentences.

To support this point of view, people might use a verse from the Bible which suggests that God cares for each person even before he or she starts to grow in the mother's womb:

> *Before I formed you in the womb I knew you.*
> **(Jeremiah 1:5)**

Roman Catholics believe that human life begins at the moment of conception, and is special and sacred to God.

There is one exception to the Roman Catholic ban on abortion, and this is known as the 'law of **double effect**'. This rule says that an abortion can only happen if it is not deliberate, but is a side-effect of some other, very necessary treatment. So if, for example, a pregnant woman was found to have a cancerous tumour and removing the tumour would mean terminating the pregnancy, then abortion could be allowed – but the abortion could not be the main aim of the treatment.

No-one wants more abortions to happen, but there are some Christians who think that there are times when abortion can be the kindest and most sensible thing to do in very difficult circumstances.

The Church of England, and some other Protestant churches such as the Methodist Church and the United Reformed Church, teaches that abortion can be a 'necessary evil'. It is never a happy choice, but in some circumstances it might be better to have the abortion than to let the pregnancy continue. For example, they might think that if doctors discovered the foetus was not developing normally and the baby would be born with serious health problems and disabilities, then it might be better for everyone's sake to end the pregnancy.

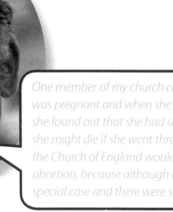

One member of my church came to see me to ask for advice. She was pregnant and when she went to the doctor for a health check, she found out that she had serious heart problems. The doctor said she might die if she went through with the pregnancy. I told her that the Church of England would support her if she chose to have an abortion, because although abortion is usually wrong, this was a special case and there were serious risks.

Exam Practice

Practise your skills in **demonstrating knowledge and understanding.**

Explain Christian views about abortion.

In your answer, show that you understand that not all Christians have the same opinions about abortion. Explain the different views Christians might have, and the reasons they might give to support their opinions. For high marks, you could include examples of teachings from the Bible.

This will help you in the exam when you answer part (d) questions.

These Christians also point out the dangers involved when abortions are carried out in secret by people without proper training or safety equipment. Before abortion became legal, many women were seriously injured because of 'back-street abortions', and some of them died. The Methodist Church campaigns against laws which might encourage illegal abortions.

Although Christians can have very different views about abortion, they all agree that:

- Abortion is a serious issue, and the people involved in making such decisions need their prayers.

- Life is a precious gift from God.

- Good sex education is important, especially for young people.

- Women who face unwanted pregnancy, whatever they decide to do about it, should be given care and support.

Attitudes to fertility treatment

This section encourages you to think about fertility treatment and Christian views about it.

EXAM FOCUS

What is fertility treatment?

The phrase 'fertility treatment' refers to a range of medical treatments that may be given to people who want children, but who are unable to conceive a baby naturally without help. Infertility problems affect about one in seven couples in the UK. Often, people look for fertility treatment because of medical problems, which might affect the man or the woman or even both. It is not always easy for doctors to work out why a couple are not conceiving; often there are no obvious health problems, but still the woman does not become pregnant.

Sometimes, couples seek fertility treatment because the woman is older than the natural age for having a baby; sometimes, a woman might want fertility treatment because she wants a baby but not a male partner. There have also been cases where women have wanted fertility treatment using the frozen sperm of a partner who has died.

▲ *In 1997, Diane Blood made legal history when she won the right to use her husband's sperm to have a baby, even after her husband was dead. When Stephen Blood became ill, samples of his sperm were kept and frozen because the couple wanted to have a baby together and thought they might need fertility treatment when he got better. Sadly Stephen died two months later, but Diane still wanted to have her husband's child. After a long legal battle, she went on to have two sons using Stephen's sperm.*

Infertility can be very upsetting for the couple, especially when their friends are having babies, and when their relations keep asking them when they plan to start a family. It can put the couple's relationship under enormous strain.

There are many different kinds of fertility treatment available, for example:

- **Fertility drugs** which help the woman to produce more healthy eggs.

- **Artificial Insemination by Husband** (AIH), which is when the husband or partner's sperm is put inside the woman using medical help.

- **Artificial Insemination by Donor** (AID), which is when sperm from an unknown donor is put inside the woman using medical help.

- **In Vitro Fertilization** (IVF), which is when eggs are taken from the woman and fertilized in a laboratory before one or more healthy embryos are placed in the woman's body to grow in her uterus. 'In vitro' means 'in glass' because the egg is fertilized in a test tube or a glass dish. Because of this, the first babies to be born with the use of IVF were known as 'test tube babies'.

- **Egg donation**, which is when an egg from an unknown donor is fertilized using IVF, and then the embryo is placed in the woman's body.

- **Freezing**, when sperm or embryos are frozen for future use.

Some couples need more than one treatment before they have a baby, and for other couples, none of the treatments are successful.

Do Christians agree with fertility treatment?

In Christianity, there are different views about fertility treatments. The Bible does not give any clear teaching because, when it was written, treatments to help people conceive were not available; so Christians have to try and work out how to apply Christian principles to the issues raised.

Some Christians, such as many Protestants, believe that if advances in medicine can help a couple to have a baby, this is a good thing. They might argue that we use other kinds of scientific and medical knowledge to help people in other circumstances. For example, if people have difficulty seeing properly, we use scientific knowledge to make the right glasses or contact lenses for them. So if people have difficulty conceiving a baby, they argue that scientific knowledge should be used to help them, too.

They might support this belief by using passages from the Bible. For example, in the book of Genesis, when God creates the first human beings, he tells them:

> *Be fruitful and increase in number; fill the earth and subdue it.*
>
> **(Genesis 1:28)**

A Christian might interpret this verse to mean that God wants all people to have children if they possibly can.

Christians might also use a verse from the New Testament called the Golden Rule. This says:

> *So in everything, do to others what you would have them do to you.*
>
> **(Matthew 7:12)**

They might think about what they would want to happen if they were the ones with infertility problems, and decide that if they would want medical help to have a baby, then they should offer this same help to others.

Thoughts on fertility treatment

Many Christians believe that fertility treatments can be an acceptable way of helping couples bring new life into the world. Other Christians believe that in fertility treatments are usually acceptable, but not always. They might argue that treatments which create 'spare' embryos should not be used, because these spare embryos might get thrown away and that would be similar to abortion. Treatments such as IVF often involve creating more embryos than are needed, so that the healthiest ones can be chosen to give the best chance of a successful pregnancy, and the others are destroyed. If a Christian believes that life is sacred and begins at the moment of conception, then they would disagree with in fertility treatments that create extra, unwanted embryos.

Some might also disagree with treatments which involve using the eggs or sperm of a third person, outside the marriage partnership. These treatments might include AID and egg donation. Some Christians might say that introducing a third adult into the conception of a baby is similar to adultery, which is forbidden in the Ten Commandments. They might also disagree with fertility treatment if it is wanted by people who are not in a married relationship, for example if it is a single woman who wants to have a baby, or a same-sex couple. They might argue that this goes against God's will for children to be the result of marriage.

There are other Christians who believe that fertility treatments can never be right. Some believe that if a couple is infertile, this is because God has made a choice that they should not have children. In the Bible there are teachings about infertile people such as Hannah, who for a long while had no children because God had decided not to let her have any:

 Peninnah had children: but Hannah had none ... the Lord had closed her womb.
(1 Samuel 1:6)

These Christians might believe that a couple is infertile because God has other plans for them – perhaps God wants them to become foster parents, or to adopt a child in need of a home, or perhaps take on some kind of work that would be difficult for parents, such as work in a developing country.

Roman Catholics often take the view that fertility treatments are wrong, because they believe that 'unnatural sex' is not permitted by God. The Church teaches that sex between a husband and wife is the only right way for a baby to be conceived. Many Catholics also believe that masturbation is wrong, so they would not accept fertility treatments which involve a man masturbating in order to produce sperm for artificial fertilization.

Roman Catholics are very much against any fertility treatments which involve creating 'spare' embryos, because they believe all human life is sacred from the moment of conception.

The Church recognizes that married couples who are unable to have children experience a lot of pain, however it views children as a gift not a right. For Roman Catholics, the life of an embryo is more important than the wishes of the couple; every embryo has the right to life, but the couple does not have the right to a child, so treatments which risk creating unwanted embryos are not allowed.

Exam Practice

Practise your skills in **demonstrating knowledge and understanding**.

Explain Christian views about fertility treatment.

In your answer, show that you understand there are different views within Christianity. Explain the different views Christians might have – for high marks, try to remember which denominations hold which beliefs. In your answer, show how a Christian might support his or her point of view with reasons.

This will help you in the exam when you answer part (d) questions

Christian attitudes towards cloning

What is cloning?

Cloning is a scientific process where cells are copied exactly, so that a new cell is made with the exact DNA of another cell.

In 1997, medical history was made when a sheep (called Dolly) was cloned from a cell taken from an adult animal. Dolly's birth was important because it showed that cloning from a single cell could be used to create a whole new animal.

Dolly the sheep was the first cloned animal to be produced. Unfortunately she developed health problems and had to be put down. ▶

Scientists are interested in cloning because it might lead to important medical breakthroughs:

- It could be used to create new organs for people who need transplant surgery. The risk of rejection of the organ would be much less, and it would overcome the problem of a shortage of donors.

- The creation of cloned embryos could lead to a better understanding of how embryos develop.

- Cloning could lead to better treatment and even cures for life-threatening illnesses such as cystic fibrosis and haemophilia.

- Some scientists think that cloning could give a better understanding of old age and the illnesses associated with ageing.

- Cloning of animals could be used to preserve endangered species, or even recreate species that have become extinct.

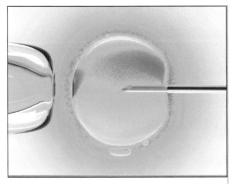

▲ *Artificial fertilization of a human egg has for some time been a medically proven method of reproduction, but it is still an area of concern for religious groups.*

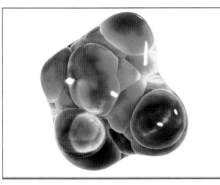

▲ *The stem cells are the first stage in the growth of a foetus, but medical research using stem cells has been a controversial issue in recent years.*

What do Christians believe about cloning?

Many people, whether religious or not, object to the idea of cloning, especially if it involves humans. In many parts of the world, human cloning experiments are illegal. Most Christians agree that this is the right position to take. They argue that each human life is a unique and special gift, created by God, and that it is wrong for people to try and create human life artificially.

Another reason why Christians might disagree with human cloning is that the process requires many human embryos to be made, before just one successful clone is formed. If people carried out cloning procedures, they would have to throw away large numbers of unsuccessful embryos. Christians who believe that life begins at the moment of conception (such as most Roman Catholics) argue that it is wrong to throw away potential human lives.

However, other Christians argue that a certain kind of cloning is acceptable. This is 'tissue cloning', where the aim is not to create an entirely new human person, but to create and develop one particular kind of cell. For example, skin cells could be cloned, so that someone who had suffered severe burns could have skin grafts made from his or her own cells, and then new skin which suited the patient perfectly could be grown to cover the damaged area. Other kinds of cell might be cloned to help people who have been injured, or to replace body organs that have stopped working properly. Cells which had an exact match to the patient would have a much better chance of working. Some Christians believe that this kind of science is an acceptable way of using medical skill to save or heal human life.

There are also some Christians who believe that human cloning experiments can take place, but only if the experiments use embryos which have already been created for fertility treatments or which are the result of abortions. They say it is wrong to make new embryos just for cloning, but if there are already unwanted embryos available, then using them for cloning is better than simply throwing them away – at least some good might come out of a bad situation.

Exam Practice

Practise your skills in **demonstrating knowledge and understanding**.

Describe what is meant by 'cloning'.

In your answer, try to give a clear but brief explanation. You could give an example of when cloning might be used.

This will help you in the exam when you answer part (b) questions.

Attitudes to euthanasia

This section will help you understand what euthanasia is, and encourage you to explore different opinions of it.

EXAM FOCUS

For **Discussion**

Consider: what sort of death do you think is a 'good' death? If you could choose how to die, what would you choose, and why?

What is euthanasia?

The word 'euthanasia' comes from two Greek words: 'eu', which means 'good' or 'gentle', and 'thanatos', which means 'death'. **Euthanasia** is not just another word for the good sort of death where people die peacefully in their sleep after a long life. Euthanasia is often known as 'mercy-killing', because the word is used to refer to deliberately ending the lives of people who suffer from painful terminal illnesses or who depend completely on others for basic care.

Euthanasia is an extremely difficult moral issue. It raises all sorts of questions about people's rights and responsibilities, the duties of the medical profession, and quality of life. In order to clarify some of the issues, people often make a distinction between different kinds of euthanasia:

Voluntary euthanasia is when someone makes a free choice to be helped to die. For example, someone who had an illness that was getting worse and who had no hope of a cure might decide that he or she wanted euthanasia.

Involuntary euthanasia is when other people make a decision that someone else should have euthanasia. For example, if someone was in a serious accident and was badly brain-damaged, the rest of the family might decide that it would be kinder to end that person's life.

Assisted suicide is a form of euthanasia where someone wants to commit suicide, but needs help. For example, someone who was unable to move because of an injury or illness might want a friend or relative to help them collect and swallow a fatal overdose of drugs.

Exam Practice

Practise your skills in **demonstrating knowledge and understanding**.

Give three statements explaining what you understand by 'euthanasia'.

Notice that the question just asks you to name key features. It does not ask you to give your opinions about them, or to explain them in detail, so you do not have to spend time giving a long answer.

This will help you in the exam when you answer part (c) questions.

Euthanasia and the law

Euthanasia is against the law in the UK, but it is allowed in some countries such as the Netherlands and Switzerland. In Britain, people who carry out acts of euthanasia, or who help people to commit suicide, can be prosecuted and sent to prison.

The subject is often debated in the media, because cases arise where people want to have the right to euthanasia, and to many it seems unfair that the law does not allow it.

Diane Pretty suffered from motor neuron disease, and wanted the courts to allow her husband to help her commit suicide when the disease became too much for her. She argued that it was a human right to be allowed to die with dignity. The courts refused, and she died aged 43 when she developed breathing difficulties. ▶

Debbie Purdy has multiple sclerosis, an incurable illness which affects the central nervous system. She raised questions about the British law on euthanasia, because she wanted to be sure that if her husband took her to another country for euthanasia, he would not be prosecuted. ▶

▲ *Dan James, 23, made the news in 2008 when he travelled to Switzerland for euthanasia. He was paralysed after an injury in a rugby training session, and decided that he would rather end his life than spend years feeling trapped inside a body that wouldn't work. He had to go to Switzerland to die, because British law does not allow euthanasia. Some people thought his decision was wrong, because he was not terminally ill or in physical pain; but others thought he should have just as much right to commit suicide as an able-bodied person has.*

Different attitudes towards euthanasia

Many people, whether they have religious beliefs or not, are against euthanasia. Here are some of the reasons used in their arguments:

1 Many people who are in a lot of pain, or who have suffered terrible injuries, are not in a state of mind where they can make sensible decisions. Perhaps, given time, they might be able to come to terms with their condition and begin to enjoy life again to an extent. They should be helped to find ways of coping, rather than being helped to die.

2 People who are ill or who need constant care often feel that they are a burden to others. They know that it costs a lot of money to look after them and that it takes a lot of other people's time. This might put pressure on ill people and make them feel they should ask for euthanasia, even if it isn't what they really want.

3 If patients are in a state where they can no longer say what it is that they want, greedy relatives might ask doctors for euthanasia in order to inherit money and property.

4 Sometimes people might think that their illness is incurable, but perhaps a cure might be found if they stay alive long enough to benefit from it.

5 Legal euthanasia would give doctors and nurses very difficult decisions to make, and some people think they should never have to make the decision to end someone else's life.

▶ *Hospices are places where patients can go when they are near to the end of their lives. They can also go there for short breaks, to give their carers a rest. Many Christians say that a hospice is a good alternative to euthanasia, because the staff there can help people to find the best quality of life available.*

Exam Practice

Practise your **evaluation** skills.

'Euthanasia should never be allowed.'

Discuss the statement. You should use different, supported points of view and a personal viewpoint. You must refer to Christianity in your answer.

This should be a longer answer. You need to think of different arguments, both for and against the view that euthanasia should never be allowed. Start by explaining why some people think euthanasia might be allowed in some circumstances. You could use examples, such as the case of Diane Pretty. Say why some Christians think that there are times when euthanasia might be right.

Then explain a different point of view. Explain why some people think euthanasia is always wrong. Give a different Christian point of view – you could refer to the teaching of the Roman Catholic Church.

Finally, decide on your personal viewpoint. Do you think euthanasia should never be allowed? Or do you think there are times when it might be the best choice? State clearly what your own opinion is, and give one or more reasons for it.

This will help you in the exam when you answer part (e) questions.

A Christian who disagreed with euthanasia might also add other arguments:

- God decides when it is right for someone's life to begin and end. Life is a sacred gift from God, not something that humans should try and control for themselves.

- If someone is suffering, perhaps God has a reason for this, even if we can't understand what that reason might be. Jesus was prepared to suffer pain for God, so people should follow his example.

- The Bible teaches:

> *Do you not know that your body is a temple of the Holy Spirit, who is in you, whom you have received from God? You are not your own; you were bought at a price. Therefore honour God with your body.*
> **(1 Corinthians 6: 19-20)**

Christians might use this verse to argue that our bodies belong to God, as a place where the Holy Spirit lives and works, and they are not our own to treat however we want.

Some people, however, believe that euthanasia can be right in some circumstances. They argue:

- A ban on euthanasia discriminates against people with health problems. People who are physically healthy are free to commit suicide if they want to, so the law should allow people with disabilities the same freedom to choose to end their own lives.

- When people are in great pain, or have lost their dignity, it is cruel to force them to stay alive. Life is only worth living if it has some quality to it.

- It costs money to keep seriously ill people alive. The money could be better spent on someone who had a chance of survival, and should not be wasted on people who have no quality of life and would prefer to be dead.

A Christian who agreed with euthanasia in some circumstances might add:

- The Bible teaches:

> *So in everything, do to others what you would have them do to you.*
> **(Matthew 7:12)**

If you wouldn't want to carry on living a life of pain and indignity, then you should allow other people the same right to die in peace.

- Christians have a duty to stand up for the weak and not let them suffer discrimination.

The Roman Catholic 'doctrine of double effect' can be used in debates about euthanasia. This rule says that it is wrong to give medicines with the deliberate intention of killing the patient, but if medicine is given to relieve pain, and is also a strong enough dose to end the patient's life, this could be acceptable. The important thing is that killing was not the intention.

Attitudes to suicide

In this section, you will learn about Christian attitudes towards suicide.

EXAM FOCUS

Suicide is the word used when someone deliberately ends his or her own life. In the past, Christians believed that suicide was a terrible sin, and the law treated it as a crime. People believed suicide was very wrong because:

* They thought it broke one of the Ten Commandments. The sixth commandment says 'Do not commit murder', and many Christians used to think that suicide was a kind of murder because it involved deliberately ending a human life, even though the murderer and the victim were the same person.

* They believed life is a gift from God, which people should appreciate.

* They believed God makes each human life for a reason, so that if a person commits suicide, he or she is refusing to do whatever it was that God intended.

Today, people have a better understanding of mental health, and are much more sympathetic towards people who feel so desperate that they want to commit suicide. Christians today recognize that when people feel suicidal, it is often because they have reached a point where they are no longer able to make a rational decision.

What might make someone suicidal?

People might feel suicidal for all kinds of reasons. Sometimes it is because they feel they are being bullied by other people at school or work, or by a partner. Sometimes, people feel like committing suicide when they lose someone they love. Sometimes financial problems, redundancy or a feeling of failure can bring about these feelings. People who have mental health problems such as depression, bipolar disorder or schizophrenia also might reach such a low point that they feel life is no longer worth living.

Christians believe that they have a duty to treat other people in the way that they would like to be treated themselves. They believe that they have special responsibilities towards people who are ill or vulnerable, which means that they should try and help anyone who is in emotional distress. They might do this by:

* making sure they are good listeners

* trying not to be judgemental when other people talk about their lives

* praying for people who are lonely or distressed

* fund-raising for organizations which support people with mental health problems

* volunteering for an organization such as Samaritans.

▲ *Fund-raising for mental health charities on the streets of East London.*

▲ *Chad Varah, who died in 2007 aged 95, was the founder of Samaritans. He put his Christian beliefs into practice by starting an organization which gives emotional support to anyone who needs it.*

Samaritans is not a Christian organization, but it was started by a Christian called Chad Varah. He was a clergyman in London, and began his work in the 1950s, when suicide was still illegal; people who attempted suicide unsuccessfully could be prosecuted. The very first funeral Chad Varah led was for a thirteen-year-old girl who had committed suicide. She had felt desperate enough to take her own life because she thought she was seriously ill, but in fact she had just started her periods and had never had any sex education, so she did not know what was happening to her. Chad Varah was very upset by this waste of a young life, because he believed that every human life is created by God. He decided to campaign for better sex education, and also to start an organization where people could go and talk if they were lonely and if they had problems where they needed support and someone to listen.

Today, Samaritans is an organization which provides emotional support to hundreds of people. It has drop-in centres, telephone helplines and online facilities, where volunteers work every day of the year, 24 hours a day.

◀ *I decided to work for Samaritans because of my Christian faith. You don't have to be a Christian, or religious at all, to volunteer, but that was my reason. A few years ago, one of my friends committed suicide after a long period of depression, and his family were devastated. It made me think about what it must be like for people who can see no way forward in their lives, so I made up my mind to volunteer. I'm not a trained psychotherapist, but Samaritans taught me how to listen to people without judging them, and how to help them feel that there are others in the world who care about them. I don't know if I've prevented anyone from committing suicide, but I hope I have.*

Exam Practice

Practise your skills in **demonstrating knowledge and understanding**.

Explain Christian views about suicide.

In your answer, show that you understand how Christian views about suicide have changed. You could include examples of teachings from the Bible, and you could show how Christians might put their beliefs into practise to help people who are feeling like committing suicide. You could mention the work of an organization such as Samaritans.

This will help you in the exam when you answer part (d) questions.

Using animals in medical research

This section encourages you to think about whether animals should be used for medical research.

EXAM FOCUS

What does the law say about using animals in medical research?

In the UK, animals are used by scientists to test new medicine and medical procedures before they are used on humans. For example, a new kind of ventilator made for premature babies might be tested first on piglets, and a new drug for treating epilepsy might be tried first on rodents and other larger animals. Research involving animals is used for all kinds of new treatments, for conditions such as Alzheimer's disease, HIV, Parkinson's disease and strokes.

The law says that medical research using animals can only be carried out when there are no reasonable alternatives, and should not be done unnecessarily. When it has to be done, it should be in a way that causes the least possible suffering to the animal. Scientists should try and reduce the number of animal experiments wherever they can, and there are some species such as chimpanzees where approval is never given for medical research.

Christian views

Many Christians believe that although causing unnecessary suffering to animals is wrong, medical research is necessary, and therefore they support the use of animals in finding cures for human illnesses. They might support this point of view by saying:

- God gave humans souls, but not animals, so human life is more precious than animal life.

- God gave people the right to rule over the animals, so animals do not have the same rights as humans:

> *Then God said: 'Let us make man in our image, in our likeness, and let them rule over the fish of the sea and the birds of the air, over the livestock, over all the earth, and over all the creatures that move along the ground.'*
> **(Genesis 1:26)**

Other Christians might disagree. They might argue that all life is created by God and that people should respect other species. They might support this view by saying:

- God told people to be 'stewards' of the earth, which means taking care of other species and not destroying them or causing them to suffer.

- God cares about all of his creation:

> *Are not five sparrows sold for two pennies? Yet not one of them is forgotten by God.*
> **(Luke 12:6)**

◀ *Peter Singer is a thinker who believes that Christianity has done a lot of harm to animals. He argues that we should recognize that we are animals too, and we should not be 'speciesist'. We should give other animals the same respect that we give to humans, he says.*

Exam Practice

Practise your **evaluation** skills.

'Animals can be used in medical research, because humans are more important than animals.'

Discuss the statement. You should use different, supported points of view and a personal viewpoint. You must refer to Christianity in your answer.

This should be a longer answer. You need to think of different arguments, both for and against the use of animals in medical research. You could start by saying why many Christians believe that animal testing is acceptable.

Then explain a different point of view. Explain why some people think animal testing is wrong. Give a different Christian point of view – you could refer to the teaching of the Roman Catholic Church.

Finally, decide on your personal viewpoint. Do you think animal testing for medical research is acceptable, or do you think it should never be allowed? State clearly what your own opinion is, and give one or more reasons for it.

This will help you in the exam when you answer part (e) questions.

Glossary

Abortion – ending a pregnancy before the baby is born

Assisted suicide – helping someone to end his or her own life

Cloning – copying the exact DNA of a living creature to create new living cells

Double effect – a Roman Catholic doctrine which says that it is wrong to kill deliberately, but that sometimes death is a side-effect of another acceptable practice such as pain relief

Euthanasia – 'mercy-killing' to allow a gentle and easy death

Fertility treatment – medical treatment to help couples who want a baby but cannot conceive naturally

Involuntary euthanasia – when the decision to have euthanasia is made on behalf of an individual by someone else

Miscarriage – when a foetus is expelled from the womb before it is able to survive independently

Procured abortion (also known as a **termination**) – when a pregnancy is deliberately ended before the birth

Samaritans – a non-religious organization providing all year round emotional support via helplines or online facilities

Suicide – the deliberate ending of a person's own life

Voluntary euthanasia – providing euthanasia when an individual asks for it

ETHICS 1

Religious views of wealth and the causes of hunger, poverty and disease

This section introduces you to Christian ideas about money.

Christians recognize that money is something people need in order to buy goods such as food and housing, and services such as healthcare and plumbing. If we are unable to earn money ourselves, other people have to provide these things for us. Christianity, like many other religions, teaches that people have a responsibility to take care of themselves and their families if they are able to do so. They should work hard, make good use of their talents, contribute something to society and help those who are unable to care for themselves.

However, money gives Christians some moral questions to consider. How much money should a Christian keep, and how much should be given away to others? Is it acceptable for a Christian to be rich? Are there right and wrong ways of earning money? How important should money be in the life of a Christian?

◀ *Could it ever be right for a Christian to have an expensive lifestyle?*

What does the Bible teach about having money?

The Bible teaches that working hard and earning an honest living is good, but that money should not be the most important part of life for Christians. In Luke's Gospel, Jesus teaches:

> 66 *Then he said to them, 'Watch out! Be on your guard against all kinds of greed; a man's life does not consist in the abundance of his possessions.'* 99
>
> **(Luke 12:15)**

Jesus went on to tell a **parable** (a story with a message) which is known as the *Parable of the Rich Fool*:

> … in the story, there was a man who owned some land where he grew crops. One year, the crop was so successful that the man had no room to store everything he had grown. He decided to build himself bigger storage barns for all the grain, and to give up work; he planned to sit around all day eating and drinking and having fun. But as soon as he had made that decision, he died the very same night.

The message of the story seems to be that the man made a foolish decision. He could have chosen to keep just what he needed, and given away the rest of his harvest to other people who were hungry. Or perhaps he could have used his wealth for the good of the community and carried on working, teaching others his skills in farming. The Rich Fool thought that being rich was going to make him happy, but he was wrong; he forgot that life is short and he did not think about trying to please God. Jesus was teaching that Christians should not measure their success by the amount they have in the bank and by their possessions, but should put God first. In Matthew's Gospel, Jesus makes a contrast between 'treasures on earth', which are material possessions, and 'treasures in heaven'.

> *Do not store up for yourselves treasures on earth, where moth and rust destroy, and where thieves break in and steal. But store up for yourselves treasures in heaven, where moth and rust do not destroy, and where thieves do not break in and steal. For where your treasure is, there your heart will be also.*
> **(Matthew 6:19-21)**

It is not completely clear what Jesus meant by 'treasure in heaven', but most Christians interpret this passage to mean things such as a right relationship with God, a good moral character, and loving relationships.

Jesus teaches that people can only have one 'master'; they can be ruled either by God or by their love of material things, but not both at the same time:

> *No-one can serve two masters. Either he will hate the one and love the other, or he will be devoted to the one and despise the other. You cannot serve both God and Money.*
> **(Matthew 6:24)**

◀ *Blessed Mother Teresa of Calcutta was a Christian nun who devoted her life to working with the poor. She said: 'Riches… can choke you if you do not use them fairly. Let us remain as empty as possible so that God can fill us up. For even God cannot put anything in a heart that is already full.'*

In the Gospels there is a story of how a rich young man asked Jesus what he needed to do in order to have eternal life in heaven with God. Jesus told him that he should love God and keep the commandments, and the young man answered that he had always done these things, ever since he was a child. But Jesus said that there was one more thing that the man needed to do:

For Discussion

Do you think it is possible for people to be 'ruled' by money? What might someone's life be like, if they were ruled by money and by collecting possessions?

> *'One thing you lack,' he said. 'Go, sell everything you have and give to the poor, and you will have treasure in heaven. Then come, follow me.' At this the man's face fell. He went away sad, because he had great wealth. Jesus looked around and said to his disciples, 'How hard it is for the rich to enter the kingdom of God.' The disciples were amazed at his words. But Jesus said again, 'Children, how hard it is to enter the kingdom of God! It is easier for a camel to go through the eye of a needle than for a rich man to enter the kingdom of God.'*
>
> **(Mark 10:21-24)**

The disciples were surprised by Jesus' teaching, because they had always thought that riches were a sign of God's blessing. If someone was very wealthy, people assumed that this must be because he or she had pleased God in some way and was being rewarded. But Jesus taught the opposite, saying that riches were not a reward from God but could be an obstacle to faith.

In the Gospel stories, especially in Luke's Gospel, God show particular concern for the poor. For example:

- Jesus was born in a stable, not in a palace or a comfortable home
- the first people who learnt about Jesus' birth were poor shepherds, not important leaders
- Jesus chose his disciples from ordinary people such as fishermen
- Jesus visited, taught and healed ordinary people.

The causes of hunger, poverty and disease

Although the world is rich in natural resources and plenty of food is produced, there are many people in the world who live in poverty. The world's supplies of food, fuel, medicines and skills are not shared out fairly. **Poverty** is difficult to define, because there are many different ways of measuring it. Most people understand poverty to mean lacking the basic essentials which give a decent quality of life, such as clean water, healthy food and medicines.

There are different ways of measuring poverty, and different ways of deciding whether a country is a developed country or a developing country. The World Bank works out the wealth of a country by dividing a country's income by the number of people who live there, because this seems a good way of knowing whether the country has enough money to look after its citizens. If a country needs more resources than it is able to produce, then it becomes poorer and gets into debt and has to borrow money from other countries. Developing countries are usually considered to be those where there are low standards of living compared with other countries. For example, there are low standards of nutrition, health, industrialization, housing, human rights and education.

According to the World Bank, 85 per cent of the world's population lives in developing countries, but they have only 21 per cent of the world's income. The richest 20 per cent in the world have more than 75 per cent of the wealth. Those who live in extreme poverty have an income of less than one US dollar per day. According to the United Nations, about 25,000 people die every day because of hunger.

These are just a few examples of the differences between rich countries and developing countries:

People in developing countries have less to spend on their food than people in developing countries spend on pet food.

In Canada, HIV and AIDS affects fewer than one in two hundred people between the ages of 15 and 49, but in Swaziland it affects one person in three in the same age group

The money that people in the US spend on cosmetics each year would be enough to pay for everyone in developing countries to receive a basic education.

The amount it would cost to provide women in developing countries with the health care they need for safe childbirth is the same amount that is spent on perfume in Europe and the US.

Some differences between rich and developing countries

The risk of dying in childbirth is 40 times greater for a woman in a developing country than for a woman in the developed world.

People who live in Eritrea are among the poorest in the world. ▶

Poverty has many causes, and often different factors are linked. These causes include:

War and conflict: when a country is at war, a lot of resources are spent on fighting instead of on development. Roads, buildings and energy supplies are destroyed. People might have to move away from their homes and live as refugees and they cannot then continue to make a living.

Bad government: when a country is not run effectively, it is harder for people to have access to education and health care. Bad government can make people feel it is not worth trying to make improvements, especially if there is a lot of crime and the people in power are corrupt.

Overpopulation: many developing countries have rapidly-growing populations, so that it becomes even more difficult for them to support themselves. Adults need to have children so that there will be a new generation to support them in their old age, because there will be no one else to care for them. They need to have several children because it is likely that not all of them will live to become adults. Also, people in developing countries often have no access to contraception.

Environmental factors: climate change often has a devastating effect on poor countries, because the people cannot afford to take steps to protect themselves from it. Droughts, floods, intensive farming and poor harvests push people even further down the poverty scale. They depend on being able to grow more than they eat, and if the crop fails, they have to borrow money and get further into debt.

Disease: developing countries often lack the resources to provide adequate health care for the people who live there. In many developing countries, diseases such as malaria, HIV and AIDS affect a large proportion of the population, so that people are unable to work to earn a living. Orphans and the elderly become particularly vulnerable because there is no one to take care of them. Each year, 15 million children are orphaned because of HIV and AIDS, this figure is roughly the same as the total number of children in the UK.

Trade laws: some people think that international banking laws work to the disadvantage of the poor. When developing countries cannot support themselves, they have to borrow money and pay it back with interest. The debt can quickly grow, and trying to pay it back makes the country even poorer. Trade laws are made by the rich countries, and they work to the advantage of the rich countries.

Poverty is an extremely difficult issue to resolve. The causes of poverty are, in many cases, also the effects of poverty: for example, poverty causes hunger, and hunger causes poor health, and poor health prevents people from working effectively so it causes more poverty. Economists often talk about poverty in terms of a 'spiral'.

This map shows the percentage of people living in poverty in different countries of the world. ▼

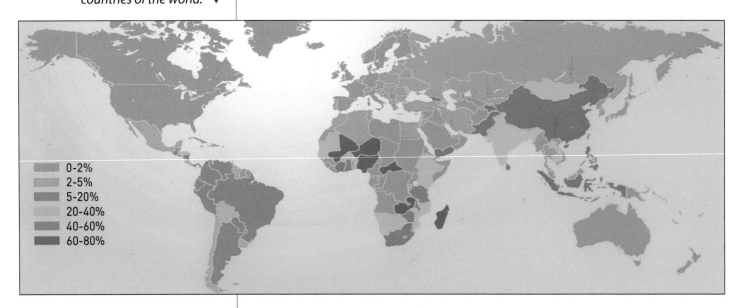

- 0–2%
- 2–5%
- 5–20%
- 20–40%
- 40–60%
- 60–80%

Exam Practice

Practise your skills in **demonstrating knowledge and understanding**.

State two of the causes of poverty.

This is a short-answer question, so you would just need to give a very brief outline of the two causes you choose, rather than going into detail.

This will help you in the exam when you answer part (b) questions.

Concern for others

This section will consider Christian views about caring for others and approaches to charity.

What does the Bible teach about caring for others?

The responsibility of people who love God to care for other human beings is one of the most important themes of the Bible.

Right from the start, where God first creates humanity in the book of Genesis, the people are given the responsibility to act as stewards of the earth. This means that they should act as God's 'caretakers' on earth. This involves taking care of the planet and becoming involved in preserving the environment; it involves caring for other species; and it also involves caring for the rest of humanity, especially those who are weak and vulnerable.

Genesis also teaches that human beings were made 'in the image of God'. Christians often interpret this to mean that all people share something of the nature of God, and so they want to care for others because they recognize other people are part of God's creation and are valuable to God.

Prophets and prophecy

The prophets of the Old Testament were people who worked as messengers; they listened to the words of God, and passed them on to the people, telling them what God wanted them to do, sharing God's promises with them and warning them of what would happen if they failed to live up to the standards God was setting for them. One of the most common themes of Old Testament prophecy is that people should stop being greedy and selfish, and should show more concern for the poor. The people were warned that God would punish them unless they behaved more fairly. The prophet Amos complained about the way the rich were behaving:

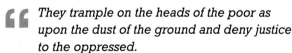 *They trample on the heads of the poor as upon the dust of the ground and deny justice to the oppressed.*

(Amos 2:7)

The prophets wanted to show their belief that God cares about the poor, and is angry when richer people ignore them.

In Matthew's Gospel, the *Parable of the Sheep and the Goats* warns Christians that God will judge them according to their attitude to the poor. Jesus says that caring for people who need help is the same thing as caring for God, and ignoring them is the same as ignoring God:

When the Son of Man comes in his glory, and all the angels with him, he will sit on his throne in heavenly glory. All the nations will be gathered before him, and he will separate the people one from another as a shepherd separates the sheep from the goats. He will put the sheep on his right and the goats on his left. Then the King will say to those on his right, 'Come, you who are blessed by my Father; take your inheritance, the kingdom prepared for you since the creation of the world. For I was hungry and you gave me something to eat, I was thirsty and you gave me something to drink, I was a stranger and you invited me in, I needed clothes and you clothed me, I was sick and you looked after me, I was in prison and you came to visit me.'

Then the righteous will answer him, 'Lord, when did we see you hungry and feed you, or thirsty and give you something to drink? When did we see you a stranger and invite you in, or needing clothes and clothe you? When did we see you sick or in prison and go to visit you?'

The King will reply, 'I tell you the truth, whatever you did for one of the least of these brothers of mine, you did for me.'

Then he will say to those on his left, 'Depart from me, you who are cursed, into the eternal fire prepared for the devil and his angels. For I was hungry and you gave me nothing to eat, I was thirsty and you gave me nothing to drink, I was a stranger and you did not invite me in, I needed clothes and you did not clothe me, I was sick and in prison and you did not look after me.'

They also will answer, 'Lord, when did we see you hungry or thirsty or a stranger or needing clothes or sick or in prison, and did not help you?'

He will reply, 'I tell you the truth, whatever you did not do for one of the least of these, you did not do for me.'

(Matthew 25:31-45)

"For I was hungry and you gave me nothing to eat, I was thirsty and you gave me nothing to drink.

(Matthew 25:42)

Activity 1

Read the *Parable of the Good Samaritan* in Luke 10:25-37. Explain in your own words:

a what happens in the story

b what message was Jesus trying to give in this story?

This will help you in the exam when you are asked to demonstrate knowledge and understanding.

The Bible teaches that showing concern for others has to include all people, whether they are friends, family, enemies or complete strangers. Jesus reminded people that the two greatest commandments were to love God, and to 'love your neighbour as yourself'; in other words, to treat other people as well as you would like to be treated yourself. When Jesus gave this teaching, he was asked to explain who counted as a 'neighbour'. Perhaps the questioner was wondering, did it mean just the people in his immediate family, or the people who lived in his street, or everyone he knew? Jesus answered by telling a parable where one man helped the victim of a robbery and assault, even though the victim was a complete stranger. The story is known as the *Parable of the Good Samaritan*, and the message is that people should treat all other human beings as 'neighbours'.

How do Christians understand the term 'charity'?

'Charity' is a word used to mean giving to people in need. It usually refers to giving money, but it can refer to giving time as well. Today, many people prefer to talk about giving 'aid' rather than 'charity'. The word 'charity' might seem to imply that the people on the receiving end are inferior to the givers.

In the Bible, charity is given an important place. Jesus talks about 'when you give to charity', assuming that this is something everyone does; he tells people that they should give in secret rather than making a big fuss about it:

> So when you give to the needy, do not announce it with trumpets, as the hypocrites do in the synagogues and on the streets, to be honoured by men. I tell you the truth, they have received their reward in full. But when you give to the needy, do not let your left hand know what your right hand is doing, so that your giving may be in secret. Then your Father, who sees what is done in secret, will reward you.
>
> **(Matthew 6:2-4)**

The person Jesus praises most for her charitable giving is a poor widow. She did not put as much into the collecting box as many other people, but Jesus said that her gift was worth the most because she gave a much bigger proportion of her income:

> As he looked up, Jesus saw the rich putting their gifts into the temple treasury. He also saw a poor widow put in two very small copper coins. 'I tell you the truth,' he said, 'his poor widow has put in more than all the others. All these people gave their gifts out of their wealth; but she out of her poverty put in all she had to live on.'
>
> **(Luke 21:1-4)**

How should Christians respond to the needs of the poor?

Christians can respond to the needs of the poor in many different ways. Some are in a better position to help than others, and can do more.

- Christians can pray about the needs of the poor. The can pray for those who are hungry, for the people who work in aid agencies, and for the people in charge of making decisions which affect the poor. Christians believe that God listens to their prayers and answers them.

- They can work politically to make changes for the poor. They might use their vote to support a candidate who shows concern for the poor. They might take part in demonstrations and protests when political decisions are made which affect people in developing countries or people on low incomes in their own country.

- They can give money to aid agencies which help the poor. Some Christians give money whenever they can spare it, while others set aside an amount every month from their wages. Some Christians keep little collecting boxes in their homes and put extra change in there whenever they remember. Christians might also consider leaving money to aid agencies when they die.

- Christians might give up their time to work for the poor. They might volunteer to help in a charity shop, or with fund-raising, or in a shelter for the homeless. They might take part in sponsored events such as walks or marathon running as a way of raising money.

- Christians might try to make sure that when they do their shopping, they think about the needs of the poor. They could make a special effort to buy goods which carry a Fairtrade mark. **Fairtrade** goods such as cotton, tea, coffee, sugar, fruit and chocolate are produced by growers who are guaranteed a fair wage, and guaranteed fair and safe working conditions. Christians could also make an effort to support the work of aid agencies by buying from charity catalogues and charity shops.

- They might make an effort to educate themselves about the needs of the poor. They could learn more about living conditions in poorer countries, and try to educate others so that other people join them in helping.

▲ *Look out for the Fairtrade logo which is a sign that the goods have been produced by people working in fair and safe working conditions in developing countries.*

Activity 2

Develop your **knowledge and understanding**.

Use the internet to find out more about Fairtrade. Read some of the stories of people whose lives have been changed because of the Fairtrade movement.

This will help you in the exam when you answer (b), (c) and (d) questions.

The work of Christian aid agencies

There are many different Christian organizations devoted to working for the poor; there are also other aid agencies which do the same sort of work but have no religious basis.

Christian Aid

One of the best-known Christian aid agencies in the UK is Christian Aid. Christian Aid began soon after the Second World War when the churches got together to help people who had been made homeless because of the war. It was known at first as Christian Reconstruction in Europe, because its aims were to help rebuild the lives and communities of people in Europe who were the victims of war. The organization rapidly grew, and started to help the poor all over the world by providing relief in times of emergency, particularly in Africa. It changed its name to Christian Aid to reflect the way in which it was working right across the world, not just in Europe. Christian Aid helps all people in need, whether they are Christian or not.

As Christian Aid expanded and took on new projects, the people who worked for the organization began to realize that giving help in times of disaster was important, but that the focus of their work should be challenging poverty and injustice all the time. Christian Aid tries to make changes in the world so that it can become a fairer place. Rather than 'giving charity' to the poor, it aims to work with them as partners, encouraging people to become more independent as they learn new skills and receive a better health care and education. Christian Aid believes that tackling poverty and injustice involves educating the rich as well as working with the poor, because it is not until rich people change their attitudes that the poor will be able to benefit. One of Christian Aid's important campaigns today is for action to fight climate change, as it believes that the greatest impact of climate change is on the poor who are powerless to do anything about it.

Christian Aid raises money in many different ways, but the focus of its fund-raising is 'Christian Aid Week' which takes place every year in May. Teams of volunteers put information about the work of Christian Aid and collection envelopes through the letterboxes of every home in their neighbourhood, in an effort to raise awareness of the work of Christian Aid and to raise funds which can be spent on helping those in most need. Christian Aid aims to put into action its beliefs that all human beings are valuable and should be treated with justice.

CAFOD

CAFOD stands for Catholic Agency for Overseas Development. It is a branch of an organization called Caritas, which is a worldwide **aid agency** run by the Roman Catholic Church. It works to bring together people in need with those who can help them, in partnership.

CAFOD began in 1962, when the Catholic Church realized that there were all sorts of small fund-raising efforts going on in different churches. They realised that there was a need for a central agency to co-ordinate all these efforts so that the money raised could be put to good use and so that people could be better-informed about the needs of the poor in other parts of the world.

We support CAFOD because we believe that God created all people to be equal. We think fighting against poverty and injustice is an important part of Christian life. In this country, we have so much, and it's good for us to take some time to stop and think about people in other parts of the world who don't have the things we take for granted. ▼

Like Christian Aid, CAFOD bases its aims on the Christian belief that all human life is valuable and deserves to be treated with dignity. It aims for social justice, so that the world can become a fairer place where everyone can share in the gifts God provides, such as food, shelter, medicine and education. CAFOD tries to give a 'voice' to the poor so they are not ignored.

One of the ways in which CAFOD raises money is through 'fast days'. These are days when supporters of CAFOD choose to go without food, or to eat only very simple food such as soup, and give the money they would have spent on meals to the poor. They experience for a short time what it feels like to be hungry, and they concentrate their prayers on those who do not have enough to eat.

Activity 3

Develop your **knowledge and understanding**.

Visit the websites of some of the Christian aid agencies to find out more about their work. Read about their aims, and also find out some details about projects they are working on at the moment.

This will help you in the exam when you answer (b), (c) and (d) questions.

The uses of money

This section will help you understand Christian teaching about the use of money.

How should Christians use their money?

Christians believe that they should think carefully about how they use their money. They believe that it is important to work hard and use well the talents that God has given. As long as they are fit and healthy and can find work, they should do their best to support their families and make a contribution to society.

They believe that the money they earn should be shared with those in need. Different Christians interpret this in different ways. Some believe that Christians should lead very simple lifestyles and do without luxuries, so that they can give as much as possible to others. Other Christians live in a similar way to their non-Christian friends, but they still try to make regular donations to the poor.

As a Christian family, we try not to be greedy. We share a lawnmower with two other Christian families in the same street, and we don't have a car. We try to buy most of our clothes from charity shops, because we think it is wrong to waste money when so many people in the world are starving. ▶

For Discussion

Practise your skills in **debate and evaluation**.

Imagine that a Christian has a choice:

* to work with old people in a care home, not earning very much and living a simple life

* or to take a job which pays a lot of money so that the Christian could give a lot to the poor, but the job is with a tobacco company.

What do you think the Christian should do? How would you support your answer?

This will help you in the exam when you answer part (e) questions.

Christian beliefs about gambling

Different Christians have different views about gambling. Some believe that as long as the gambling is not taken too seriously, and as long as it is only occasional rather than a habit, there is not much wrong with it. Christians might hold raffles when they are fund-raising; some Christians might buy lottery tickets, or apply for lottery funding when they want to raise money for a church project. Schools can benefit from lottery funding, especially for IT projects, and the governors of church schools do not want their students to miss out.

However, there are many Christians who are uncomfortable about gambling and who do not think Christians should take part in it or encourage it. They believe that gambling is wrong because:

- it can become addictive – some people who gamble find it difficult to maintain self-control and get into serious debt

- it gives some people money they have not earned, at the expense of others who are unlucky

- it can encourage people to look for easy, 'get-rich-quick' methods of making money, where they lose sight of what is important.

Exam Practice

Practise your **evaluation** skills.

'Christians should never take part in gambling.'

Discuss this statement. You should include different, supported points of view and a personal viewpoint.

Begin by giving a Christian viewpoint – you could show that you realize not all Christians think the same way about gambling. Then give a different point of view – what might a non-Christian think? Finally explain your own viewpoint with reasons.

This will help you in the exam when you answer part (e) questions.

Christian beliefs about lending

There are many different reasons why people might want to lend money or goods to other people. They might want to do it out of generosity, because they can see that the other person is in need. A Christian might lend a friend a good book, or some extra plates to help cater for a big party, or lend some money to help someone who is struggling; they think there is nothing wrong with letting other people borrow from you in order to help them.

However, some Christians believe that it is wrong to lend if you are doing it in order to make a profit. Some people make a business out of lending money, where the money has to be paid back with interest (this means that the borrower has to pay back an extra percentage, on top of the original amount). Christians might feel that this kind of lending is wrong, because it is taking advantage of people in need and making a profit out of them.

Moral and immoral occupations

This section will help you understand Christian beliefs about what is moral and immoral.

What do Christians believe about right and wrong?

Christians believe that something is morally right if it obeys God's commandments, and it is wrong if it disobeys God. They believe that they can find out what God wants them to do by:

- reading the Bible

- following the teachings of the Church

- praying for God to guide them

- asking for the advice of other Christians.

Teachings about moral and immoral occupations

Although Christianity does not have strict rules about how people earn their living, there are several different questions a Christian might want to consider when choosing a career. Ideally, Christians prefer to have jobs which help others and avoid harm. However, not everyone is in a position to choose what they do for a living; many people have to make decisions based on the wages, the journey to work, the hours and the needs of the rest of the family. Christians believe that whatever work is done, they should put their Christian principles into action in the workplace. They should treat other people fairly, be honest in the way that they deal with customers, and show respect to the people with whom they work.

Many Christians try to choose careers where they can be involved in helping others. ▶

Helping others – many Christians prefer to choose jobs which directly help other people in some way. They might become health care workers, social workers, teachers, or workers for an aid agency.

Avoiding harm – Christians might want to avoid jobs where some people are treated badly in order to help make a profit. For example, they might look at the ethical record of the company to see if it pays its workers a fair wage and to see whether it cares about environmental issues. They might also want to avoid jobs in industries such as making tobacco or alcohol.

I'm a Christian and I work as a computer programmer. I chose this career because it's something I'm good at, and I believe that God gave me my talents for a reason. I think it's a good career. I earn quite a good salary, and this means I can support myself and also set aside quite a bit of money every month to give to Christian Aid.

I'm good at chemistry, and I was offered quite a well-paid job with a cosmetics company. Because I'm a Christian, I looked on the Internet to find out more about the company. I discovered that they still do a lot of testing on animals, and I don't really agree with that. I also wasn't sure whether I wanted to spend my life making lipsticks. I decided in the end to work for a company that makes medicines, because it seems a better use of my skills.

I work as a classroom assistant in my daughter's primary school. I'm a Christian, and I think this is a good job for me, because I'm helping others. It doesn't pay very well, but it's good for our family life and that's important to me.

I used to work for a clothing company, but when I became a Christian, I decided to change my job. My company employed a lot of machinists in developing countries and paid them a very low wage, and it also didn't have a good record on care for the environment. So I decided to move to a company which showed more concern for others.

For **Discussion**

Look at the following list of jobs. For each one, discuss whether you think a Christian would consider it to be a moral or immoral way of earning money. Try to give reasons for your choice:

- running a betting shop

- working in a charity shop

- being a teacher

- being a journalist for a men's magazine

- running a pub

- working for a tobacco company

- being a soldier.

This activity will help to develop your skills in **evaluation**.

Glossary

Aid agency – an organization which works on behalf of people in need

Fairtrade – a movement which aims to give all people a fair price for the goods they produce and safe working conditions

Parable – a story with a message

Poverty – lacking the basic essentials needed for a decent quality of life

ETHICS 1

The roles of men and women in the family

This section will help you understand Jewish ideas about gender roles.

In Judaism, as in many other religions, there are different views about the roles of men and women. Some Jews believe that men and women are entirely equal and that each gender should be allowed exactly the same opportunities at work, in the home and in places of worship. Others believe that although men and women are equally valuable as God's creations, they have different natures, different purposes and different talents, and therefore their roles should be different.

The Bible teaches that God made humanity, both male and female. In the book of Genesis, God made man first:

> *The Lord God formed the man from the dust of the ground and breathed into his nostrils the breath of life, and the man became a living being.*
> **(Genesis 2:7)**

God then made woman, to keep the man company and to help him:

> *The Lord God said, 'It is not good for the man to be alone. I will make a helper suitable for him.*
> **(Genesis 2:18)**

> *So the Lord God caused the man to fall into a deep sleep; and while he was sleeping, he took one of the man's ribs and closed up the place with flesh. Then the Lord God made a woman from the rib he had taken out of the man, and he brought her to the man.*
> *The man said,*
> > *'This is now bone of my bones*
> > *and flesh of my flesh;*
> > *she shall be called 'woman',*
> > *for she was taken out of man.'*
> *For this reason a man will leave his father and mother and be united to his wife, and they will become one flesh.*
> **(Genesis 2: 21-24)**

Jews believe that God made all people 'in his own image'. It is difficult to understand exactly what this means, but it is often understood to mean that everyone has the ability to develop a relationship with God, everyone is valuable to God, and everyone has a responsibility to recognize that value in each other.

Because it says in the Bible that God created the man first, some people think that the male should be the leader in the world, and that the female should follow, supporting men by looking after them. Other people think that this is a wrong interpretation of the story, and that both male and female can be leaders.

Within Judaism there are different groups whose ways of understanding Jewish laws and the right ways to lead a Jewish life differ. Two important groups are **Orthodox** and **Reform**, and these two groups have some quite different opinions about human relationships and family life. There are other groups in Judaism too.

Orthodox Judaism

Orthodox Jews are traditional in the way that they understand the Jewish laws. They believe that the Torah (the Jewish law in the Bible) comes directly from God. The 613 laws of Judaism are all equally important to Orthodox Jews, and they apply in all countries and at all times of history, including in the modern world. Some aspects of modern life make it difficult for Orthodox Jews to keep to the laws of the Bible, but they believe that it is their religious duty to keep to the rules as far as they possibly can and not allow the pressures of society to turn them away from their faith. Jewish teachers, who are known as rabbis, help members of the community to understand how the laws of the Torah should be interpreted. Because of their beliefs, Orthodox Jews will try hard to keep the Sabbath separate as a special day. They will try to obey the laws in every way they can, for example by sticking to kosher food laws, and by understanding the roles of men and women in the way that the Bible teaches.

◀ *Orthodox and Reform Jews have different ideas about how the laws of the Torah are to be understood by modern people.*

Reform Judaism

Reform Jews are another group within Judaism. They believe that Judaism needs to be able to change and develop as society changes and develops. They consider that the Torah comes from God, but that it needs to be reinterpreted by every generation, and some laws might be more important than others in different situations. Many Reform Jews think that some of the traditional Jewish ideas about the roles of men and women are not so appropriate for the modern world. They believe that the rules worked well at the time the Bible was written, but that modern society is different and so perhaps the rules need to be adapted.

Men and women in the home

Traditionally, men and women have had very different roles in a Jewish family. From the beginning of life, different customs apply to boys and girls. When a male baby is born there are special ceremonies to welcome him into the Jewish community and prepare him for the role he will take on as an adult man. When a boy reaches the age of 13, the bar mitzvah ceremony celebrates the fact that he has become an adult, and he can take his place alongside the other men at important religious occasions. In the Orthodox Jewish tradition, girls do not have the same kind of celebrations. Some people think this is unfair, and that this treats girls as if they are not as important as boys. Others say it is simply that males and females have different strengths and qualities which need to be recognized in different ways.

In the past, and in many Orthodox homes today, Jewish women have been expected to support their husbands by staying at home and taking care of the family. However, in Judaism the home is very important, and the woman rules it, so she is not seen as inferior but has a very special role to play in religious life. Her duties include bringing up the children in the Jewish faith by setting them a good moral example and teaching them the laws of the Torah, as well as teaching them the customs of the Sabbath and of the festivals. She helps the whole family to fulfil their religious duties by making sure that the food she buys and prepares is kosher (fit to eat, according to Jewish law). By looking after the home and the children, she makes it possible for her husband to have the time to study the Torah and other Jewish teachings.

Obeying Jewish laws

Each week, it is traditionally the role of the woman to welcome the Sabbath into the home by preparing the house, the food and the table, and by lighting candles to mark the beginning of the most important day of the week. In the Orthodox Jewish tradition, the woman does not have to keep any of the laws that depend on being available at a fixed time, because she might find, for example, that the baby needs to be fed or that another responsibility has to come first. Some Jewish teachers argue that women are naturally more spiritual than men and have a better sense of self-discipline, so men need to have more rules than women. Men have to wear special religious clothes and symbols when they pray at fixed times of day, but the women do not have to do this. Women can choose to pray at any time of day that is convenient for them.

The Bible teaches that it is a great privilege for a man to have a good wife. In the Book of Proverbs, there is a description of a wife who supports her husband and her home, not as an inferior person but as someone who is to be greatly admired:

> *A wife of noble character who can find?*
> *She is worth far more than rubies.*
> *Her husband has full confidence in her*
> *and lacks nothing of value.*
> *She brings him good, not harm,*
> *all the days of her life.*
> *She selects wool and flax*
> *and works with eager hands.*
> *She is like the merchant ships,*
> *bringing her food from afar.*
> *She gets up while it is still dark;*
> *she provides food for her family*
> *and portions for her servant girls.*
> *She considers a field and buys it;*
> *out of her earnings she plants a vineyard.*
> *She sets about her work vigorously;*
> *her arms are strong for her tasks.*
> *She sees that her trading is profitable,*
> *and her lamp does not go out at night.*
> **(Proverbs 31: 10-18)**

In contrast, the man's main duties are outside the home. His major responsibilities are to provide for his family and to support the Jewish faith in public life, by taking an active part in his community. Within the family his role is to help his wife raise the children by teaching them how to become responsible Jewish adults. Traditionally, the

In the Orthodox tradition, there are different ceremonies for boys and girls when they become adults, such as the bar mitzvah. ▼

Traditionally, Jewish women have the honour of welcoming the Sabbath into the home by lighting candles. ▼

On the Sabbath, the father prays for his children. ▼

For **Discussion**

Do you think that women are better suited for home and family responsibilities than men? Talk about your opinions and try to give reasons to support them.

man should teach his children practical skills they can use to support themselves in later life, and also how to keep safe by giving them swimming lessons and advice about being streetwise.

The rabbis teach that the man should help with household duties such as cooking when he is available, rather than expecting his wife to be his servant. When the Sabbath comes each week, the father of the house has the responsibility of giving each of his children a special blessing.

Less traditional forms of Judaism usually do not have such noticeable differences between the roles of men and women. In Reform Judaism, for example, women as well as men go out to work, both might take similar responsibilities for housework and childcare, and the women might have a more active role in public life without always feeling that family life has to come first. Reform Jews point out that not all women have husbands and children to look after. They might be in a position to take a more active part in public life, and should be allowed the opportunities to choose this if they want to.

I think people are wrong when they say that Orthodox Jewish women are badly treated in the home. Raising children and looking after the family is a great privilege, not a punishment.

Men and women are different, and there is no point in pretending they are the same. They don't need to have the same roles.

Making women stay at home and look after the family is wrong, I think. They should be able to go out and earn money, have high-status jobs and have their say in the community in just the same way as men.

Men and women in the synagogue

A **synagogue** is a Jewish place of worship. It is the place where Jews meet for services on the Sabbath and on festival days, and also it often works as a meeting-place for the Jewish community, where people can get together for clubs, for education and for social events.

In Orthodox Judaism, men and women have very clear, separate roles in the synagogue.

Some Jewish teachers (called rabbis) explain that women do not need to go to the synagogue as often as men do. They can choose to go whenever they like, but they do not have to go if their other responsibilities to the family need to come first.

Men have a responsibility to worship together in a community group. This group has to have a minimum of ten men, and is known as a minyan. Women do not have the same responsibility, but they also do not count towards a minyan.

An Orthodox synagogue is arranged so that women sit separately from men. This might be upstairs in a gallery, or at the back behind a screen. The idea is not to make the women feel excluded, but to stop the men from being distracted as they should be concentrating on their prayers, not looking at the women. In the Orthodox tradition, women do not become rabbis, and they do not lead worship or read from the Torah in services. The reason is that these responsibilities would require them to be available at fixed times of day, which is not always possible for a woman.

▲ *In Reform Judaism, women have the same opportunities as men to become rabbis (religious teachers).*

Reform Jews, however, disagree. They argue that separating men from women in the synagogue is a rule which belongs in the past. In a Reform synagogue, men and women sit together, and women can lead the services and read from the Torah. They can also become rabbis, receiving the same training as men and having the same opportunities to teach and to lead.

In my synagogue, which is Orthodox, women sit upstairs, away from the men. If we have small children, they sit with us too. We do this to support the men in their prayers, so they are not distracted. I think this tradition should be kept, because it shows respect to men and women, and most importantly to God. We should be thinking about God as we pray, not trying to catch the eye of someone attractive!

I go to a Reform synagogue, where I can take a full part in worship. I sit with my husband and we worship together, side by side. Sometimes he has the honour of reading from the Torah during the service, and sometimes, I do. We are equal at the synagogue, just the same as we are at home.

In the Bible, there are examples of women who have taken a leading role in religious life:

- Huldah was a prophet (someone who tells the people messages given by God) and King Josiah asked her for advice rather than listening to the men.

- Deborah is described as a prophet and was also a leading poet. People asked her for advice, and took what she said very seriously.

- Esther was a brave queen who defended her people and took them to victory.

Jews use examples such as these to show that women are valued in religious life and are clearly important to God.

Exam Practice

Practise your skills in **demonstrating knowledge and understanding**.

Explain Jewish beliefs about the roles of men and women in religious life.

For this answer, it would be good to show that you realize there are different groups within Judaism, and these different groups have different ideas about the roles of men and women. You could give some different examples to illustrate the points you make, such as whether women can sit with men during worship and whether they can train to be rabbis.

This will help you in the exam when you answer part (d) questions.

Marriage and marriage ceremonies

In this section, you will learn about the importance of marriage in Jewish life, and about Jewish weddings.

Judaism teaches that marriage is given by God, in order for men and women to find fulfilment and happiness as couples and as parents. It teaches that marriage should be a lifelong commitment where two people are faithful to each other and do their best to make each other happy. According to Judaism, when men and women get married, they are following the example God gave to Adam and Eve, and they are helping Judaism to survive and flourish for future generations.

Most Orthodox Jews believe that Jews should marry other Jews, rather than people from another religious tradition or from no religion ('marrying out').

The Bible teaches:

> *Do not intermarry with them. Do not give your daughters to their sons or take their daughters for your sons, for they will turn your sons away from following me to serve other gods, and the Lord's anger will burn against you and will quickly destroy you.*
>
> **(Deuteronomy 7:3-4)**

The home is very important in Judaism, so Orthodox Jews feel it is important that both partners should care about keeping the Jewish laws, keeping traditions alive and bringing up any children to practise the faith of their ancestors. It is possible for a non-Jew to convert to Judaism, and sometimes people do this when they want to marry, but it is a long and difficult process which not all Jews encourage. Some Orthodox Jews feel so strongly about 'marrying out' that if one of their children chooses to marry a non-Jew, they treat that child as if he or she were dead.

Other groups within Judaism are less strict about this rule, and they believe that if two people love each other and want to commit themselves to each other in marriage, they should be encouraged to do so, even if one of the couple is not Jewish.

Marriage ceremonies

Jewish weddings are very happy occasions where not only two people, but two families, are joined together to begin a new life. Weddings can take place on any day of the week except the Sabbath (Saturday) or a festival; in the UK, they are often on a Sunday because it is easier for the guests to attend at a weekend.

In the week leading up to the wedding, the groom goes to the synagogue for a special ceremony, and there is often a celebration with refreshments after the service and sweets. In the Orthodox tradition, the bride will take a ritual bath to make herself pure for the wedding.

Before the marriage can begin, a marriage contract called the ketubah is signed. This is an ancient tradition which is very much like the modern 'pre-nuptial agreement': the couple agree in advance their responsibilities towards each other, and agree about what should happen if the marriage does not work. The groom places a veil over the bride's face, as a way of showing that he intends to provide her with clothing.

For **Discussion**

Some people think that it is a good idea for a couple to agree, while they love each other, about what should happen if they separate. Other people think this is not very romantic! What do you think? Talk about your ideas and try to support them with reasons.

The bride and groom traditionally fast on the day of the wedding, as a way of showing that they are putting their past lives behind them and entering into the marriage in a new way.

The actual wedding ceremony is quite short. The bride and groom marry underneath a canopy called a **chuppah**, which represents their new home together. It is often a special structure with four poles to hold it up, decorated with flowers, but it can just be a prayer shawl held over the couple. The bride and groom are escorted to the chuppah by friends and family, with music and singing. Usually, the chuppah is indoors in the synagogue so that the weather does not spoil the ceremony, but it can be anywhere, such as an open field, or a non-religious building such as a hotel.

In some traditions, the bride walks around the groom a certain number of times, while the groom says prayers. This walking around is different for Jews from different cultures, but it represents the idea that a man's wife will surround him and protect him. The groom is believed to be especially close to God at this moment, and he will pray for friends and relations who are not yet married, and for people who are ill. Sometimes he might be passed notes from other people at the wedding, asking for his prayers for something special. When the circling is over the bride and groom share some wine as a symbol of their joy together, and the rabbi gives special blessings.

The chuppah (canopy) represents a Jewish couple's new home. ▼

The most important part of the wedding is when the groom places the wedding ring on the bride's finger. Because it is a circle the ring represents the eternity of the relationship. When the groom gives the bride the ring, he says the words:

'Behold, thou art consecrated to me by this ring, according to the law of Moses and of Israel.'

At this point, the couple commit themselves to becoming husband and wife for the rest of their lives. Sometimes the bride also gives the groom a ring.

After this, the marriage contract is often read out loud so that everyone can witness it, and then there is a blessing over a cup of wine. In some wedding ceremonies, the rabbi gives a sermon (a speech) where he gives the couple advice about married life and encourages them in their new life together. At the end of the wedding, the groom breaks a wine glass under his foot. This reminds everyone present that although a wedding is a happy occasion, there are many people in the world who have suffered and who are suffering. It reminds Jews that their Temple in Israel was destroyed and that they are still waiting for it to be rebuilt.

Everyone congratulates the couple, and then they have some quiet time alone together before the wedding party begins, with plenty of food, wine and music.

Exam Practice

Practise your skills in **demonstrating knowledge and understanding**.

Explain key elements of a Jewish wedding ceremony.

For this answer, you need to give an accurate outline of what happens during a Jewish wedding. For high marks, try to use key Jewish terms such as 'chuppah'.

This will help you in the exam when you answer part (c) questions.

The groom breaks a wine glass under his foot as a reminder of the suffering in the world. ▼

Divorce

EXAM FOCUS

This section will help you to understand Jewish rules and beliefs about divorce.

Not all marriages turn out to be as happy as the couple hoped. For many different reasons a marriage can fail, and the husband and wife realize that they are making each other unhappy. This could be because:

- One of the couple is attracted to someone else, and wants to start a new relationship with that person.

- There might be disagreements about money.

- The couple might find that as they get older they have less in common than they used to have.

- They might find that they irritate each other and argue a lot, and that they can't resolve their differences.

- Sometimes circumstances such as illness and disability put a lot of strain on a marriage.

- Sometimes there is domestic violence and cruelty.

Jewish teachings recognize that marriages do not always work, and they agree that divorce might sometimes be necessary. The couple are encouraged to try hard to make their marriage work, perhaps by going to counselling, and they are encouraged not to take divorce lightly. But if their efforts fail and they really do not want to stay together, then divorce is allowed.

The Bible teaches that a man is allowed to divorce his wife, but it is not completely clear about the circumstances:

> *If a man marries a woman who becomes displeasing to him because he finds something indecent about her, and he writes her a certificate of divorce, gives it to her and sends her from his house …*
>
> **(Deuteronomy 24:1)**

Rabbis have argued about what this 'something indecent' might mean. Some argue that it refers only to adultery, so a man can only divorce his wife if she has been unfaithful to him. Others think that it covers other circumstances too, for example if the wife argues with her husband a lot, or does not support him when he makes decisions.

Orthodox Jews believe that, because the text talks about the man divorcing his wife, but not about the wife divorcing her husband, the decision has to come from the man. Jewish law says that for a couple to have a religious divorce, the man must give the woman a certificate of divorce, called a get. He has to do this for a good reason; he cannot just divorce her when she has done nothing wrong, simply because he prefers someone else. If the woman refuses to take the get, then the man is not allowed a divorce. The get is a legal document in Jewish law, and the couple cannot marry anyone else without it.

In Orthodox Judaism, the wife cannot choose to divorce her husband, whatever he has done. She has to wait for him to decide to give her a get. This custom can cause problems, for example if the man leaves his wife and she does not know where he is. One day, she might meet someone else and want to remarry, but without a get, she cannot do this and have her marriage recognized. If she did marry someone else without having a get, and then she had children, they would be considered illegitimate.

A woman in this position, whose husband is missing and who has no get, is called **agunah**, which means 'chained wife'. She has a lot of sympathy from the Jewish community, but they cannot change the rules.

Reform Jews are not as strict about divorce, and if they feel that the woman is being treated unfairly, then the Beth Din, which is a court of rabbis, can choose to give her a get if her husband refuses or is unavailable.

The divorce happens at a ceremony, where at least three rabbis from the Beth Din are present to witness the man giving the get to his former wife, so that both have the freedom to remarry if they want to. Jews believe that it is important to have the ceremony rather than just dealing with it by post. It gives the couple the chance to close their relationship face to face in a dignified way. However, if they really feel unable to see each other again, they are allowed to send someone else to represent them at the ceremony.

Exam Practice

Practise your skills in **demonstrating knowledge and understanding**.

Explain Jewish teaching about divorce.

For high marks in this answer, try to use key Jewish terms such as 'get', and show that you understand not all Jews have the same rules about divorce.

This will help you in the exam when you answer part (c) questions.

Sexual relationships and contraception

EXAM FOCUS

This section will help you understand Jewish beliefs about sexual relationships.

Sex within marriage

Unlike many religions, Judaism has quite a lot to say about sexual relationships. It teaches that sex is given by God, not just for the purposes of having children, but also for enjoyment. Married couples are encouraged to strengthen their relationship by having sex often, and the rabbis teach that a man has a responsibility to make sure that his wife gets as much pleasure from sex as he does. If his job demands that he works away from home a lot, he has to make sure that he comes back as often as he can so that his wife does not have to go without sex for too long.

In the Orthodox tradition, there are quite strict rules about the times when sex is allowed and when it is forbidden. These rules are known as the 'laws of niddah', and they are also called 'family purity laws'. When a woman has her period, and for seven days afterwards, the couple should not have sex or any other kind of physical contact. Once this time is over, the woman should go to a special bath at the synagogue called a mikveh, which is filled with a mixture of tap water, rainwater and disinfectant. She has to immerse herself completely under the water, and after this she is considered to be pure again and can have sex with her husband until the time her next period starts.

Jews who keep the laws of niddah say that the discipline helps to keep their marriages alive, and helps them to respect each other and to appreciate the times when they can have sex. Reform Jews consider these laws to be unnecessary, and so there are no mikvehs in a Reform synagogue.

▲ *The mikveh is a special ritual bath used by Orthodox Jewish women when they keep 'family purity laws'.*

Exam Practice

Practise your **evaluation** skills.

'People cannot be expected to stay faithful to just one sexual partner for life.'

Discuss this statement. You should include different, supported points of view and a personal viewpoint. You must refer to Judaism in your answer.

You might want to start by giving a Jewish point of view. Perhaps a Jew would argue that marriage should be for life – how might this opinion be supported?

In your next paragraph, explain a different point of view. Perhaps, now that people often live for a long time, faithfulness to one partner is too difficult. Explain why some people might not agree with Jewish teaching.

Finally, give your own opinion – you might want to agree with one of the ideas you have already explained, or you might have another view. Remember to support your view with reasons.

This will help you in the exam when you answer part (e) questions.

Adultery and sex before marriage

The Jewish law teaches that sexual relationships should only happen within a marriage. Adultery (cheating on a husband or wife) is forbidden in the Ten Commandments; the Bible is very clear about it.

> *You shall not commit adultery.*
> **(Exodus 20:14)**

Jews believe that faithfulness is extremely important between a husband and wife, and they argue that when married people are unfaithful to each other, they destroy the trust God has given to married relationships.

Not all Jews agree about sex before marriage. Most Orthodox Jews believe that sex should only happen within a marriage, and that having sex without being married is bad for a person's self-respect. Others might be less strict in their views, but most Jews argue that having a lot of sexual partners can be damaging and can spoil something which God intended to be special.

Homosexuality

Jewish law forbids sexual activity between two men:

> *Do not lie with a man as one lies with a woman; that is detestable.*
> **(Leviticus 18:22)**

For Orthodox Jews, this means that homosexual activity of any kind is not allowed. Although the Bible does not say anything about lesbian relationships, Jews think that the same rules apply to women as well as to men. Orthodox and other traditional Jews believe that God made sexual activity in order for it to enhance the relationship between a married couple, so using sex in other ways is degrading and disrespectful.

▲ *Individual Jews have different opinions about whether homosexuality can be acceptable.*

Traditional Judaism is against homosexual acts, but not against homosexual people. God loves all people, whatever their sexuality, but the Torah clearly teaches that homosexual acts are wrong. As an Orthodox Jew, I believe that even homosexual people might be able to find a fulfilling relationship within a heterosexual marriage, with the help of God.

I think the Bible was written when people understood less about homosexuality. As a Reform Jew, I believe that God loves everyone, whatever their sexuality, and wants everyone to enjoy a full life. I think that if two people love each other and want to have sex together, even if they are the same sex, that should be accepted by the Jewish community and those people should not be made to feel bad.

Activity 1

Do you think homosexual relationships should be respected just as much as heterosexual relationships? Talk about your opinion and then write about it in your notes. Try to give reasons to support your view.

However, other Jews argue that **homosexuality** is more acceptable in modern times than it was when the Bible was written. They argue that today, people have a better understanding of human sexuality. Today, we realize some people are naturally attracted to the same gender and are not just choosing to be homosexual. If homosexuality is seen as wrong and forbidden, then some people are left without being able to have loving sexual relationships at all. In Judaism, some people campaign to make homosexuality more acceptable to the Jewish community. The most liberal movements within Judaism have rabbis who are openly homosexual, and they are supporting same-sex marriages.

Contraception (birth control)

Judaism welcomes children and sees them as a gift from God. The Bible teaches that God wants couples to have children to populate the planet:

> God blessed them and said to them, 'Be fruitful and increase in number; fill the earth and subdue it.'
>
> **(Genesis 1:28)**

This does not mean that Jewish parents must have as many children as they can. Large families are popular in Judaism, because they help the faith to survive into the future, and they provide a new generation to take care of the elderly. However, the rabbis teach that people should be given the choice to limit the size of their families; they should not feel they must have more children than they can afford to bring up, and women should not feel forced to become pregnant if this would affect their health. Orthodox Judaism suggests that the commandment to 'be fruitful and multiply' would be obeyed if a couple had two children, or more if they want more.

▲ *Judaism celebrates large families, but teaches that couples may use contraception if this is their choice.*

Exam Practice

Practise your skills in **demonstrating knowledge and understanding**.

Explain Jewish teaching about contraception (birth control).

For this answer, you need to show that you understand what contraception is, and also that you can give a clear explanation of Jewish teaching about it.

This will help you in the exam when you answer part (d) questions.

Judaism allows artificial **contraception** (birth control) as long as it is used appropriately, so that couples can decide how many children they want to have and when to have them. Rabbis have studied the Bible to work out which methods of contraception are acceptable in Jewish law, and decided:

- Contraception should not spoil the pleasure of sex – so if a couple find that they get less pleasure if they use condoms, they should find another method instead.

- Contraception should prevent the egg from being fertilized. It should not allow fertilization but then prevent the embryo from growing. So the 'morning-after pill' would not be encouraged.

- The female contraceptive pill is probably the best kind of contraception for most couples to use.

- Sterilization is where the man or the woman has surgery to prevent pregnancy when the couple have decided that they definitely do not want more children. This is only allowed in Judaism when there are medical reasons for it.

Exam Practice

Practise your **evaluation** skills.

'Married people have a duty to have children.'

Discuss this statement. You should include different, supported points of view and a personal viewpoint. You must refer to Judaism in your answer.

For this answer, you need to consider different points of view. Why might some people think that married people have a duty to have children, and why might other people think differently?

You might start by giving a Jewish point of view; you could support this with reference to the Bible. Try to explain why Jews might hold this opinion.

Then give a different point of view; what might someone say who disagreed with Judaism? What reasons might they give?

In your conclusion, give your own opinion. It does not have to be a third point of view – you can agree with one of the views you have already given. Explain the reasons why you hold this opinion.

This will help you in the exam when you answer part (e) questions.

Glossary

Agunah – a 'chained wife' who cannot be divorced because her husband is missing

Chuppah – a canopy used at a Jewish wedding to represent the new home

Contraception – birth control; methods used to deliberately prevent pregnancy

Homosexuality – being emotionally and sexually attracted to members of the same sex

Mikveh – a special ritual bath used by Orthodox Jews

Niddah (Family purity laws) – Orthodox Jewish laws about the times of the month when a couple may have sex

Orthodox – a branch of Judaism which teaches that the laws of the Bible should always be followed

Prophet – someone who passes on messages from God

Reform – a branch of Judaism which says that the Bible needs to be interpreted for modern life

Synagogue – a Jewish place of worship

ETHICS 2

Christians generally believe war should be avoided. ▶

Attitudes to war

EXAM FOCUS

This section will introduce you to different Christian beliefs about the ethics of war.

Most Christians believe that war should be avoided, but some think that it is sometimes acceptable, while others believe that it is never acceptable.

In the Bible, there are passages which seem to conflict with each other on the subject. Some biblical teachings suggest that sometimes war is acceptable, because God instructs it, while other teachings imply that violence is wrong.

- Generally, Christians believe war should be avoided.
- Some Christians believe war is never acceptable.
- Some Christians believe war is acceptable if it is holy (God wants it).
- Some Christians believe war is acceptable if it is just (fair).

Holy war

'Holy war' means war on behalf of God. Some Christians believe that although war should generally be avoided where possible, it is acceptable if it is holy. Sometimes Christians believe that God wants them to make war.

The idea of holy war goes back to the Old Testament, where there are examples of God ordering war:

> " *I will punish the Amalekites for what they did to Israel when they waylaid them as they came up from Egypt. Now go, attack the Amalekites and totally destroy everything that belongs to them.* "
>
> **(1 Samuel 15:2-3)**

> *Proclaim this among the nations: Prepare for war!*
> **(Joel 3:9)**

Some people believe that holy war can just be used as an excuse, a convincing argument.

The Crusades were wars waged by Christians to recover the Holy Land of Palestine (Israel) from Muslims. They were criticized for bringing destruction, devastation and mass slaughter.

Just War

The word 'just' means fair or right. A war is considered to be a 'Just War' if it is for just/right reasons and if it is carried out justly/fairly.

Many Christians today believe that war should be avoided where possible, but that sometimes it is necessary and the Just War conditions should be used.

The idea of a Just War concerns:

- justification – reasons and rights to go to war
- conduct – the right behaviour within the war.

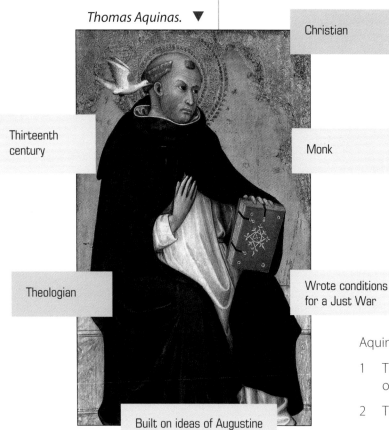

Thomas Aquinas. ▼

Christian

Thirteenth century

Monk

Theologian

Wrote conditions for a Just War

Built on ideas of Augustine from fourth century

Aquinas' conditions for a Just War:

1   The war must be started and controlled by the authority of the state or ruler.

2   There must be a just cause.

3   The war must be for good or against evil. Law and order must always be restored afterwards.

Later Christians added extra conditions:

4   The war must be the last resort.

5   The war must be fought proportionally.

6   The good gained by the victory must be greater than the evil which led to the war.

Why were the conditions created?

- Prevent war.
- Limit effects of war.
- As guidelines for those in charge.

War is never acceptable

Some Christians believe that war is never acceptable. Here are some examples of reasons why Christians may be against war:

War causes mindless destruction of God's creation – the earth and everything on it. We should be stewards and protect the earth, not waste and damage it.

Modern war causes a lot of people to suffer, including many innocent people. No reason for war is enough to justify this pain and suffering.

War is a negative way of dealing with things, and encourages people to hate each other.

As it says in the Bible, 'Love your enemies, and pray for those who persecute you, that you may be sons of your Father in heaven. (Matthew 5:44-45)'

Violence and pacifism

In this section, you will be considering whether it can ever be right to use violence, and looking at Christian ideas.

There are many different types and levels of violence, such as fighting, hitting, kicking, throwing things, use of weapons. Some violence happens over a period of time, or on a large scale as in wars.

Christian beliefs about violence and pacifism

Although Christians generally believe that violence should be avoided where possible, different Christians have different beliefs about whether violence is ever acceptable.

Acceptable	Unacceptable
Jesus used violence when he threw the money changers out of the temple. Some Christians believe that this implies violence is sometimes acceptable. *So he made a whip out of cords, and drove all from the temple area, both sheep and cattle; he scattered the coins of the money-changers and overturned their tables. (John 2:15)*	The Bible teaches the importance of peace, love and forgiveness. Many Christians try to live their lives according to these principles, and believe that violence goes against them. *Blessed are the peacemakers, for they will be called sons of God. (Matthew 5:9)* *But I tell you, do not resist an evil person. If someone strikes you on the right cheek, turn to him the other also. (Matthew 5:39)* *But I tell you: Love your enemies and pray for those who persecute you, that you may be sons of your Father in heaven. (Matthew 5:44)*
Some Christians believe that violence can sometimes be acceptable if it is for a greater good, such as fighting against oppression. *… he has anointed me to preach good news to the poor. He has sent me to proclaim freedom for the prisoners … to release the oppressed. (Luke 4:18)*	God created humans in His own image, so many Christians believe that all humans are sacred and it is wrong to use violence against anyone.
The Old Testament contains many references to violence and wars being ordered by God.	One of the Ten Commandments is 'Do not kill'. Although some Christians translate it as 'Do not murder', others believe that it refers to any type of killing, including wars.
	So God said to Noah, 'I am going to put an end to all people, for the earth is filled with violence because of them. I am surely going to destroy both them and the earth'. (Genesis 6:13)
	Jesus said… 'all who draw the sword will die by the sword.' (Matthew 26:52)

Religious beliefs may be a reason why conscientious objectors refuse to take part in war. ▼

The **Quakers (Religious Society of Friends)** are a Christian denomination who:

- are **pacifist**
- believe violence is wrong
- won the Nobel Peace Prize in 1947
- *'We work for peace and justice and to alleviate suffering and seek positive social change'* (from www.quaker.org.uk)
- current examples of the Quakers' work for peace and justice include a 'Dialogue for a nuclear weapon-free world' initiative and a 'Peace and disarmament' (getting rid of weapons) campaign.

The Roman Catholic Church

'Respect for and development of human life require peace. Peace is not merely the absence of war, and it is not limited to maintaining a balance of powers between adversaries. Peace cannot be attained on earth without safeguarding the goods of persons, free communication among men, respect for the dignity of persons and peoples, and the assiduous practise of fraternity. Peace is 'the tranquillity of order'. Peace is the work of justice and the effect of charity.'

(Catechism of the Catholic Church, 2304)

Conscientious objectors

During the First World War (1914–1918) conscription was introduced, which meant that all eligible men were required to join the army. There were 16,000 **conscientious objectors** recorded who refused to participate in war because of their beliefs. Some refused to participate in the war in any way, while others agreed only to take non-fighting roles. Tribunals were set up to decide what would happen to each conscientious objector. Their reasons varied from religious or political to personal circumstances or medical issues. Thousands were sent to prison. Many of those who objected because of religious reasons were Quakers, who are pacifists.

Alternatives to violence

In situations where pacifists do not agree with something, and want to do something about it without resorting to violence, there are alternative ways of speaking out or taking action, which are sometimes called 'non-violence'.

Non-violent protest can involve:

- speeches, writings or art
- petitions,
- peaceful demonstrations, gatherings of people or marches
- boycotts
- peaceful non-cooperation.

Crime and punishment

This section considers different ideas about what justice is, and about how people who break the law should be punished.

What is justice?

Justice generally means fair treatment. Where crime is concerned, justice means dealing fairly with the crime. It should be dealt with in a way that is fair to both the criminal and their society, including any direct or indirect victims of their crime.

Laws provide objective rules for managing behaviour and keeping order in our society. A crime is committed when someone 'breaks the law': does something which a law forbids. When a person is convicted (found guilty) of a crime, they are sentenced, which means that their punishment is decided.

In the UK, we have a Criminal Justice System, which is responsible for detecting crime and dealing with it through justice.

The Criminal Justice System aims to bring justice for all by convicting and punishing criminals and protecting society.

What are the main aims of punishment?

Deterrence	To deter (put off) criminals from reoffending. To deter others from committing crimes.
Authority	To show the authority of the law. To command respect of the law.
Protection	To protect society from criminal behaviour. To prevent effects of further crime on the community.
Payback	As retribution (payback, revenge) for a crime, by punishment. To take revenge on the criminal for their actions.
Even the score	To get back at the criminal for what they have done. To retaliate against the crime.
Reform	To try to reform (change) the criminal, so that they are less likely to reoffend.

There are many different types of punishment given to criminals in today's world. Some examples are:

- prison
- community service
- fine
- probation
- corporal punishment (bodily punishment)
- capital punishment (death penalty).

The treatment of criminals

Attitudes towards how criminals should be treated vary a great deal from person to person, and many people have very strong feelings about the issue. The issue of how criminals should be treated is often highlighted in the media, and one topic which is regularly examined is prisons.

Prison overcrowding reaches a new high

Prisoner dies of heart attack as staff accuse her of 'trying it on'

Does prison work? Why do so many criminals reoffend?

Prison is the lap of luxury, boasts murderer

▲ *Prison conditions throughout the world mean overcrowding for many.*

Christian beliefs about the treatment of criminals

Different Christians have different beliefs about how criminals should be treated. Here are some examples of Christian beliefs about the treatment of criminals:

Forgiveness

- The Bible teaches forgiveness of people who have done wrong.

> *Be merciful, just as your father is merciful...*
> *Forgive, and you will be forgiven.*
> **(Luke 6:36-37)**

Activity 1

Look back at 'What are the main aims of punishment?' earlier in this unit, and consider how they might apply specifically to prisons.

- *(At his crucifixion) Jesus said:*

  " *Father, forgive them, for they do not know what they are doing.* "

  (Luke 23:34)

- " *Then Peter came to Jesus and asked, 'Lord, how many times shall I forgive my brother when he sins against me? Up to seven times?' Jesus answered, 'I tell you, not seven times, but seventy-seven times.'* "

  (Matthew 18:21-22)

- Many Christians believe that it is necessary to forgive criminals, because the Bible teaches the importance of forgiveness, Jesus demonstrated through his actions and teachings, and it is an important part of faith in action.

- Sometimes even Christians who have been victims of crime forgive the criminals because of their faith. For example, the mother of murdered Christian teenager Anthony Walker publicly forgave her son's killers in 2005.

- Some Christians find themselves in situations where they struggle to forgive, even though they believe that it is the right thing to do. For example, a vicar resigned in 2006 because she could not forgive the terrorists responsible for her daughter's death in the London bombings of 7 July 2005.

- Forgiving is not the same thing as excusing the crime – most Christians still believe that justice should be done.

Punishment

- Many Christians believe that punishments are necessary, in order to protect the innocent and help to keep society safe.

- The Bible says that the punishment should fit the crime:

  " *... eye for eye, tooth for tooth ...* "

  (Deuteronomy 19:21)

Change

- Many Christians believe that criminals should be allowed to reform (change), and that we should help criminals to change, by giving them support, counselling, opportunities and so on.

- In the Bible, Jesus encourages an adulterous woman to change:

  " *Go now and leave your life of sin.* "

  (John 8:11)

Making amends

- Community service allows criminals to try to make amends for their crimes and give something back to the community they have wronged.

- Many Christians believe this is a positive way to treat criminals for certain crimes, because it punishes them while still allowing them to do good things for society.

- It can help to rehabilitate the criminal (get them back on track) and also benefits the community.

Fair treatment

- Sanctity of life: Christians believe that God made humans in his own image, and so they are sacred. This includes people who have committed crimes. Therefore most Christians believe that criminals should be treated fairly, without any violation of their human rights.

- "Love your enemies, do good to those who hate you, bless those who curse you, pray for those who ill-treat you."

  (Luke 6:27-28)

- "Remember those in prison as if you were their fellow-prisoners, and those who are ill-treated as if you yourselves were suffering."

  (Hebrews 13:3)

The Church of England view

That this Synod

a welcomes Her Majesty's Government's commitment to the development of restorative justice programmes which enshrine the biblical principles of holding offenders responsible for their crimes, addressing the needs of victims, and enhancing the protection of the public;

b welcome efforts to prevent 15 and 16 year olds being remanded into prison custody by offering constructive alternatives in the community;

c note the continuing public concern about the effect of crime in our communities;

d record its unease at the disproportionate number of black offenders in our prisons, and welcome initiatives to eradicate racism throughout the judicial and penal system;

e request Her Majesty's Government to reassess the situation whereby mentally ill people are often held in prison when they would be better treated in a secure hospital environment;

f recognise the need to reintegrate offenders into the community through prison and community based programmes and in partnership with employment and accommodation schemes;

g affirm the role of prison staff, chaplains, Boards of Visitors and volunteers and the part they play in supporting the families of people in prison; and

h urge dioceses, deaneries and parishes to promote the study of *Prisons: A Study in Vulnerability* (GS Misc 557) through criminal justice groups and other means.

Quoted from the Church of England website www.cofe.anglican.org.uk.

Practise your skills in **demonstrating knowledge and understanding**.

Describe three Christian beliefs about the treatment of criminals.

Remember that this type of question is not opinion-based, so you should not spend too much time giving a long answer.

This will help you when you answer part (c) questions.

Many organizations provide chaplains in prisons in the UK, and aim to care for prisoners in a practical and non-judgemental way. ▼

Christian responses to the treatment of criminals

Work

Rehabilitation of criminals (getting them back on track) is an important issue for many Christians. Therefore some Christians work with criminals, both in and out of prison, as volunteers for organizations, or as part of their Christian ministry.

Campaign for changes

Some Christians believe that criminals are treated unfairly, in a way that infringes on their human rights. One way of putting this belief into action is by campaigning for changes in the way criminals are treated.

Prayer

Prayer is very important in the Christian faith, as it is a way of communicating with God. Christians may pray to God about criminals. For example, they might ask God to look after them, or to help them to repent (be sorry) and reform (change).

Capital punishment

Capital punishment, the death penalty, means that a criminal is killed as punishment for their crimes. In the United Kingdom capital punishment was abolished in 1965, under the Murder (Abolition of Death Penalty) Act 1965 and made permanent in 1969. The last person to face the death penalty was executed in 1964 for murder.

Capital punishment is currently* retained as a punishment for ordinary crimes in 58 countries, including the United States of America (in 35 out of 50 states), Afghanistan, China, Egypt, India, Iraq, Pakistan, Vietnam and Singapore. There is a slow trend towards abolishing the death penalty, with Uzbekistan and Argentina getting rid of it in 2008 and Burundi and Togo in 2009. The European Union is against the death penalty, and in order for countries to join the EU they must abolish the death penalty. *

Amnesty International recorded that at least 2390 people were executed and at least 8864 sentenced to death around the world in 2008. Of these death penalty executions, 72 per cent took place in China. *

* (see www.amnesty.org /July 2009)

Forms of capital punishment

Once a person is tried for a capital offence (a crime which carries the death penalty) ... what happens next? This varies a great deal from country to country: sometimes a criminal is executed fairly soon after being convicted, but often they are held in prison for months or years before being executed. Public executions are held in some countries, to deter (put off) others from committing capital offences.

Saddam Hussein, the former leader of Iraq was hanged in December 2006, as punishment for crimes against humanity. ▼

For **Discussion**

Do you think it was right that Saddam Hussein was executed for being a murderer?

Prisoners are held in cells, referred to as 'death row.' ▼

Here are some examples of forms of execution still used around the world:

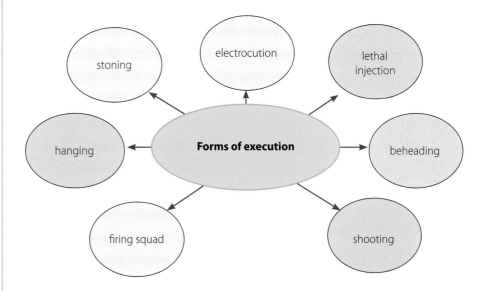

Responses to capital punishment

For capital punishment	Against capital punishment
Protection	Against human rights
Justice	Promotes and encourages violence in society
Revenge	Two wrongs don't make a right
Deterrent	No stronger as deterrent than life imprisonment
Kinder than life imprisonment	More expensive than life imprisonment*
Cheaper than life imprisonment*	Discrimination against mentally ill
	Biased against the poor

* Due to the extensive trial process required to bring the death penalty in some countries, some statistics show that life imprisonment actually costs less. However, other statistics show that the death penalty is cheaper than life imprisonment. Therefore the money argument can be used to support either case.

Christian responses to capital punishment

Different Christians have different beliefs about whether capital punishment is acceptable.

Church of England

In July 1983 the General Synod debated capital punishment and the following motion was carried:

'That this Synod would deplore the reintroduction of capital punishment into the United Kingdom sentencing policy.'

This subject has not been debated by Synod since 1983.

(from www.cofe.anglican.org)

The Roman Catholic Church

'Assuming that the guilty party's identity and responsibility have been fully determined, the traditional teaching of the Church does not exclude recourse to the death penalty, if this is the only possible way of effectively defending human lives against the unjust aggressor.

If, however, non-lethal means are sufficient to defend and protect people's safety from the aggressor, authority will limit itself to such means, as these are more in keeping with the concrete conditions of the common good and more in conformity with the dignity of the human person.

Today, in fact, as a consequence of the possibilities which the state has for effectively preventing crime, by rendering one who has committed an offence incapable of doing harm – without definitively taking away from him the possibility of redeeming himself – the cases in which the execution of the offender is an absolute necessity "are rare, if not practically non-existent."'

(Catechism of the Catholic Church, 2267)

The Bible

The Bible contains some passages that seem to be in favour of the death penalty (although not all Christians think they should be taken literally), but other parts seem to be against it.

What the Bible says about capital punishment. ▼

For	Against
Old Testament	**Old Testament**
Whoever sheds the blood of man, by man shall his blood be shed. (Genesis 9:6) In Leviticus 20:2-27, God tells Moses lots of situations where people must be put to death, including cursing their parent and committing various sexual acts. *Show no pity: life for life, eye for eye, tooth for tooth, hand for hand, foot for foot.* (Deuteronomy 19:21)	One of the Ten Commandments that God gave to Moses is: *'Do not kill' (Exodus 20:14)*
New Testament	**New Testament**
For rulers hold no terror for those who do right, but for those who do wrong. Do you want to be free from fear of the one in authority? Then do right and he will commend you… He is God's servant, an agent of wrath to bring punishment on the wrongdoer. (Romans 13:3-4) While Pilate decided whether or not Jesus should be punished with crucifixion: *Jesus answered, 'You would have no power over me if it were not given to you from above.'* (John 19:11)	*If someone strikes you on the right cheek, turn to him the other also.* (Matthew 5:39) Jesus' response to the stoning of an adulteress: *'If any one of you is without sin, let him throw a stone at her.'* (John 8:7) *Do not judge, or you too will be judged.* (Matthew 7:1) *Do not take revenge, my friends, but leave room for God's wrath, for it is written: 'It is mine to avenge; I will repay,' says the Lord.* (Romans 12:19) *Do not be overcome by evil, but overcome evil with good.* (Romans 12:21)

Different Christians interpret the Bible's teachings in different ways. For example, the commandment 'Do not kill' is sometimes interpreted as 'Do not murder', which completely changes the meaning, and implies that it might allow for other types of killing, such as executions.

Here are some examples of Christian beliefs against capital punishment:

- Christians believe that God created humans in His own image, and because of this many Christians believe that human life is sacred and only God should have the authority to destroy it.

- Some Christians disagree with capital punishment because it usually causes great suffering to the criminal's family and friends.

- Some Christians do not like the fact that capital punishment does not give the criminal any opportunity to reform (change).

- Because of the possibility of 'miscarriage of justice' (executing someone innocent), some Christians believe that capital punishment is unacceptable.

- Many Christians and non-Christians alike believe that the death penalty goes against human rights. They may support organizations like Amnesty International, who are working to completely abolish capital punishment.

Some Christians believe that capital punishment is acceptable, because it protects the innocent and helps to keep society safe. They believe that it was established by God (as written in the Old Testament).

Exam Practice

Practise your skills in **demonstrating knowledge and understanding**.

What are Christian attitudes towards capital punishment?

Explain the different views Christians might have, and the reasons they might give to support their opinions. For high marks, you could include examples of teachings from the Bible.

This will help you in the exam when you answer part (d) questions.

Exam Practice

Practise your **evaluation** skills.

'The death penalty is a fair punishment for some crimes.'

Discuss this statement. In your answer, you need to show that you have thought about different responses to the statement and that you have thought about your own opinion. Start by explaining how a Christian might respond – you might be able to give an example from the Bible or from real life to support this. Then give a different opinion – it could be a different Christian opinion, or it might be a view that someone with different beliefs might hold. Finally explain your own views, and make sure you reach a conclusion. You can say in your conclusion that you don't know, if this is your view, but you need to explain what makes it difficult to decide.

This will help you in the exam when you answer part (e) questions.

Social injustice

EXAM FOCUS

This section will help you understand what Christians think about fairness in society.

Social injustice basically means unfairness in society. Sometimes people are treated unequally and they may have fewer rights, opportunities and rewards. They may also have more burdens or be discriminated against because of, for example, race, sex, age, disability, or poverty.

Social justice means fair treatment in society, for example equality of opportunity, fairness of criminal justice, social rules and processes and social and political rights.

Christian beliefs about social injustice

> *But let justice roll on like a river,*
> *righteousness like a never-failing stream!*
> **(Amos 5:24)**

Christians generally believe that social justice is important, and social injustice is wrong. The Bible contains many teachings on the subject:

- Christians believe that God created humans in his own image, and therefore each individual life is sacred and should be respected and protected from injustice.

- The Bible teaches that people should not place importance on becoming rich or favour the rich over the poor.

> *If you show special attention to the man*
> *wearing fine clothes and say, 'Here's a good*
> *seat for you,' but say to the poor man, 'You*
> *stand there' or 'Sit on the floor by my feet,'*
> *have you not discriminated among yourselves*
> *and become judges with evil thoughts?*
> **(James 2:3)**

- Many Christians try to follow the example of Jesus, who wanted to help the poor and oppressed.

> *The Spirit of the Lord is on me, because he*
> *has anointed me to preach good news to the*
> *poor. He has sent me to proclaim freedom*
> *for the prisoners and recovery of sight for the*
> *blind, to release the oppressed, to proclaim*
> *the year of the Lord's favour.*
> **(Luke 4:18-19)**

Exam Practice

Practise your skills in **demonstrating knowledge and understanding**.

What is 'social injustice'?

Try to make your answer clear, short and to the point.

This will help you when you answer part (b) questions.

- The Bible teaches that it is important to love others, and look after each other. Many Christians believe that helping the needy and making society fairer are part of this.

> *Love your neighbour as yourself.*
> **(Leviticus 19:18)**

- Christians generally believe that Jesus' example and teachings show that it is important to serve others. For example, in the account of the feeding of the five thousand (Matthew 14:13-21), Jesus provides food for the hungry crowd.

Because of Jesus' example, many Christians believe that they should act against social injustice and help those in need.

> *Come, you who are blessed by my Father; take your inheritance, the kingdom prepared for you since the creation of the world. For I was hungry and you gave me something to eat, I was thirsty and you gave me something to drink, I was a stranger and you invited me in, I needed clothes and you clothed me, I was sick and you looked after me, I was in prison and you came to visit me.*
> **(Matthew 25:34-36)**

> *Remember those in prison as if you were their fellow-prisoners, and those who are ill-treated as if you yourselves were suffering.*
> **(Hebrews 13:3)**

- The Bible says that racial inequality is wrong.

> *When an alien lives with you in your land, do not ill-treat him. The alien living with you must be treated as one of your native-born. Love him as yourself, for you were aliens in Egypt. I am the Lord your God.*
> **(Leviticus 19:33-34)**

- The Bible implies that the criminal justice system should be fair.

> *Hate evil, love good;*
> *maintain justice in the courts.*
> **(Amos 5:15)**

Christian responses to social injustice

Since many Christians believe that social justice is necessary and important, sometimes they put this belief into practice and do something about it.

Examples of how some Christians respond to issues of social injustice are:

Prayer

Prayer is an important part of the Christian faith, because it is a way of communicating with God. Christians may pray about specific issues of social injustice. They might ask God to help with a situation, or ask God for guidance about what they should do themselves.

Treating people fairly

Because of their beliefs about social justice, many Christians try to treat everyone fairly in their everyday lives. This might include not discriminating against people or favouring people because of things such as race, sex, age, physical ability, or money.

Helping the needy

Some Christians try to help people in need. For example, they might give money or food to someone who needs it, or they might stand up for someone who is being bullied.

Volunteering or working

Christians might decide to volunteer or work to make society fairer. They might work in the community, or for charities or larger organizations such as Amnesty International.

Christians believe social justice is important. ▲

Exam Practice

Practise your **evaluation** skills.

'Social injustice is not ideal, but it is not my responsibility to fight against it.'

Discuss this statement. You should include different, supported points of view and a personal viewpoint. You must refer to Christianity in your answer.

For this answer, you need to demonstrate that you understand different points of view. Start by giving an explanation of Christian responses to social injustice – you might be able to support this with teachings from the Bible. Then explain why other people might agree with the statement. Finally, give your own view and remember to use the word 'because'.

This will help you when you answer part (e) questions.

Campaigning

Some Christians believe that it is necessary to speak out or fight against social injustice, through campaigns to make society fairer. This can gain support, raise awareness and influence changes to political and social systems.

Supporting organizations who work for social justice

Christians may choose to support organizations who work for social justice by donating money, supporting campaigns, signing petitions, or becoming members. Organizations involved with working for social justice include Catholic Agency for Overseas Development (CAFOD), Tearfund, Christians Against Poverty (CAP) and Amnesty International.

Liberation Theology

This is a Christian movement (particularly in the Roman Catholic Church) whose basic beliefs are that:

- Christians have a responsibility to fight against poverty, oppression and injustice
- Christians should take action to protect people's basic human rights.

Liberation theologians have fought against issues such as poverty as a result of government corruption, and imprisonment without trial.

Glossary

Capital punishment – the death penalty

Conscientious objector – someone who refuses to participate in war because of their beliefs

Pacifism – the belief that war and violence should always be avoided

Principle of equality

This section will help you understand Christian beliefs about prejudice and discrimination.

All people have the same rights in society regardless of physical ability. ▶

For Discussion

What kinds of discrimination can you think of?

Is discrimination ever acceptable?

Equality is the state of being equal or being treated equally. Some people believe that everyone should receive equal rights, treatment and opportunities because everyone is equally important. They want social justice, which means fairness in society. They believe in equality for all people, regardless of their race, gender, sexuality, age, religion or physical or mental ability.

Other people argue that since everyone is different, it is impossible and unnatural to give everyone complete equality. There are physical, mental, and social differences between people, and so everyone cannot be treated equally.

Sometimes we treat people unequally because they are different. This can be for good reasons, such as giving one person a job instead of another because they performed better in an interview, which is fair. However, sometimes people unfairly treat others unequally, because they are prejudiced against them. This unfair unequal treatment is **discrimination**.

Article 1
All human beings are born free and equal in dignity and rights. They are endowed with reason and conscience and should act towards one another in a spirit of brotherhood.

The Universal Declaration of Human Rights

States the following in relation to equality and discrimination in the first two of its 30 articles.

Article 2
Everyone is entitled to all the rights and freedoms set forth in this Declaration, without distinction of any kind, such as race, colour, sex, language, religion, political or other opinion, national or social origin, property, birth or other status. Furthermore, no distinction shall be made on the basis of the political, jurisdictional or international status of the country or territory to which a person belongs, whether it be independent, trust, non-self-governing or under any other limitation of sovereignty.

What do Christians believe about equality?

- Equality – everyone is equal

The Bible teaches that everyone is of equal value, and being different does not ever mean being better or worse than other people. Christians believe that everyone was made in the image of God, and the Bible teaches that it is important to treat everyone fairly.

> *If you show special attention to the man wearing fine clothes and say, 'Here's a good seat for you,' but say to the poor man, 'You stand there' or 'Sit on the floor by my feet,' have you not discriminated among yourselves and become judges with evil thoughts?*
>
> **(James 2:3-4)**

- Love – we should love each other

Christians believe it is important for people to love one another and treat each other well. The Bible teaches the importance of love, and it is emphasized through the example of how Jesus treated others, as well as his teachings.

> *A new command I give you: Love one another. As I have loved you, so you must love one another.*
>
> **(John 13:34)**

> *Love your neighbour as yourself.*
> **(Matthew 22:39)**

- Justice – everyone should be treated fairly

The Bible shows the importance of social justice, of people being treated fairly regardless of their race or position in society.

> *Do not deprive the alien or the fatherless of justice.*
>
> **(Deuteronomy 24:17)**

- Sanctity of life – all human life is sacred

Christians believe that all humans were made in God's own image. They believe that God gave humans a special status in life, and that every human is sacred and should be treated accordingly.

- Not judging – we should not judge others

The Bible says that only God has the authority to judge people. Christians believe we should not judge others to be better or worse than ourselves, because we do not have the authority to judge. Since none of us is perfect, we should try to think about our own faults rather than criticizing others.

Many Christians believe that the principle of not judging others means that we should not condemn people who show discrimination or prejudice to others, but try to help them to treat people equally.

Exam Practice

Practise your skills in **demonstrating knowledge and understanding**.

Describe the main Christian beliefs about equality.

Remember that this type of question is not opinion-based, nor do you need to explain the concept in detail, so you should not spend too much time giving a long answer.

This will help you in the exam when you answer part (c) questions.

Attitudes towards racism

This section helps you to understand Christian beliefs about racial prejudice.

EXAM FOCUS

Racism means prejudice or discrimination because of race (colour, culture and ethnic group). Sometimes people believe that a certain race is better or worse than others, and this is racial prejudice. When these beliefs are acted upon, and people are treated differently because of their race, this is racial discrimination.

Racial discrimination was made illegal by the Race Relations Act of 1976. This is not only for deliberate discrimination, but also for indirect discrimination (where the discrimination is not deliberate or obvious). It includes racial harassment (bullying, threats, 'jokes', and hostility) and victimization.

Racial prejudice refers to beliefs and attitudes in people's minds. Reasons for racial prejudice include lack or understanding, fear of what is different, the influence of family, peers and role models, historical traditions.

What do Christians believe about racism?

Christians generally believe that racism is wrong, because it goes against Christian principles of equality and love. Racism does not fit in with the Christian principle of love, because it involves treating people badly and not showing them love and respect. Racism is a form of inequality, so all of the Christian beliefs in the previous section about equality can be applied to racism.

The Bible on racism

The Bible teaches that everyone was created equally, which implies that no race is better than another.

> *From one man he made every nation of men, that they should inhabit the whole earth; and he determined the times set for them and the exact places where they should live.*
>
> **(Acts 17:26)**

The Bible says that there should be no racial barriers in Christianity.

> *There is neither Jew nor Greek, slave nor free, male nor female, for you are all one in Christ Jesus.*
>
> **(Galatians 3:28)**

> *Talking with him, Peter went inside and found a large gathering of people. He said to them: 'You are well aware that it is against our law for a Jew to associate with a Gentile or visit him. But God has shown me that I should not call any man impure or unclean. So when I was sent for, I came without raising any objection…'*
>
> **(Acts 10:27-29)**

For **Discussion**

Why do you think racism still exists in contemporary twenty-first-century society?

▲ *Sport provides an opportunity for people of different races to play together.*

Jesus' example and teachings

Although Jesus was a Jew and Jews did not normally associate with Samaritans because they were a different race, the Gospel of John shows Jesus talking with a Samaritan woman (see John 4), and the Gospel of Luke records a story Jesus told where a Samaritan is praised for his kind actions (see Luke 10).

The Parable of the Good Samaritan

> In reply Jesus said: 'A man was going down from Jerusalem to Jericho, when he fell into the hands of robbers. They stripped him of his clothes, beat him and went away, leaving him half-dead. A priest happened to be going down the same road, and when he saw the man, he passed by on the other side. So too, a Levite, when he came to the place and saw him, passed by on the other side. But a Samaritan, as he travelled, came where the man was; and when he saw him, he took pity on him. He went to him and bandaged his wounds, pouring on oil and wine. Then he put the man on his own donkey, brought him to an inn and took care of him. The next day he took out two silver coins and gave them to the innkeeper. 'Look after him,' he said, 'and when I return, I will reimburse you for any extra expense you may have.'
>
> 'Which of these three do you think was a neighbour to the man who fell into the hands of robbers?'
>
> The expert in the law replied, 'The one who had mercy on him.'
>
> Jesus told him, 'Go and do likewise'.

(Luke 10:30-37)

What would you do if someone from a different race needed your help? ▶

The Methodist Church sums up a Christian response to racism like this:

'We submit that racism exists, overtly and covertly, in our country, of which the Methodist Church is a part. It is of vital importance that the Church should give an unmistakably clear lead as to where it stands in this matter. As an institution, which is an integral part of national life, it must continually be giving signs and signals declaring its abhorrence and utter rejection of this incipient evil.'

from the Methodist Church website: www.methodist.org.uk

For **Discussion**

What do you think Jesus would teach about racism if he was preaching today?

How do Christians respond to racism?

There are many examples in history of when Christians have been responsible for racial injustice (for example, during the Crusades). In modern society there are still some instances of racism in the Christian Church, but in the majority of cases Christians try to put Jesus' teaching about treating all people equally into action.

In their everyday lives

Many modern Christians try not to be racist themselves.

- Christians generally try to treat people of all races fairly.
- They try to respect everyone equally, regardless of race.
- If they find that they have racial prejudice, they often repent and try to change.
- This can bring challenges such as people making fun of them.
- Christians often have to not join in with others' racist behaviour.
- Christians often try to make a positive effort to welcome ethnic minorities.

Christians may try to encourage racial equality

- By setting a positive example to others.
- By creating an atmosphere of equal respect for everyone (at work or school, or in a social situation) regardless of race.
- By educating children about equality and the importance of respecting everyone. This can happen at home, in school, or at church.
- By sharing their beliefs about racial equality and social justice.

Some Christians take action against racism

Many Christians believe that simply believing that racism is wrong is not enough – they believe that they must take real action against racism, and do something to stop racial injustice. The Bible teaches that Christians should not just stand by and do nothing.

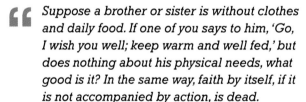

Suppose a brother or sister is without clothes and daily food. If one of you says to him, 'Go, I wish you well; keep warm and well fed,' but does nothing about his physical needs, what good is it? In the same way, faith by itself, if it is not accompanied by action, is dead.

(James 2:15-17)

Action against racism can include:

- challenging or reporting any racist behaviour
- supporting anti-racist organizations
- campaigning for equal opportunities
- protesting against racist policies.

Christians often respond to racism through practices of their faith

Prayer is very important to Christians, because it is a way of communicating with God. Christians may pray to God for guidance in how they should fight racism, or they sometimes pray for God to help in certain situations.

◄ *Prayer is important to Christians.*

This Christian prayer was used in the Racial Justice Sunday 2009 campaign:

Statement of affirmation

Let us affirm together

- WE pledge to examine our own biases and positions of privilege through self reflection and earnestly work to resolve them.

- WE pledge to live by compassion and be consciously inclusive of all people.

- WE pledge to affirm the value of diversity.

- WE pledge to promote understanding, inclusion and mutual respect, and thus build community within all ethnicities and cultures.

- WE pledge to transform our institutions into authentically anti-racist and anti oppressive communities of action.

- WE pledge to advocate for justice, demand equal opportunity for all and so help create a beloved community for everyone to share.

God of all people,

May the things we do, always include everyone

For in the example of Jesus no one was excluded from his circle of life.

Create in us renewed and reinvigorated hearts and minds

That, rooted in your love, our lives may continue to bear fruit

As we live these commitments

In the name of Jesus, we pray.

Amen

Exam Practice

Practise your **evaluation** skills.

'People are not the same so there is no need to treat them equally.'

Discuss this statement. You should include different, supported points of view and a personal viewpoint. You must refer to Christianity in your answer.

For this answer, you need to consider different opinions. Start by explaining what a Christian might say about people being equally valuable to God. Then try and explain what a person who disagreed might say, and give reasons to support it. After this, explain your own point of view. You might agree with one of the opinions you have already explained, or you might want to give another point of view.

This will help you in the exam when you answer part (e) questions.

The church

Many Christian churches respond to racism. For example:

- The church programme can include education and information to promote racial justice.
- Church leaders can lead and work in the community towards racial equality.

The Christian responses of not judging and of forgiveness

The Bible teaches that only God has the authority to judge, and that we should not judge others. Therefore many Christians believe that it is important not to judge racist people and label them as 'bad'. Some Christians find this difficult, particularly if they personally experience racism.

This does not mean that Christians do not believe that racism is wrong, but that they should respond without judging people. The principle of **forgiveness** means that many Christians believe it is important to offer forgiveness to those who are responsible for racism.

Apartheid

- In South Africa between 1948 and 1994 there was a legal system of apartheid (separation) of black people and white people.
- White people were given better rights, education, health care, opportunities and treatment than black people.
- Black people were often treated badly, for example being forced out of their homes and made to live in poor conditions, and even being treated with violence.

The Dutch Reformed Church supported apartheid for several decades, believing that the Bible supported the idea of racial separation and that it was God's will. They eventually publicly repented for this support in the 1980s.

Other Christians protested against apartheid, some through non-violent protest (e.g. Archbishop Desmond Tutu), while others used violence.

◀ *Dr John Sentamu became the Archbishop of York in 2005. He has worked to raise awareness about racism within the Church of England and in society in general. He aims to bring God's love and grace to everyone. In response to being sent racist hate mail (including some with human excrement on), he prayed for those responsible, and talked publicly about forgiveness of the past and hope for the future. Rather than judging their racism, he focused on his vision for a loving Christian society. Many people, both Christians and non-Christians, were shocked by his response.*

Attitudes towards gender

This section will help you understand Christian ideas about equality between genders.

EXAM FOCUS

Gender discrimination

Sometimes people are treated unfairly because they are male or female. This is called gender discrimination or sex discrimination.

Historically, men and women were treated differently and were expected to take on different roles in society. In today's society, it is acceptable to recognize that there are differences between men and women, but the Sex Discrimination Act of 1975 made sex discrimination illegal in the UK.

However men and women are still not always treated equally. Examples of unequal treatment at work include:

- Women being unfairly given less challenging work.
- Sexual harassment in the workplace.
- Unfair promotion of one gender instead of another.
- Different pay for the same job.
- Not enough support for women balancing parenthood and a job.
- Men being allowed less time off work than women after having a baby.

Should men and women be treated equally in society?

Yes	No
Differences do not mean that one sex is better than the other.	Men and women are physically different – for example, men overall are physically stronger than women.
Equality is an essential human right.	Women can have children, so it is natural for them to care and nurture.

Christian attitudes towards gender equality

The traditional view

Traditionally, most Christians believed that men were in charge, and the role of women was to support men. Today there are some Christians who still believe that men should be the leaders in the family and in society, while women should take on the supporting roles.

For **Discussion**

Do you think men and women are treated fairly today?

Do you think equality between the sexes is improving? Try to support your answer with reasons.

For **Discussion**

Look at the table opposite. Which arguments are the most convincing? What is your own opinion? Can you think of any other arguments not shown here?

◀ *Are men and women really equal?*

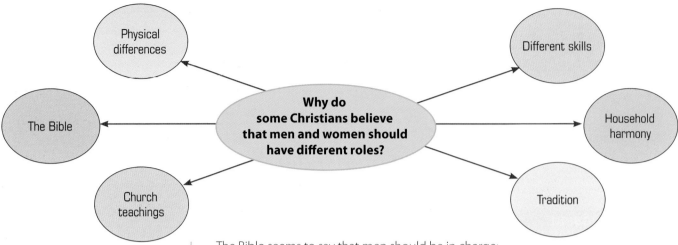

The Bible seems to say that men should be in charge:

- Jesus' disciples were all men.

- The first woman, Eve, was created as man's companion.

> *Wives … be submissive to your husbands … . Husbands, in the same way be considerate as you live with your wives, and treat them with respect as the weaker partner.*
>
> **(1 Peter 3:1,7)**

The liberal view

Many modern Christians believe that men and women should be treated equally, and that they should both be in charge together.

Some Christians believe:

- The Bible was written a long time ago, in a male-dominated society, and its references to the roles of men and women reflect this. Jesus' Apostles were all men, but this was because that was how things worked at that time. Modern society has progressed and today men and women should be treated equally.

- There are principles of equality in the Bible that should be applied to gender, for example:

> *There is neither Jew not Greek, slave nor free, male nor female, for you are all one in Christ Jesus.*
>
> **(Galatians 3:28)**

- Although there are differences between men and women, it is unfair to limit opportunities and treat people differently because of this. Some Christians believe that gender inequality goes against the Biblical principles of love and social justice.

The Roman Catholic view

The Catholic Church teaches that men and women are equal but different:

'Man and woman have been *created*, which is to say, *willed* by God: on the one hand, in perfect equality as human persons; on the other, in their respective beings as man and woman.'

(Catechism of the Catholic Church, 369)

Gender and equality within churches

The Church of England has allowed female vicars since 1994. Currently women can not become Bishops in the Church of England, but that looks set to change as soon as measures for those who don't agree with women as Bishops are agreed.

The decision to allow women as priests has divided opinion in the Church of England. Some people have criticized the decision because they believe it's a response to culture and the pressure of political correctness rather than being based on God and the Bible. Others believe it reflects the Christian principles of equality, justice and love.

The Catholic Church does not allow women to be priests, bishops or pope, because

- the hierarchy of the Church reflects Jesus and his Apostles

- the priest represents Jesus, who was a man, and therefore the priest should be male

- bishops are descendants of Jesus' Apostles, who were also male

- the Pope (head of the Catholic Church), is always a man because he is the successor of Peter, the foundation of the Church (see Matthew 16:18).

For more information about the roles of men and women in the Christian family and Church, see the section on Religion and human relationships, page 126.

Exam Practice

Practise your skills in **demonstrating knowledge and understanding**.

Give two different Christian views about the treatment of men and women.

This will help you in the exam when you answer part (b) questions.

Attitudes to religion

This section looks at the ways Christians view members of other religions, and encourages you to think about your own opinions.

▲ *Most Christians respect people who follow other religions.*

The majority of Christians around the world believe that 'Christianity is the only true faith'. However, most Christians try to show respect for people who follow other religions.

Other religions should be respected

Although Christians do not generally accept the beliefs of other religions as being equal to their own, most Christians believe in religious freedom. They believe that everyone has the right to their own beliefs, and everyone deserves respect and love, regardless of religion.

In the UK today, we are part of an increasingly multi-cultural society, enriched with a great wealth of different cultures and religious beliefs. Many Christians believe it is right to respect the beliefs of others and live together in harmony whilst appreciating the right to practise one's own faith.

Inter-faith work

There are a number of different organizations with the specific purpose of encouraging a positive relationship between Christianity and other religions.

For example:

The Inter Faith Network for the UK

Founded in 1987, the Inter Faith Network for the UK aims to promote a strong interfaith relationship based upon respect and mutual understanding. It recognizes that 76.8 per cent of the UK population (census 2001) admit to having a religious faith, and believes that it is important for us all to get along.

The Council for Christians and Jews (CCJ)

This is Britain's oldest national interfaith organization. Its aims are to promote mutual understanding and respect. It also has dialogue with the other faiths in the UK.

Many Christian organizations are affiliated to these movements and work alongside their neighbours from other faiths.

Only Christians can know God and enter heaven

Christians are taught that only a Christian, who accepts Jesus as the Son of God and the Saviour, can know God. Followers of other religions which do not recognize the full importance of Jesus can not enter heaven.

> *Jesus answered 'I am the way and the truth and the life. No-one comes to the Father except through me.'*
>
> **(John 14:6)**

> *For us men, and for our salvation, he came down from heaven.*
>
> **(From the Nicene Creed)**

There is only one true God

Christianity is a monotheistic religion which means that it only has one God.

Some other religions are polytheistic which means they believe in more than one God. Christian teachings do not accept that there can be more than one God, and therefore disagree with the teachings of some other religions on this subject.

> *I believe in one God, the Father Almighty, maker of heaven and earth, of all that is seen and unseen.*
>
> **(From the Nicene Creed)**

Other religions may have part of the truth and be searching for the whole truth

Although Christians generally believe that only Christianity is based on the whole truth, some Christians believe that some other religions may have part of the truth.

Many Christians recognize that by following other religions, people are searching for the truth, and this should be respected.

The Catholic Church:

'The Catholic Church recognizes in other religions that search, among shadows and images, for the God who is unknown yet near since he gives life and breath and all things and wants all men to be saved. Thus, the Church considers all goodness and truth found in these religions as "a preparation for the Gospel and given by him who enlightens all men that they may at length have life."'

(Catechism of the Catholic Church, 843)

▲ *Only Christians who accept Jesus can know God.*

For **Discussion**

There are different opinions amongst Christians when it comes to the roles of other religions. Read the comments below and discuss your views.

Some Christians believe that other religions have equal value to Christianity

Although most Christians believe that Christianity is the only true faith, some Christians believe that other religions can have equal value.

In the Bible, Jesus says:

> **In my Father's house are many rooms.**
>
> **(John 14:2)**

Some Christians interpret this as meaning that other religions are an equal and valid path to God and heaven. However, other Christians interpret this as meaning that heaven is a big and complex place.

> The Bible makes it very clear that only Christians can know God through Jesus. Therefore other religions are simply not compatible with Christianity.

Vaughan, aged 21

Toby, aged 29

> God is loving. He will welcome people of all faiths to heaven. It is not possible for all people on Earth to have heard of Jesus. What about them?

Missionary work

Missionary means someone sent on a religious or charitable mission (job or assignment), often abroad, or someone who attempts to convert people.

The main aims of Christian missionary work are:

- To carry out the will of God: Christian missionary workers generally believe that they have been 'called' by God. They also believe they are carrying out the teachings of the Bible, by telling people about Christianity and helping the needy.

- To evangelize (spread the news of the Christian faith) or convert (help people to become Christians): for Christians, missionary work is strongly linked to **evangelism**. Before his ascension to heaven, Jesus instructed his followers to go forth and make disciples of all nations. Missionaries often devote their whole lives, or make significant sacrifices, for their work. Missionary work includes community work, church planting (founding new churches), and building new relationships, often overseas.

- To act out the Christian principle of love: the Bible teaches that Christians should care for those in need. Lots of missionary work includes helping people to overcome situations, challenges or problems. Many Christians believe that missionary work is the work of God, and that it shows God's love for the world.

Evangelism

The Great Commission

Therefore go and make disciples of all nations, baptising them in the name of the Father and of the Son and of the Holy Spirit, and teaching them to obey everything I have commanded you.

(Matthew 28:19)

These words of Jesus in the Bible are considered by Christians to be an instruction to all his followers, including modern Christians, to evangelize. For Christians, evangelism is the idea of going to tell people about Jesus and encouraging them to convert to the faith.

Jesus gave this instruction just before His ascension to heaven, and so many Christians believe that this makes it an even more important instruction. Some Christians believe that evangelism is the most important task they have to do.

The Catholic Church expresses the need for all Christians to evangelize:

'Although in ways known to himself God can lead those who, through no fault of their own, are ignorant of the Gospel, to that faith without which it is impossible to please him, the Church still has the obligation and also the sacred right to evangelize all men.'

(Catechism of the Catholic Church, 848)

Many evangelists believe that by telling people about Jesus and encouraging them to convert to Christianity, they are helping people and showing love towards others. They believe that everyone needs the true God, and by converting people to Christianity they are helping them to be able to go to heaven when they die.

◀ *The Alpha course*
The Alpha course is run by many different Christian churches.
It is mainly aimed at people who do not regularly go to church.
Evangelism is one of the aims of the course.
Millions of people in the UK participate every year, and millions more worldwide.
The course is designed to allow people to explore the meaning of life.
It is mainly based on exploration and discussion in small groups.

Some Christians do not focus on evangelism. They may believe that religion is a personal choice, and while it is okay to share your beliefs if asked, it should not be something that should be pushed on others. They may also believe that God decides who will be in His Book of Life so it is not up to humans to convert people.

Ecumenism

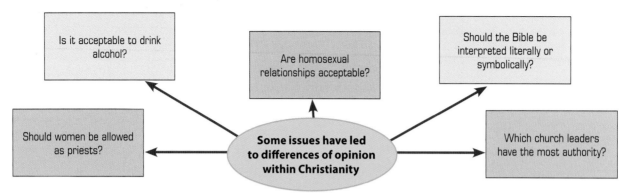

Is it acceptable to drink alcohol?	Are homosexual relationships acceptable?	Should the Bible be interpreted literally or symbolically?
Should women be allowed as priests?	**Some issues have led to differences of opinion within Christianity**	Which church leaders have the most authority?

Ecumenism is the concept that all the different Christian denominations should be united together. Believers in ecumenism encourage Christians to unite and worship God and forget their differences. ▶

An ecumenical organization: The World Council of Churches

- The World Council of Churches was set up in 1948.

- It believes that arguing damages the Christian message of love, and there are more important problems in the world to deal with than church squabbling.

- It aims to help restore peace in the world and amongst Christians.

- It aims to promote unity, to help relieve social injustices and to be the voice for Christians.

- The World Council of Churches aims for the representatives of all churches to meet regularly to talk through theology, how to tackle problems in the world, and generally to remain friends rather than for poor communication to lead to further isolation.

Other groups

There are other ecumenism groups around the world that encourage unity. The Taizé Community is one such group based in Burgundy in France which is made up of Christians from many different denominations. Each year it is estimated that over 100, 000 young people go there to visit the community for communal work, prayer and Bible study.

Forgiveness and reconciliation

This section will help you understand Christian beliefs about forgiving other people and making peace with them.

Forgiveness means the act of excusing a sin or wrongdoing. Forgiveness is necessary in order to restore relationships.

What do Christians believe about forgiveness?

Forgiveness is an important principle of Christianity. There are many teachings in the Bible about forgiveness, which many Christians believe still apply today.

The Lord's Prayer, which the Bible says Jesus gave to his followers, says:

> *And forgive us our sins, as we forgive those who sin against us.*

This shows that:

- Christians admit that they are not perfect.

- Christians believe that God can forgive their sins.

- Christians ask for God's forgiveness of their sins.

- Christians forgive other people for their sins.

God's forgiveness

One important Christian belief about forgiveness is that God forgives their sins.

Christians do not believe that God forgives them because they deserve it, but rather because:

- God is loving – God loves everyone no matter what they have done in the past.

- God is forgiving by nature – there are examples of God's forgiveness throughout the Bible.

- God is perfect – He does not have human weaknesses to stop Him forgiving.

Our forgiveness of others

> *Then Peter came to Jesus and asked, 'Lord, how many times shall I forgive my brother when he sins against me? Up to seven times?' Jesus answered, 'I tell you, not seven times, but seventy-seven times.*
> **(Matthew 18:21-22)**

For Christians, the principle of forgiveness is closely related to the principle of love. Forgiveness is a way of showing love to others, which the Bible teaches is important. Christians believe that if people do bad things, they should respond with love.

> *But I tell you who hear me: Love your enemies, do good to those who hate you, bless those who curse you, pray for those who ill-treat you. If someone strikes you on one cheek, turn to him the other also.*
>
> **(Luke 6:27-29)**

Christians believe that forgiveness is good, as opposed to hatred or grudge-holding, which are the works of evil.

> *Do not be overcome by evil, but overcome evil with good.*
>
> **(Romans 12:21)**

Christians believe that they must forgive other people in order for them to be forgiven by God for their own sins. This is important, because it emphasizes the two-way street of forgiveness, and links to the teaching that Christians should treat others as they would like to be treated themselves.

> *For if you forgive men when they sin against you, your heavenly Father will also forgive you. But if you do not forgive men their sins, your Father will not forgive your sins.*
>
> **(Matthew 6:14-15)**

> *Blessed are the merciful, for they will be shown mercy.*
>
> **(Matthew 5:7)**

Jesus' example of forgiveness

Christians believe that Jesus is their ultimate example, and they should try to be like him and follow his example.

Jesus' example is highly significant when it comes to forgiveness. Although he did nothing wrong, he was crucified along with criminals. Before he died, he forgave those responsible for his death:

> *Father, forgive them, for they do not know what they are doing.*
>
> **(Luke 23:34)**

Many Christians believe that we should try to follow Jesus' example, and forgive people who sin against us, whatever the amount suffering they may have caused us.

How do Christians respond to the issue of forgiveness?

Through prayer

Many Christians believe it is important to pray for forgiveness when they sin. Most Christians admit that they are not perfect – it is human nature to sin and although they try to avoid sin wherever possible it is important to admit their wrongs and pray to God for forgiveness.

For **Discussion**

What do you think about forgiveness? Would you always be prepared to forgive?

Exam Practice

Practise your skills in **demonstrating knowledge and understanding**.

Describe the main Christian responses to forgiveness.

Remember that this type of question is not opinion-based, nor do you need to explain the concept in detail, so you should not spend too much time giving a long answer.

This will help you in the exam when you answer part (c) questions.

Christians might pray for God to help others to be able to forgive each other, as this can resolve conflict, stop suffering and bring about peace and love.

The Archbishop of York, Dr John Sentamu, famously prayed for those who sent him racist hate mail.

Through repentance

Repentance basically means being sorry or asking forgiveness for sins. It also represents change – from an old life to a new one, away from sin and towards God.

Most Christians believe that repentance is not necessary to be forgiven by God, because God forgives their sins as a gift of grace. However, Christians do believe that God wants them to repent:

> *In the past God overlooked such ignorance, but now he commands all people everywhere to repent.*
>
> **(Acts 17:30)**

The Bible teaches that repentance is necessary in order to gain eternal life:

> *But unless you repent, you too will all perish.*
>
> **(Luke 13:5)**

Through forgiveness in practice

Christians generally believe that they should forgive people who sin against them. Most Christians try to put this into practice in their everyday lives, with varying degrees of success. There are often situations where Christians find it really difficult to forgive someone, and this can lead to a 'crisis of faith', where they think 'How can I be a Christian if I can not do what God wants?'

Some Christians believe that someone has to show repentance in order for you to forgive them. However, most Christians believe that they should forgive people regardless, because Jesus did so when he forgave those who crucified him and the Bible emphasizes responding to evil with good (i.e. responding to unrepentant sin with love and forgiveness) and the principle of loving your enemy.

An example of Christian forgiveness in action: Gee Walker, the mother of Anthony Walker who was the victim of a racist murder, publicly forgave those responsible. She admitted that it was not easy, but referred to the teachings about forgiveness in the Bible and talked about how she tries to practise what she preaches.

Beliefs about reconciliation

Reconciliation basically means the bringing back of friendly relations, bringing things or people back together, or settling something. For Christians, reconciliation means getting a relationship back on track – a relationship between people, or a relationship with God.

The Bible teaches the importance of reconciliation, resolving situations and restoring relationships with one another and with God. When someone has done something wrong, reconciliation requires forgiveness.

Christians generally believe that blame is not important. It is not the issue whose fault a problem or situation is, they must try to resolve it and do everything they can to bring reconciliation.

The importance of reconciliation is emphasized in the Bible:

> *Therefore, if you are offering your gift at the altar and there remember that your brother has something against you, leave your gift there in front of the altar. First go and be reconciled to your brother; then come and offer your gift.*
>
> **(Matthew 5:23-24)**

The Roman Catholic Church – The sacrament of reconciliation

The sacrament of reconciliation is often also called confession or penance.

Catholics believe it frees people from their sins. God forgives their sins through the priest, who conducts the sacrament. A person confesses sins, and the priest says words including 'I absolve you from your sins.'

Glossary

Discrimination – unfair treatment based on prejudice

Ecumenism – the idea that all different Christian groups should be united together

Evangelism – sharing beliefs and trying to persuade others to follow them

Forgiveness – the act of excusing a sin or wrongdoing

Prejudice – prejudging something or someone without good reason or without full knowledge of a situation

Reconciliation – bringing opposing people or groups back together again

Relationship with the media

In this section, you will be introduced to ideas about the relationship between Christianity and different forms of media.

What is the media?

The word **media** refers to any type of mass communication. There are many different forms of media, and the main examples are television, radio, newspapers and magazines, Internet, and leaflets and posters. The media plays a very important role in modern society, and can often be accessed all day, every day. It also allows communication on a local, national and global scale.

How are we influenced by the media?

It is mass communication. This means that one television programme or publication can reach a huge audience.

Efficient modern technology and transport mean that it is relatively quick and easy to transmit or circulate media broadcasts and publications.

Why is the media so influential?

The media has wide appeal because it is very varied, with many different types, and a wide variety within each type. Therefore it reaches a large number of people.

There is lots of money involved in today's media. For example, £19.4 billion was spent on advertising in the UK in 2007 (according to the Advertising Association). As a result, the media is increasingly powerful.

In modern society the media is an extremely powerful means of communication. Think about how much time people spend watching television, listening to the radio, reading papers, or surfing the web. The media has a massive influence on society, in both positive and negative ways.

Education: the media can teach us things

- TV channels such as the Discovery Channel shows specifically educational science and history programmes.

- Through daily crosswords or soduku puzzles the media can teach us and test our mental skills.

Information: news, facts and opinions about many different subjects

The media enables us to find out about different cultures. Because the media reaches so many people around the world, it often gives information, opinions and ideas that people would not otherwise have access to.

▲ *The news tells us about current events from around the world, such as when the World Trade Center in New York was attacked in 2001.*

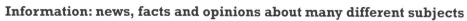

Role models: the media provides both positive and negative role models

Anyone who appears in the media can be seen as a role model – including presenters, actors, singers, subjects or writers of newspaper or magazine articles, sports players, and even fictional characters. They may be role models because people can relate to their personality or circumstances, or because they have inspiring traits. The influence of role models can be positive, providing inspiration, encouragement and ambition. For example, Olympic gold medallist Chris Hoy is represented in the media as a role model for sport, health and achievement. However, the effect of role models can also be negative, and is sometimes blamed for encouraging violence, coarse language, bad attitudes and so on. Often celebrities are in the media for bad behaviour, such as alleged drug taking or getting drunk.

Global citizenship

Media coverage of certain events and situations can spread moods and reactions more widely, and promote global citizenship. For example, during the build-up and result of the American presidential elections of 2008, the international media coverage encouraged everyone around the world to take an interest.

Advertising: the media can influence what we buy

Companies spend millions of pounds on advertising so that we buy their products – and it often works! Sometimes this can be either a conscious influence, e.g. 'Which chocolate bar should I buy? Ooh, that's the one that looked really creamy on the telly – I'll try that one' or subconscious influence, where people might buy a product they have seen advertised without realizing it. As well as influencing purchases through advertising, the media can also strengthen or weaken brand images by mentioning them in programmes or articles, or on websites.

Politics: the media can influence people's political views

Sometimes the media provides political facts, or allows politicians to communicate with the public. Certain newspapers are biased towards different political parties, and many readers are unaware of this bias. So when newspapers publish articles which say good things about politicians they support, and bad things about their opposition, this can influence readers and can even persuade them who to vote for.

Society: the media can influence the actions and words of individuals and groups in many ways

- A magazine providing ideas for using fair trade fashion outlets, adapting clothes and growing your own vegetabtles might inspire readers to live in a more environmentally friendly way.

- The behaviour of fictional characters in popular soap operas can affect what people think is right or wrong.

Exam Practice

Practise your **evaluation** skills.

'The media has a positive influence on society.'

Discuss this statement. You should include different, supported points of view and a personal viewpoint. You must refer to Christianity in your answer. In this answer you need to demonstrate that you understand different points of view (including Christian beliefs), and also that you have thought about your own view. Christians might think that the media has positive and negative influences, and so might other people for different reasons. Try to think of different examples to support different ideas.

This will help you in the exam when you answer part (e) questions.

▲ *Dawn French in her role as the vicar of Dibley.*

For **Discussion**

How do you think Christianity is portrayed in the media?

How is Christianity portrayed in the media?

Christianity often comes under the spotlight in the media, and it is portrayed in lots of different ways, both positive and negative. Although many people in the UK call themselves Christians, church attendances have decreased in recent years. Statistics vary, but all show a significant decline. Therefore the media plays an important role in how Christianity is viewed by the public, as it may be the only regular source of experiences of Christianity for many people. Headlines are seen such as "1 in 10' attends church weekly' (BBC NEWS website April 2007).

The media sometimes portrays contemporary Christian issues. In 1994, the Church of England ordained the first group of female vicars. In response, the BBC made a controversial television comedy called *The Vicar of Dibley*, which played on the idea of whether it is acceptable to have a female vicar when the Church had traditionally been opposed to the idea. In the first episode, many of the characters were shocked that their new vicar was female, and wrote a letter of complaint to the bishop. When they got used to the idea, they later came to accept her role.

In 2008, MPs debated the controversial Human Fertilisation and Embryology Bill in the Houses of Parliament, which included issues of abortion and hybrid embryos that conflicted with Christian ethics about the sanctity of life. Three Roman Catholic members of the Cabinet, including Ruth Kelly, voted in line with their religious beliefs rather than their Prime Minister's view. This caused a mixed reaction in the media – some commended that they had stood by their religious morals, while many portrayed Christianity as opposing the advancement of science and freedom of choice.

There is often a focus in the media on the history of Christianity. From biblical documentaries to references to religion in period films, there is a strong sense that Christianity is part of the heritage of our nation.

One way in which the media portrays Christianity is through its varied representation of fictional Christian characters. Many are stereotypically respectable Christian characters with real Christian values such as treating others as you would like them to treat you, or turning the other cheek, regularly used as a basis. Fictional Christians are often shown as upright members of society who are honest and kind. Sometimes they are also shown as naive and easy to take advantage of, or as smug goody-goodies. For example, the character of Ned Flanders from the American cartoon show *The Simpsons* is portrayed as a goody-goody who is often taken advantage of because of his Christian morals.

Sometimes the media presents fictional Christians who do not uphold the values of Christianity. They may be heard to undermine biblical teachings, or despite calling themselves a Christian live a lifestyle that does not reflect this.

How are important religious figures portrayed by the media?

Religious figures are presented by the media in a variety of ways, depending on the circumstances, context and whether bias is involved. Sometimes they are portrayed factually, in a matter of fact way. Other times they might be represented from a certain angle or with a specific focus.

The media often represents religious figures as positive role models, living a morally good lifestyle, helping others, being kind, and putting biblical teachings into practice.

However, some areas of the media, such as tabloid newspapers, contrast the 'bad' things they get up to with the 'good' life you might expect. Things such as extra-marital relationships, debt, and ill treatment of others are often presented in the media as scandal when they concern church leaders.

Important religious leaders are often portrayed as sources of moral authority. Many people living in the UK regard themselves as Christian and as a result look to religious leaders when they need direction on issues of morality. This is also true for the media. When an ethical issue is raised in society, such as cloning, abortion or capital punishment, religious leaders are asked for their thoughts, and the media portrays their opinions about what is morally acceptable.

Other important religious figures are often portrayed in a respectful way. The Queen is the Head of the Church of England. As a result, she is often shown in the media attending church and meeting with religious people. In this context she is always shown in a courteous and respectful way. This is also true with other religious figures such as Pope Benedict XVI, the leader of the Roman Catholic Church since April 2005. The media is often said to reflect the views of society, and although not everyone supports the Queen or the Pope, their positions do command a level of respect.

Sometimes important religious figures are shown in a fun, charismatic way. Dr John Sentamu, a high-ranking minister in the Church of England, is often in the news, for example, when he does something unusual to raise awareness for a cause.

◀ In 2006 Dr John Sentamu camped in a tent in York Minster as a public witness to encourage peace in the Middle East. He lived on a liquid-only diet and gave up a family holiday in Austria for his campaign.

Activity 1

Explain in your own words how the media portrays religious figures.

Jesus is portrayed by the media in many different ways, he is sometimes presented in a factual way, where the media reflects his character and actions in the Bible.

There are regularly documentaries and articles about Jesus, particularly at religious festivals. In fact, the media in this country focuses a lot of attention on Christmas and Easter, which are festivals to remember Jesus' life, death and resurrection. This shows Jesus as a uniquely positive, praiseworthy figure.

However, Jesus is sometimes depicted in a more controversial way, such as in the American cartoon show *South Park*, where Jesus is shown as having his own TV show called 'Jesus and Pals' and is killed fighting Iraqis when trying to rescue Santa on Christmas Eve, This was seen by some as entertaining and funny, but by others as offensive and blasphemous.

I was offended by the portrayal of God in Bruce Almighty. *In the film God gave some of his powers to a human to teach him a lesson, and this is something that I believe God would never do. The Bible teaches us that we should love God with all our heart, mind and strength (Matthew 22:37). Therefore I think that films which disrespect God are wrong.*

I thought that the character of God in Bruce Almighty *was OK. Of course, I don't think that everything God did and said in the film matches what Christians believe about God. However, I think that it is great to have a film which might makes people think about God and prayer. Sparking people's interest might lead to people realizing how important God is and becoming Christians.*

Morgan Freeman as God in Bruce Almighty. ▶

Responses and attitudes towards films and books which focus on religious/philosophical messages

What is a religious/philosophical message in a film?

A religious or philosophical message is when a film tells or shows us something about religion or philosophy.

For example, the way a film shows religious characters, events or activities gives ideas and meanings about them. Or films which focus on issues such as beliefs, morals, truth and the meaning of life can give philosophical messages.

The film *The Matrix* focuses on a philosophical message. It tries to make the audience question the reality of life. In the film, humans really exist inside a computer programme called the Matrix, and the computers that rule the earth secretly use the human bodies to generate power to exist.

What is the Christian response to films with religious/philosophical messages?

Christians may respond in different ways. Here are two examples of how Christians might respond to the film *Bruce Almighty*.

The Passion of the Christ is a film about Jesus' final days. It was directed by Mel Gibson, who is a Catholic. He aimed to make the film as truthful as possible. The film had a mixed response from Christians. Some Christians were pleased that there was a famous film about Jesus, in which many of the important details were the same as the stories in the Bible, because it helped to praise Jesus and 'advertise' the Bible. Other Christians were very unhappy with the film because some of the storyline varied from accounts in the Bible. Some Christians believed that it contained unnecessary graphic violence, such as in the scene where Jesus was flogged.

Books which focus on religious and philosophical messages

In Christianity, a wide range of books are available for people to learn more about their faith, and to read the stories of other Christians. There are books for children, which retell Bible stories in simple language or which give Christian messages. *The Chronicles of Narnia* series was written by a Christian writer, C.S. Lewis, who used a fantasy genre to tell a Christian story of the battle between good and evil. There are biographies and autobiographies of Christian lives; for example *A Life For God* tells the story of Mother Teresa and her Christian work among the poor. Christians might read these to give themselves new ideas about how they could put their faith into practice. There are books which teach Christians about the Bible and explain its history and interpretation, and there are books about different aspects of Christian life, such as how to bring up children and how to cope with loss.

Not all books about Christian ideas are written by Christians, and not all of them encourage people to develop Christian faith. *The God Delusion*, for example, is a book by the scientist Richard Dawkins, in which he explains why he believes religious belief is wrong and damaging. Some Christians welcome books like this because they encourage people to talk about religion and they provide opportunities for Christians to talk about their faith with their friends; but others think that they can harm religious belief.

Use of the media

This section considers the advantages of the media for Christians.

EXAM FOCUS

The media is used to communicate about Christianity to both Christians and non-Christians. It can be used to educate, to inform, to provide moral or ethical guidance, and also to support Christians in their faith.

Most Christians believe that it is important to spread the gospel and show other people what Christianity is all about. **Evangelical** Christians believe that they should spread the gospel as wide and far as they can, in order to convert as many people as possible to Christianity. In modern society, media is considered to be a really effective form of communication with people on a local, national and global scale. Therefore, some Christians use the media to educate people about their faith, sometimes leading to people becoming Christians. Through the media, they can also strengthen the faith and understanding of people who are already Christians.

> *Therefore go and make disciples of all nations.*
> **(Matthew 28:19)**

As well as spreading the gospel, the media can be used to communicate Christian beliefs in a moral or social context. Some Christians may even attempt to influence people's behaviour by communicating through the media, while others prefer to provide help, advice and compassion without any attempt to indicate right and wrong.

Praise and worship are very important aspects of Christianity. The media is a way of sharing and promoting praise and worship. This enables people who are unable to go to church, and those who choose not to attend, to participate in praise and worship. It also educates non-Christians about that aspect of their religion.

▲ *Musical worship group on the God TV channel*

Christian churches and organizations often use the media to convey information to people. This can include details of what is going on in a particular church and its community, such as services or social events. The information could also be about what a particular Christian organization does. This can be useful in helping people to know where to look for specific help and advice, services, contacts etc. Also, it can be used for fund-raising and recruiting volunteers for Christian charities, through explaining to people what they do and how people can help.

The media has such a huge presence in the UK today – just think about how much time we all spend watching television, listening to radio, surfing the web, reading newspapers, magazines, leaflets and posters. According to the 2001 census, over 42 million people in the UK consider themselves to be Christian, and the media is often said to reflect society, so it is natural that the faith is represented by the media.

What types of media are used to represent Christianity?

Television

There are some dedicated religious programmes on terrestrial channels. They are specifically religious, which means that they are factual (rather than made-up soap operas, comedies etc.) and are officially classed as religious by the television authorities. The majority of dedicated religious programmes on terrestrial television in the UK are Christian.

As there is variety within the different denominations of Christianity, not all programmes reflect the beliefs or attitudes of every Christian.

There is a wide variety of religious programmes used to represent Christianity on television, and they usually fall into three main categories:

▲ *Volunteers from* Make Me a Christian *TV show.*

- **Documentaries**
  'Documentary' is a broad genre of television broadcast which usually refers to a creative factual programme, or literally a programme that aims to 'document' (meaning record or verify) fact or reality. There are a wide variety of types of religious documentary through which Christianity is represented. The subject matter ranges too greatly to list every possibility, but examples can be historical, biblical, biographical, ethical, educational, thought-provoking, comparative, or narrative.

  Reality TV is a fairly recent development in the world of television documentaries. Although it is often questionable whether they are true documentaries or works of 'contrived' reality, they are often highly popular. In summer 2008, Channel 4 broadcast a controversial three-part series called *Make Me a Christian*, in which a reverend and his team of mentors try to promote a Christian way of life by convincing a group of non-Christian volunteers to live according to biblical teachings for three weeks.

- **Praise and worship**
  Some religious programmes focus on bringing Christian praise and worship to viewers. There are different types of worship programme on terrestrial television. They sometimes show hymns sung in churches, or religious songs performed by professional singers. They are often aired on a Sunday, but there are also special programmes at times such as Christmas, Easter and other religious festivals. They are aimed at both Christians and non-Christians, and allow viewers to join in with the worship, watch and listen, and learn about the worship aspect of Christianity. Modern worship programmes often feature interviews and stories throughout, as well as songs, as this generally attracts a wider audience.

The Florida 'healing revival' in 2008 was regularly shown live on God TV (available on UK satellite television) and included scenes of people being 'knocked over by the Holy Spirit', as well as live 'miraculous healings'. The broadcasts received mixed reactions around the world. ▼

Songs of Praise is the most popular religious worship programme, watched by millions of people – both Christians and non-Christians. As well as hymns from a different church each week, it features human interest stories and historical articles.

- **Discussion**
  Also known as magazine programmes, discussion shows often have an informal set-up with varied content. They sometimes involve presenters interviewing guests, discussions between two or more people, or debates with a studio audience. They may also have viewer input by email, text message or phone. The subject matter on religious discussion programmes varies greatly, and topics can include aspects of faith, theology or ethical and moral issues. They often represent different faiths within the same show, as well as different denominations of Christianity. Secular discussion programmes are popular and accessible to the masses, so the use of the same type of programme to represent religion is an effective way of attracting a variety of viewers. The BBC show *The Heaven and Earth Show* is an example of this genre.

Satellite television is a rich source of specialist television, and as well as religious programmes such as documentaries on mixed channels, there are also whole channels dedicated to religion, including Christianity. They are often more controversial than religious programmes on terrestrial television, and are commonly evangelical.

Radio

There are regular religious broadcasts on the radio, which include worship, documentaries, discussion and prayer. As the radio is the only form of the media which is purely auditory, it is particularly useful in representing Christianity through music and talk. Examples include: *Thought for the Day* on BBC Radio 4, which offers 'reflections from a faith perspective on issues and people in the news;' *The Moral Maze*, a live radio debate about moral issues; and *Choral Evensong*, which has been broadcast from cathedrals, churches and chapels every week since 1926.

Internet

The Internet is an extremely important form of media, and is widely used in the representation of Christianity. It is the most varied resource of communication and information about Christianity, which can be both a positive and a negative thing. There are official websites produced by Christian denominations, organizations and churches. They are reliable, factual representations of their branch of Christianity. There are also pages about Christianity on information websites from widely trusted sources such as *BBC Religion & Ethics*. However, anyone can put a website on the Internet, so there are also many sites with unreliable information, or which give an unfair representation of the Christian faith. Social networking websites such as Facebook and MySpace, as well as online message boards and chat rooms, allow Christians to communicate globally.

Newspapers and magazines

There are a variety of local, national and international newspapers and magazines, and these can be highly effective in representing Christianity. As well as general publications which sometimes contain specifically religious material, there are also specialist religious newspapers and magazines. Newspapers sometimes contain information about local churches, including details of services and events, to encourage attendance, support and awareness. National and international publications sometimes communicate specifically religious news or views from a Christian perspective. There are also a wide variety of specialist religious newspapers and magazines, often associated with a particular denomination or organization, or aimed at a specific reader, for example, young people.

Here are some examples:

Church Times is the world's leading Anglican weekly newspaper. It is independent of the Church of England and 'it now attempts to provide balanced and fair reporting of events and opinions across the whole range of Anglican affairs'. (www.churchtimes.co.uk)

The War Cry is an evangelical newspaper from The Salvation Army, published in several countries including the UK.

Youthwork Magazine is a monthly evangelical Christian magazine, which aims to support the Church with effective youth work and ministry.

Leaflets and posters

These are often used locally to advertise Christian events or meetings. They are also an effective tool for fund-raising for churches and charities. Most large religious organizations also produce and distribute this type of media to inform the public about what they do and how people can get involved or use their services.

How can the media educate both Christians and non-Christians about Christianity?

The media can be an effective tool in educating both Christians and non-Christians about Christianity:

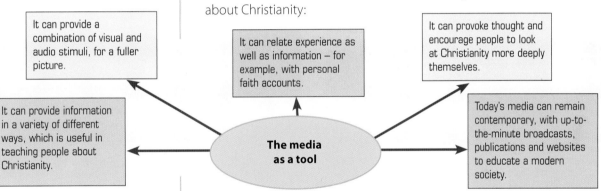

Christians and non-Christians are educated about Christianity by the media in different ways.

Christians usually have a certain amount of information and experience already, and the media can develop this further by providing varied and in-depth information about things they might not already know, or helping them to experience different aspects of Christianity that are outside their personal experience of their faith (for example, different denominations or customs).

Some non-Christians know a certain amount about Christianity, but others may know little or nothing. Therefore the media can provide an excellent introduction to their education about Christianity. This may be because they have chosen to learn about the religion, or because they happen to watch, listen to or read something that teaches them about Christianity. Most religious media does not assume that the public already know about Christianity, so it often includes basic information or explains what is happening.

The media does have its limitations with educating people about Christianity. Despite being varied, it does not give a full picture of every aspect of the faith. Also, it might possibly misrepresent the religion, due to bias or inaccuracy.

Activity **1**

List four ways in which the media can educate both Christians and non-Christians.

Christian beliefs and attitudes towards the portrayal of violence and sex in the media

What do Christians believe about violence in the media?

◀▲ Films and soap operas portray violence in many different ways.

> He overturned the tables of the money-changers and the benches of those selling doves.
>
> **(Mark 11:15)**

> If someone strikes you on the right cheek, turn to him the other also.
>
> **(Matthew 5:39)**

Some Christians believe that these passages suggest Jesus thought violence was sometimes OK.

> 'Put your sword back in its place,' Jesus said to him, 'for all who draw the sword will die by the sword.'
>
> **(Matthew 26:52)**

> Blessed are the peacemakers.
>
> **(Matthew 5:9)**

Some Christians believe that these passages suggest Jesus did not agree with violence.

Christians have many different opinions about violence in the media

Here are some examples:

The Bible teaches that violence is wrong, so I believe that having violence in the media is wrong.

People should be encouraged to lead good lives, but violence in the media provides a bad example, and makes violence seem acceptable, which is a bad thing.

As a Christian, I don't think people should behave violently because Jesus taught us to love one another. However, I don't mind fictional violence in the media if is for entertainment or information – that doesn't hurt anybody.

There are many examples of violence in the Bible, and that is the Word of God. Look at the story of Jesus' torture and crucifixion for example! Therefore, I don't see why violence in the media would be a problem for any Christian.

I don't like it when the media glamorizes violence. It is often portrayed in the media as 'cool' or 'tough' like when rock stars punch photographers, or in the soaps with all the fights.

I boycott violent TV programmes and films, to avoid exposing myself to them, as I think they can be emotionally damaging. If more people respond in the same way then violence in the media will be less common.

News reports and documentaries containing violence can raise awareness about related causes and organizations, or help people to understand situations such as riots or wars.

Sometimes violence in the media can actually have a positive impact. By showing the consequences of violence, for example, people might see that it is a bad thing and be put off doing violent things.

How is sex represented in the media?
Sex is represented in the media in a variety of ways. It appears on television and film, is discussed on radio, posted on the Internet, and written about in newspapers and magazines. Sometimes it is used in an obvious way and people are actually portrayed 'in the act'. More commonly sex is implied more subtly, such as with partial nudity or representation of bodies as 'sexually attractive', or the portrayal of relationships and behaviour.

These are some examples of sex in the media:

- soap opera characters kissing and going home together
- films which contain sex scenes
- song lyrics about sex on the radio
- newspaper 'advice' column containing sexual problems
- magazine articles about sexual technique
- advertisement showing a man wearing just boxer shorts
- Internet pornography
- suggestive talk within a programme
- discussion about sex or related issues, for example, virginity, intimacy, homosexuality
- leaflets about using condoms to avoid STIs and pregnancy.

Sex is used by the media for many reasons:

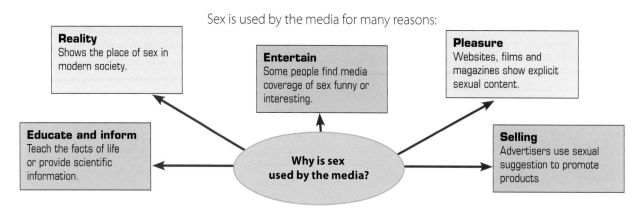

Reality
Shows the place of sex in modern society.

Entertain
Some people find media coverage of sex funny or interesting.

Pleasure
Websites, films and magazines show explicit sexual content.

Educate and inform
Teach the facts of life or provide scientific information.

Why is sex used by the media?

Selling
Advertisers use sexual suggestion to promote products

The question is often asked in today's world, 'Does the media reflect society, or does society reflect the media?' This is very important in relation to the issue of sex and the media. The media shows that certain things are 'normal' or 'right', and this can have an impact on how people behave.

Activity 2

What do Christians believe about sex in the media?

- The media sometimes shows promiscuity, where someone has lots of different sexual partners.

- The media often shows sex as a part of a loving marriage.

- The media often shows unmarried people having sex outside of marriage.

- There are sometimes homosexual relationships in the media.

- Contraception is sometimes referred to in the media.

- The media often focuses on sexual attractiveness as an important quality to have.

- The media sometimes portrays rape and sexual violence. (When these occur in the media, they are generally condemned as being wrong.)

Some Christian beliefs about sex in the media

I do not like to see nudity and sex on TV and in newspapers and magazines – the Bible teaches that sex should happen within a loving marriage, so I don't think it is right to show it in the media.

God created all people in his own image, and so everyone should have the freedom to communicate whatever they want, including sexual morals. It is up to those in control to realize for themselves that they should represent good things rather than bad.

It is not the media that is at fault for representing sex in a certain way, but rather it is the world that needs to realize what morals people should uphold. The media reflect society, and it is important for Christians to show good examples, but it is not for us to judge or control what others do.

Morals in the media are a bad influence and make people think that it is normal to commit adultery or be promiscuous. The Bible teaches that these things are wrong, and I do not think the media should 'teach' them through example, because it goes against how God wants us to live.

Pornography is dangerous, because it can lead to addiction and destroy people's relationships with their families. Therefore I think it should be banned completely, because this would help people, and God wants us to show love for our neighbours.

Censorship and freedom of speech

In this section, you will consider whether there should be controls over what is allowed to be published in the media.

Censorship means:

- The act of controlling what is said or written.
- Removal of offensive, harmful, inappropriate or sensitive material.

Examples of material which may be censored:

- graphic sexual or violent material
- terrorist messages
- material which incites (stirs up) hatred.

Examples of censorship in the media

On terrestrial television, programmes aired before the 9pm watershed must be suitable for both adults and children, and their content is restricted. After 9pm there is more freedom to broadcast things aimed specifically at adults, which may contain strong language, scenes of a sexual nature, or violence. In addition radio or television programmers may bleep out swear words.

Films are regulated by the film classification system which enables audiences to be controlled.

In 2005 when *Jerry Springer: The Opera* was shown by the BBC, it received 63,000 complaints by Christians offended by its portrayal of Christian icons (including Jesus). One Christian group tried to prosecute the BBC for blasphemy, but the charges were rejected because they specifically did not apply to stage productions and broadcasts.

Censorship of the media

Many people believe censorship is important because it gives a level of protection to the public. It restricts the use of offensive material, and seeks to maintain a minimum level of morality in the media.

Most forms of the media aim at attracting wide audiences, so they are happy to restrict material that might offend and turn viewers, readers or listeners away.

▲   *In October 2008, there were over 37,000 complaints about a BBC radio show in which Jonathan Ross and Russell Brand telephoned an actor to tell him lewd details about his granddaughter's relationship with one of the presenters. They were suspended, and the show's producer resigned over the matter.*

Racial and Religious Hatred Act 2006 (UK)

This makes it an offence to incite ('stir up') hatred against a person on the grounds of their religion (or lack of religious belief).

(It applies to threatening words, behaviour or written material.)

'It remains our firm intention to give people of all faiths the same protection against incitement to hatred on the basis of their religion. We will legislate to outlaw it and will continue the dialogue we have started with faith groups from all backgrounds about how best to balance protection, tolerance and free speech.'

(Labour Party manifesto *Forward not back* (2005), p111–112).

Obscene Publications Acts

These legal acts

- define the limits of obscenity in England and Wales
- enforce the censorship of obscene material.

In 2008, a man was prosecuted under the Obscene Publications Act because he posted on a website a fictional (made up) story which was allegedly about the kidnap, rape and murder of pop group Girls Aloud.

The common law offence of blasphemy was abolished in 2008. It had been illegal since the seventeenth century, but the Criminal Justice and Immigration Act of 2008 abolished the offence of blasphemy.

The media often censors terrorist organizations, in order to discourage further terrorism (as terrorists often aim to get lots of publicity and reaction for their actions).

Censorship is not always a positive influence. Sometimes it can be used to restrict freedom of expression or to control the way things are represented. In some countries access to websites by the public is restricted in order to control what its citizens think about certain issues. For example, the BBC News website could recently not be accessed legally in China.

Censorship can also be done in a biased way, such as negative feedback being conveniently omitted from an online product review, a magazine refusing to print articles that might reflect one of its financial backers in a bad light, or a television producer cutting out parts of a documentary that go against his own religious beliefs.

Some Christian responses to censorship of the media

- It is a good thing that some censorship exists to ensure a minimum moral standard, and restrict things such as swearing, and sexual and violent content.

- Censorship of incitement of racial and religious hatred is a good thing because the Bible teaches us to be kind to people from different cultures. Jesus helped people from different backgrounds, such as Samaritans, and Christians should follow Jesus' example.

- Censorship of pornography is a good thing because it can be a negative, addictive influence that can cause people harm.

- Swearing is wrong, and should be restricted. Therefore censorship of swearing before certain times is a good thing.

> *But I tell you, Do not swear at all.*
> **(Matthew 5:34)**

- Portrayal of graphic violence is wrong, and personally offends many Christians. Therefore they may agree that it should be censored.

> *If someone strikes you on the right cheek, turn to him the other also.*
> **(Matthew 5:39)**

- Although censorship of the media does exist, it is enforced by secular (non-religious) authorities. Therefore, many Christians believe that the existing censorship is ineffective, and could be greatly improved if it were more in line with Christianity. They believe that a lot of things which are permitted to be printed or broadcast should not be allowed – for example, any sexual content or any violence.

OFCOM (The Office of Communications) is the independent regulator and competition authority for the communication industries in the UK.	The Press Complaints Commission is a regulatory body for British printed newspapers and magazines, consisting of representatives of the major publishers. It is self-regulating.

- Some Christians believe that, although they do not personally agree with offensive content, the media should not be censored at all because it is important for people to have free will to choose for themselves what they say or do, as this was what God intended.

Explain in your own words what is meant by 'freedom of speech.'

What is freedom of speech?

Freedom of speech is the belief or principle that people have the right to voice opinions freely and without restriction.

Although many countries permit freedom of speech, there are always some restrictions (censorship).

In the past there have been times when people did not have freedom of speech. Before the fall of the Soviet Union, there were huge restrictions placed on people living in Russia including their right to religious freedom. In the 1940s, Russian Bibles were smuggled into the country so people could have a copy.

Imagine if you did not have the freedom to say what you wanted? You might be scared of the consequences if you said something that was not allowed, or feel like you were not in control of your own life.

There are many different people in the world, with a wide variety of opinions and beliefs. Freedom of speech allows us to communicate these different ideas to each other. This helps people to develop a better understanding of the cultures, beliefs and views of others, and leads to understanding.

The Human Rights Act 1998 supports the use of the European Convention on Human Rights in the UK. These rights include the right to Freedom of Expression, subject to certain restrictions that are 'in accordance with law' and 'necessary in a democratic society'. This right includes the freedom to hold opinions, and to receive and impart information and ideas.

Freedom of speech is important because it enables people to be individuals and to have their own identity. It allows people to live in a way that is acceptable to them without worrying about persecution from authorities.

Freedom of speech lets people speak their mind. People can for example criticize important political leaders without fear of being arrested. This is very important because sometimes governments need to be told that their policies do not work. This could be seen as a form of constructive criticism!

Some Christian responses to freedom of speech:

* Many Christians believe that all humans were made in the image of God and should all therefore have the same rights.

> **" So God created man in his own image ...**
>
> **(Genesis 1:27)"**

* But other Christians believe that some of the things communicated with full freedom of speech contradict Christian beliefs and morals, and should not be communicated by the media.

The Bible makes several references to freedom, and the responsibility that it brings:

> *Live as free men, but do not use your freedom as a cover-up for evil.*
>
> **(1 Peter 2:16)**

> *Be careful, however, that the exercise of your freedom does not become a stumbling block to the weak.*
>
> **(1 Corinthians 8:9)**

> *You, my brothers, were called to be free. But do not use your freedom to indulge the sinful nature.*
>
> **(Galatians 5:13)**

Many Christians believe that such teachings mean that everyone should have the freedom to say or write whatever they want, but that they should ensure that they use that freedom for good.

Some Christians believe that people should not decide whether the things that others say are right or wrong – it is only God who can judge:

> *Do not judge, or you too will be judged.*
>
> **(Matthew 7:1)**

Therefore, people do not have the right to judge whether what others are broadcasting or publishing is right.

Activity 2

Summarize what you know by listing as many points as you can, then expand your list by adding a sentence to each point explaining it more fully.

Glossary

Censorship – restrictions on the things people are allowed to publish

Evangelism – sharing beliefs and trying to persuade others to follow them

Media – different forms of mass communication

ETHICS 2

Attitudes to war

This section introduces you to Muslim beliefs about war and peace.

EXAM FOCUS

For most people, peace is an important aim that we should be striving towards. Although sometimes unavoidable, war is not normally something that is sought, and peaceful methods of solving conflict are usually explored before military action is taken.

British troops fighting in Afghanistan, 2009 . ▼

After the enormous loss of life and casualties in the two world wars in the first half of the twentieth century, the United Nations (UN) was founded in 1945. The aim of the UN is partly to try and keep the world's nations at peace and to provide an arena for international discussions and collaboration. Its work has been largely successful although in recent years there have been foreign military activities involving countries such as America and the United Kingdom in Afghanistan and Iraq. Nevertheless, these countries speak of the need for peace and co-solidarity and justify their military attacks as a small step to achieving peace.

For Discussion

What do you think of war? Is it avoidable? Is it always a good solution to our problems?

Much of the British public also support peace. According to a report in *The Independent*, July 2009, a poll showed that the majority of the public (52 per cent) think 'the war in Afghanistan is unwinnable and British troops should be withdrawn immediately.'

Muslim attitudes towards war

On the whole, Muslim attitudes towards war are largely negative. Despite its often negative and hostile portrayal in the media, Islam is actually a peaceful religion; in fact, one understanding of the word 'Islam' is peace. This is a concept that is transmitted through Muslim customs. For example, it is traditional for a Muslim to greet someone with the words 'Peace be with you' to which one would normally reply 'and with you'.

The often violent stereotype of a war-like religion is not a fair reflection of Islam on the whole. However, there are sometimes people that claim to be Muslims who go to war in the name of Islam and Allah, but usually they do not follow the strict Qur'anic rules for jihad. In the early stages of the twenty-first century, there have been a number of Islamic extremists that have been involved in terrorism because they believe to be following the will of Allah. These 'wars' have largely been condemned by the Islamic world.

For most Muslims, unnecessary war is undesirable and goes against the teachings of both the Qur'an and those of the Prophet Muhammad. It is Allah's plan for our communities to live in harmony with one another and not to fall out and be angry with one another.

> O mankind! We created you from a single (pair) of a male and a female, and made you into nations and tribes, that ye may know each other (not that ye may despise each other).
>
> **(Qur'an 49:13)**

Despite its overall peacefulness, Islam is a realistic religion and recognizes that sometimes war is unavoidable. Muslims are permitted to get involved in war but there are very strict regulations regarding it:

- *It must be for a just cause* – it is not right for Muslims to go to war if the circumstances are not right. More often, war is justified for self-defence including the protection of Islam. It is also permitted to fight for the innocent if they are suffering.

- *War must be the last resort* – war isn't desirable but can lead to a desirable end. Every other means of solving the problem has to be tried before war is considered. It is also believed that war should never be started by the Muslim and can only be in self-defence.

- *It must be an Islamic decision* – only Muslim leaders can authorize war. This does not include political leaders because they may have other motives than fighting in the name of Allah.

- *Preventing extra suffering* – the only casualties of war should be those on the battlefield. For the Muslim, the innocent must not be attacked or hurt.

- *Control* – as war should be the last resort, if the opposition decides to re-enter peaceful negotiations, or if they cease to attack, the fighting must not continue. War should also be balanced and any fighting should not be excessive as it should be self-defence.

> Fight in the cause of Allah those who fight you, but do not transgress limits; for Allah loveth not transgressors.
>
> **(Qur'an 2:190)**

> Think not of those who are slain in Allah's way as dead. Nay, they live, finding their sustenance in the Presence of their Lord.
>
> **(Qur'an 3:169)**

Despite its message that peace is best, Islam encourages all Muslims to take up arms and fight if a war is necessary and that all fit Muslim men should fight if called upon. The reasons for this are:

Allah – says that Muslims must fight to defend themselves if they are attacked. It is also written in the Qur'an that all those that fight in a just war will go straight to heaven.

Prophet Muhammad – he often spoke of the need for Muslims to fight in just wars. The first war involved Muhammad (see the Battle of Badr).

Exam Practice

Practise your skills in **demonstrating knowledge and understanding**.

Describe Muslim attitudes to war.

Remember that this type of question is not opinion-based, nor do you need to explain the concept in detail, so you should not spend too much time giving a long answer.

This will help you in the exam when you answer part (c) questions.

The Battle of Badr

The first Muslims believed that it was never right to fight in wars even in self-defence. In the later stages of his revelation from Allah, the Prophet Muhammad was taught that it was in fact permissible to fight in the defence of Islam. The Muslims that lived in the Muslim community in Medinah were often in conflict with the people from Makkah. This led to the first Muslim war. Three hundred Muslims were involved here in 624CE in a battle against 1000 soldiers. Despite being outnumbered, Allah was on the Muslim's side and Muhammad led them to victory. Muslims believe that because they prayed for help, and Allah helped them, then it must be acceptable to go to war if all else fails.

Concept of jihad

Jihad is a very important part of Islamic faith, and it is even considered by some to be the sixth pillar of Islam. The term literally means 'struggle' or 'struggle against evil'. It is essentially about every individual's fight against evil so that they can live according to Allah's way. Sometimes this could result in war but in most cases does not. In the early years after the Prophet Muhammad died, the leaders of Islam fought to make their religion stronger by conquering the groups that left their faith. This led to Muslims ruling a large area including North Africa and parts of India.

> " *The person who struggles so that Allah's word is supreme is the one serving Allah's cause.* "
> **(Hadith)**

Jihad is controversial in the non-Muslim world and many people confuse it as a holy war, partially due to the misuse of the term by modern day Muslim fanatics or by political leaders to justify war. Islam encourages peace between people but if war is necessary and just, the religion urges every Muslim to fight. Mujahid is the name given to a person performing jihad. There are regulations for a true jihad.

War is not jihad if:

- The war is started by a political leader – only a religious leader can authorize a jihad
- The Muslim community does not support it
- The war is aggressive rather than defensive
- Peaceful solutions haven't been tried first
- The purpose of the war is to force conversion
- It is to gain land or power
- Innocent people are endangered
- Animals and the environment aren't protected
- The fighting damages homes/place of worship

> *The most excellent jihad is the uttering of truth in the presence of an unjust ruler.*
>
> **(Hadith)**

There are two forms of jihad – greater jihad and lesser jihad.

Greater jihad refers to the individual's personal struggle in life to live according to Allah's Shari'ah laws. This struggle lasts for the whole lifetime and success is rewarded with paradise in the afterlife.

Lesser jihad refers to the struggle to transform the world into a better place. This can be achieved through eliminating problems in the world such as enemies against Islam, as well as social problems like poverty and injustice. The Prophet Muhammad taught:

> *Hate your enemy mildly; he may become your friend one day.*
>
> **(Hadith)**

Therefore one main concern is how to eliminate enemies against Islam. Islamic extremist terrorist groups such as Al Qaeda use lesser jihad to justify their attacks on America and the United Kingdom, but most Muslims argue that killing is wrong (haram) and goes against the idea that jihad should only be in self-defence.

Generally, the aims of jihad should only be to maintain a society where people are free to worship Allah in peace without politics restricting them. Fighting should never be an act of revenge or driven by hatred. Once peace is restored, all differences must be resolved.

For **Discussion**

Discuss the term 'jihad'.

Do you think the Muslim understanding of the term is understood in the non-Muslim world? Why do you think differences in understanding sometimes occur?

Exam Practice

Practise your skills in **demonstrating knowledge and understanding**.

What is meant by 'jihad'?

Just give a simple definition for this answer.

This will help you in the exam when you answer part (a) questions.

Violence and pacifism

This section encourages you to consider whether violence can ever be right, and introduces you to Muslim views about violence.

EXAM FOCUS

Attitudes towards the use of violence

There are many different types and levels of **violence**, such as fighting, hitting, kicking, throwing things, and the use of weapons. Some violence happens over a period of time, or on a large scale as in wars.

As we have read earlier, the word 'Islam' can be translated as peace and as such, the vast majority of Muslims are not violent and seek peace.

> *For without doubt, in the remembrance of Allah do hearts find satisfaction.*
>
> **(Qur'an 13:28)**

Shari'ah law defends the rights of all human beings. As a result, any violence or unjust action against Muslims and 'People of the Book' (Christians and Jews too) is something to which Islam is totally opposed. Islam is based upon moderation and its morality is grounded upon keeping to the middle ground.

> *Nor take life – which Allah has made sacred – except for just cause.*
>
> **(Qur'an 17:33)**

Violent acts of terrorism are very much condemned by the vast majority of Muslims around the world. The Prophet Muhammad once declared that those that murder will be the first people to be judged by Allah on Judgement Day. For a Muslim to strike terror into the hearts of innocent people, to destroy buildings such as those on 11 September 2001 in New York, and to deliberately cause death injury to women and children, would be to go against everything that they are taught by Allah, and breach a number of Islamic laws. Muslims are taught to live a life that is pleasing to Allah and as such violence does not normally apply.

> *Every time they kindle the fire of war, Allah doth extinguish it. But they (ever) strive to do mischief on earth. And Allah loveth not those who do mischief.*
>
> **(Qur'an 5:64)**

Sometimes Muslims are deliberately violent towards themselves: during the Ashura celebrations, Shi'ite Muslims remember the death of Al-Hussein by self-harm. It is quite common for Shi'ite men and boys to be seen whipping themselves to mark the event. In this Islamic denomination, there is huge respect given to those people that are prepared to suffer or die for their religion.

Khan Abdul Ghaffar Khan's close association with Gandhi earned him the nickname 'Frontier Gandhi'. ▶

Attitudes towards pacifism

Pacifists believe that peace is favourable and war is wrong: on the whole Islam is a pacifistic religion.

In situations where pacifists do not agree with something, and want to do something about it without resorting to violence, there are alternative ways of speaking out or taking action, which are sometimes called 'non-violence'.

Non-violent protest can involve:

*   speeches, writings or art
*   petitions
*   peaceful demonstrations, gatherings of people or marches
*   boycotts
*   peaceful non-cooperation.

Khan Abdul Ghaffar Khan

Khan Abdul Ghaffar Khan was arguably the world's most famous Muslim pacifist who led by example, and went about non-violent methods to achieve his goal of freedom.

Ghaffar Khan worked in India during the twentieth century to oppose British occupation of India; this was eventually achieved in 1947. In what was a hugely violent area at the time, Ghaffar Khan ignored the threat of bullets and prison to endure his own jihad, or struggle, to fight for his cause in a non-violent way.

The Khudai Khidmatgar, or Servants of God, was set up by Ghaffar Khan and was most active in the 1920s–30s. Its 100,000+ members opposed the British police and military in non-violent ways. Ghaffar Khan said they had a greater weapon and 'that weapon is patience and righteousness. No power on earth can stand against it'. Many lost their lives in their struggle and Ghaffar Khan spent 52 years of his life imprisoned or in exile.

Crime and punishment

This section considers what justice is and how those who break laws should be punished.

Concept of justice

Justice generally means fair treatment. Where crime is concerned, justice means dealing fairly with the crime in a way that is fair to both the criminal and their society, including any direct or indirect victims of their crime.

In Islam, justice (al-adl) is understood as putting things into their correct place and this includes equality of people. Justice forms part of human morality to try and enable us live the way Allah wants us to. After all, Muslims believe that Allah is the ultimate judge and will weigh up our good and bad deeds when we die. Therefore, it is important that we should live accordingly. Justice is the supreme virtue, according to the Qur'an. Injustice is forbidden although Muslims are reminded that Allah is merciful and we should be too.

▲ *Islamic justice is the supreme virtue according to the Qur'an.*

> *Allah commands justice, the doing of good, and liberality to kith and kin.*
> **(Qur'an 16:90)**

> *O ye who believe! Stand out firmly for Allah, as witnesses to fair dealing.*
> **(Qur'an 5:8)**

> *We sent aforetime our messengers with Clear Signs and sent down with them the Book and the Balance (Of Right and Wrong), that men stand forth in justice.*
> **(Qur'an 57:25)**

For all people, justice is an important step in creating a secure society where people can feel free to conduct their daily lives. It is the same for Muslims. Islam offers a justice system based upon the welfare of society and the way in which criminals are punished concentrates primarily on the protection of it rather than punishing the offender.

According to Islam, Shari'ah law, the basis of the Islamic justice system, was passed down from Allah through the Prophet Muhammad. Muslims believe that the laws are flexible enough to be translated from society to society and the changing shape of humans. They contain detailed rules on how to deal with particular life circumstances and fixed punishments that will discourage crime. Muslims believe these rules make for a more stable society.

For **Discussion**

What you think justice means? Should anyone ever be let off punishment because they are sorry for their crimes?

▲ *Wrongdoers must be punished according to Islam.*

Aims of punishment

All issues of crime and its punishment are based closely on Shari'ah law. Muslims do not believe that people have the right to forgive people for their wrongdoings as this is the job of Allah when the person seeks forgiveness.

There are three main aims of punishment in Islam:

- To protect society – punishment is seen only as a way in which to protect the community from the criminal. In Islam, the aim of punishment is to protect the welfare of society. This should be to provide a society that can prosper and worship Allah. Everyone should be given the opportunity to develop spiritually and intellectually.

- To reform the criminal – the Qur'an is full of writing about how to deal with criminals. It also explains that forgiveness is available to those who truly repent of their crimes.

> *It they repent and amend leave them alone; for, Allah is Oft-Returning Most Merciful.*
>
> **(Qur'an 4:16)**

- To make up for the crime that has been committed – it is considered by most people that criminals should never be treated lightly if they are a threat to society. Think back at those people that have committed violent crimes having been released early from prison, or even by mistake.

> *The punishment of those who wage war against Allah and His Messenger, and strive with might and main for mischief through the land is: execution or crucifixion, or the cutting off of hands and feet from opposite sides or exile from the land.*
>
> **(Qur'an 5:33)**

Overall, Islam's concept of the justice system based upon the welfare of society is based upon the five universal principles:

1. The preservation of life.
2. The preservation of religion.
3. The preservation of reason.
4. The preservation of lineage or family.
5. The preservation of property.

It is considered that if these five principles are preserved, then so will the welfare of our society. The grid below gives examples of crimes that break each of the five principles.

Type of preservation	Associated crimes or laws
Life	Law of retribution or revenge
Religion	Crime of apostasy
Reason	Crime of drinking
Lineage or family	Crime of fornication
Property	Crime of theft

The main aim of punishment is prevention and deterrence and it is important that there is equality in measure for the crime.

How Shari'ah laws on justice are carried out depends upon the country they are in. For example, according to a *Daily Mail* report, 29 June 2009, there are 85 Shari'ah courts operating in the UK but their jurisdiction is not on an equal level to the regular British courts. In an Islamic country such as Iran, where religion and state are merged, all courts are based on Shari'ah law and therefore it is much easier for Muslim beliefs to be reflected in punishments of criminals.

Beliefs about the treatment of criminals

Where Shari'ah law is applicable, criminals are treated in a way that is in the best interest of the society. As such, the punishment does not always fit the crime. Punishments in Islam are known as **hudu** – these are more like balancing the right and wrong than punishments. Hudu relates to crimes that are mentioned in the Qur'an or Hadith such as murder.

The main belief about the treatment of criminals is that justice prevails. According to Shari'ah law, punishments of criminals fit into three categories:

Firstly, Islam has prescribed punishments for crimes associated with the five principles of life (murder, assault), property, lineage, reason, and religion. Here are some examples of crime and their punishment.

Crime	Punishment
Life (such as murder or assault)	Death
Lineage or family (such as adultery/fornication)	Whipping/flogging: *The woman and the man guilty of adultery or fornication – flog each of them with a hundred stripes. Let not compassion move you in their case, in a matter prescribed by Allah, if ye believe in Allah and the Last Day: and let a party of the Believers witness their punishment. (Qur'an 24:2)*
Defamation (destroying someone's character)	Whipping/flogging: *And those who launch a charge against chaste women, and produce not four witnesses (to support their allegations) – flog them with eighty stripes; and reject their evidence ever after: for such men are wicked transgressors. (Qur'an 24:4)*

On 6 January 2008, the Iranian Students' News Agency reported that some armed robbers were punished with the cross-amputation of the left foot and right hand in Iran.

Secondly is retribution or revenge. Here, the criminal can be punished in the same way they treated their victim. For example, if the criminal has chopped off a limb of their victim, then they can face the same punishment. It is common practice for specialists to be consulted to see if it is possible to remove certain limbs without resulting in death. Retribution is only possible for crimes associated with murder or deliberate injury.

▲ *Whips may be used to punish someone found guilty of a crime.*

For **Discussion**

Do you think any particular crimes would receive a more harsh punishment? Are there any crimes you would be willing to forgive?

For **Discussion**

How do you think British society would react if the laws regarding punishment of criminals were changed and the victims could affect the punishments of the offenders?

> *O ye who believe! The law of equality is prescribed to you the cases of murder.*
> **(Qur'an 2:178)**

As retribution is considered the right of the victim, Islam permits and even encourages the criminal to be completely pardoned by the victim. Heavenly rewards can be gained for the victim. This is an opportunity to perform a good deed if you let them have a less severe punishment.

> *If anyone remits the retaliation by way of charity, it is an act of atonement for himself.*
> **(Qur'an 5:45)**

> *… the remission … is the nearest to righteousness.*
> **(Qur'an 2:237)**

Thirdly are discretionary punishments. This is the largest and most flexible category of punishment and takes into account the needs of the community. These can also be the most effective punishment for reforming the criminal as the most appropriate punishment can be selected from within the Islamic framework. The punishments are usually a fine, flogging, or imprisonment.

Responses to the treatment of criminals

Forgiveness is an important part of crime and punishment for Islam. It is believed that when a criminal seeks forgiveness from Allah and is genuinely sorry for the crime that is committed, then no further punishment is necessary.

Attitudes towards capital punishment

Capital punishment means the death penalty – a criminal's life is taken away for the most severe crimes. According to Amnesty International (www.amnesty.org), at least 2390 people were executed and at least 8864 sentenced to death around the world in 2008; 72 per cent of these death penalty executions took place in China.

Exam Practice

Practise your skills in **demonstrating knowledge and understanding**.

Explain why Muslims treat criminals in the way that they do.

Give reasons for your answer and try to refer to the Qur'an where possible.

This will help you in the exam when you answer part (d) questions.

For the most severe crimes a person may be hanged. ▶

Shari'ah law has three main aims of punishment to protect the welfare of society. Capital punishment is permitted, although in reality this is rarely carried out and usually only in cases of murder. Islam would prefer forgiveness and peace over the death penalty.

> ❝ *Take not life, which God hath made sacred, except by way of justice and law.* ❞
>
> **(Qur'an 6:151)**

The three crimes for which capital punishment is permitted are:

- Murder

- Sexual misconduct (including making false allegations)

- **Apostasy** (crimes of giving up or insulting religious faith)

There are various means of capital punishment carried out in the Islamic world including hanging, beheading and stoning. In some places executions take place in a public square to act as a deterrent for other people from committing the same crimes in the future.

In February 2008, the President of Iran, Mahmoud Ahmedinejad, suggested that there should be the death penalty in Iran for anyone who converted from Islam to another religion.

For Discussion

What do you think of capital punishment?

Should people around the world agree to get rid of the death penalty?

Social injustice

This section will help you understand Muslim views about fairness in society.

EXAM FOCUS

Social injustice basically means unfairness in society. Sometimes people are treated unequally and they may have fewer rights, opportunities and rewards. They may also have more burdens or be discriminated against because of, for example, race, sex, age, physical or mental ability, or poverty.

In society not all people are equal and some suffer through poverty. ▼

For Discussion

What kind of social injustices can you think of?

Do you think we have a duty to help people who are less fortunate?

Social justice means fair treatment in society, for example equality of opportunity, fairness of criminal justice, social rules and processes and social and political rights.

Beliefs about social injustice

Injustice is arguably the biggest concern for Muslims. It is believed that balance in the universe comes from Allah and Muslims have a duty to preserve this by making all people live in equality. This can range from standing up for the oppressed, giving aid to the needy, and even protecting wastage of the world's resources.

> *And be fair: For Allah loves those who are fair (and just).*
>
> **(Qur'an 49:9)**

Exam Practice

Practise your **evaluation** skills.

'Everyone has a duty to help make the world a fairer place.'

Discuss this statement. You should include different, supported points of view and a personal viewpoint. You must refer to Islam in your answer.

In your answer, you need to consider different points of view. Start with the answer you think a Muslim would give – you might be able to give some examples of Muslim action for social justice, to support your ideas. Then give a different point of view, explaining why some people might disagree. End with your own view, which might be the same as one of the ideas you have already explained or could be something different again.

This will help you in the exam when you answer part (e) questions.

> *Serve Allah, and join not any partners with Him and do good – to parents, kinsfolk, orphans, those in need, neighbours who are near, neighbours who are strangers, the Companion by your side, the wayfarer (ye meet)... For Allah loveth not the arrogant, the vainglorious.*
>
> **(Qur'an 4:36)**

> *Whoever relieves a human being from a grief of this world, Allah will relieve him from a grief on the Day of Judgement.*
>
> **(Hadith)**

As you can see from the scripture passages above, Islam teaches that relieving grief in the world is of utmost importance. It is not the Muslim way to live in luxury whilst others are suffering. This would not be living a life of life that Allah would approve of. Good deeds (Sadaqah) are important when it comes to Judgement Day.

Some Muslims believe that tackling societies' injustices is jihad, or struggle. This is because there are a lot of things in society that are not ideal and that go against Allah's plans on earth. It is important for us to live in a just world and Muslims should do all they can to help achieve this. This jihad involves sacrifice. It could be connected to your time, money, skills and in extreme circumstances could cost you your life.

> *Every good action is a charity and it is a good action to meet a friend with a smiling face.*
>
> **(Hadith)**

Muslims can do little things to help too. Exploitation is not allowed in Islam and this is contrary to many modern capitalist points of view. It is quite normal for Muslims not to use ordinary banks that make money from other people's debt. Some Muslims arrange any interest they earn to get paid directly to a charity.

Responses to social injustice

Muslims respond to social injustice in a number of different ways depending upon the circumstances. Simple good deeds, or Sadaqah, can be carried out for the sake of Allah, and help those in need. The Prophet taught that this could be simple things such as picking up litter or trying to cheer people up, or it could be donating money to charity or praying about a particular issue. Muslims believe that they should help all people whether they are Muslim or not because we are all part of Allah's creation, and all should live a life of equality.

> *Sadaqah is the responsibility of every Muslim...to give to charity...help a distressed person... [and] do good deed.*
>
> **(Hadith)**

Islamic society has a history of trying to create a fair and just society. Around 1000 years ago, Muslim rulers went to great lengths to ensure that their people had clean water. In the tenth century, Muslim countries had running water with drains, well- planned towns with streets, schools, libraries and street-lamps at night. It would be hundreds of years afterwards before Europeans copied these ideas. In Cairo, even ordinary people were allowed to visit the palace library free of charge and were even provided with complimentary pens and paper!

Islamic Relief

There are a number of Islamic charities that help to relieve the social injustices of the world. Founded in the UK in 1984 by Dr Hany El Banna, Islamic Relief is a non-governmental charity that helps support the world's poorest people, and concentrates on issues causing poverty and suffering. Their mission is centred around the Qur'anic quote:

> *And if anyone saved a life, it would be as if he saved the life of the whole people.*
> **(Qur'an 5:32)**

For Islamic Relief, working hand-in-hand with local communities is paramount to develop sustainable economic and social development.

Islamic Relief works in six main sectors:

- Overview
- Sustainable livelihoods
- Education
- Health and nutrition
- Orphans and child welfare
- Water and sanitation

Zakah (almsgiving)

Zakah, one of the Pillars of Islam, is arguably the strongest way Muslims respond to social injustice. Zakah requires Muslims to donate 2.5% of their wealth to charity. This is not jut a simple charity donation, or an expression of kindness, it is something Allah inspired to help society as a whole. An unequal society is not the kind of world that Allah desires and it is a Muslim's role to help bring balance through Zakah. As such, this kind of giving is considered to be a form of worshipping Allah. It is also a test for the Muslim, as all wealth belongs to Allah anyway and one must trust in Him to provide whether or not they think they are able to give.

One understanding or the term Zakah is purity. This kind of giving helps purify the givers heart from greed and selfishness, and also the receiver of jealousy or hatred. Muslims are encouraged to create more opportunities for the less fortunate such as providing jobs. The Prophet Muhammad once said:

> *Whoever relieves a human being from a grief of this world, Allah will relieve him from a grief on the Day of Judgement.*
> **(Hadith)**

▲ *Muslims believe in working for others.*

In Islamic countries, Zakah is sometimes taken as a tax. In the UK, most Muslims give Zakah as an offering in the mosque and a committee decides how it would be best spent. Many Muslims donate annually at the festival Eid ul-Fitr, as this is connected with fasting, and a time has been spent considering what it would like to be poor during the preceding month of Ramadan.

Activity 2

Practise your skills in **demonstrating knowledge and understanding**.

What is Zakah? Explain why Muslims like to give so generously.

For Discussion

Would you be willing to give regularly to a charity? Who would you give to? Why?

Glossary

Apostasy – renouncing or giving up your religion and principles

Hudu – punishments in Islam, which are concerned with balancing the right and wrong (relates to crimes that are mentioned in the Qur'an or Hadith such as murder)

Jihad – literally means 'struggle' or 'struggle against evil'

Pacifism – the belief that war and violence should always be avoided

Violence – an act of aggression that is intended to cause destruction or suffering